PENGUIN BOOKS
SONIA: A BIOGRAPHY

Rasheed Kidwai, forty-three, is Associate Editor of the *Telegraph*, Calcutta. He graduated from St. Stephen's College, New Delhi, and holds a master's degree in mass communication from UK's Leicester University where he went on a Commonwealth India scholarship. Kidwai is a regular political commentator on various television networks, radio programmes and newspapers. He is a guest lecturer at several journalism schools, universities and media organizations.

SONIA
A Biography

Rasheed Kidwai

PENGUIN BOOKS

An imprint of Penguin Random House

PENGUIN BOOKS

USA | Canada | UK | Ireland | Australia
New Zealand | India | South Africa | China | Singapore

Penguin Books is part of the Penguin Random House group of companies
whose addresses can be found at global.penguinrandomhouse.com

Published by Penguin Random House India Pvt. Ltd
4th Floor, Capital Tower 1, MG Road,
Gurugram 122 002, Haryana, India

Penguin
Random House
India

FFirst published in Viking by Penguin Books India 2003
Revised edition published in Viking by Penguin Books India 2009
This updated edition published in Penguin Books 2011

ISBN 9780143416869

Not for sale in Pakistan

Typeset in Aldine by Mantra Virtual Services, New Delhi

Printed at Repro India Limited

www.penguin.co.in

MIX
Paper from
responsible sources
FSC® C047271

This is a legitimate digitally printed version of the book and therefore might not
have certain extra finishing on the cover.

For

my wife Farah

CONTENTS

PREFACE TO THE PAPERBACK EDITION

The first edition of *Sonia: A Biography* was released in December 2003 just days after the Congress' crushing defeat in the party-ruled states of Madhya Pradesh, Rajasthan and Chhattisgarh. The period had marked an all-time high for the then prime minister Atal Bihari Vajpayee and the ruling National Democratic Alliance (NDA). Buoyed by the electoral success, Vajpayee had called for early general elections in April–May 2004.

The outcome of the general elections, however, surprised everyone. The Congress-led alliance emerged as a winner and Sonia Gandhi was suddenly at the centre of every power equation.

In 2009, the opposition closed ranks, spent colossal amounts in projecting veteran L.K. Advani as a prime ministerial candidate, questioned Dr Manmohan Singh's integrity in the context of the Indo-US civil and defence nuclear deal. Throughout the election campaign, the N-deal was portrayed as India succumbing to US pressure and compromising the national interest, but the electorate reposed its faith in the Sonia–Manmohan combine. The 200-plus Lok Sabha seats verdict in favour of a Congress-led coalition gave rise to the speculation that Sonia would project son Rahul Gandhi as future prime minister. However, during 2004–10 Rahul continued to deny that his sole purpose in politics was to become prime minister. The Congress general secretary carried out his stated aim of learning politics 'brick by brick'. This period also saw Sonia confronting many battles, ranging from the issue of corruption to a decline of the party organization.

Here is my modest attempt to piece together some of the most extraordinary and dramatic events in Indian politics in the last decade. As an independent and unauthorized biography, this work attempts to offer a perspective on events till December 2010 and seeks to examine Sonia's new role.

I take this opportunity to once again express my deep sense of gratitude to numerous Congress party members who continue to provide insight into the finer aspects of Sonia's personality, her style of functioning and Congress party politics. I am also grateful to leaders of other political parties, academicians, intellectuals, opinion-makers and bureaucrats who went out of their way to help me.

No words can express my gratitude to Aveek Sarkar, my editor and guide. Manini Chatterjee, Deepayan Chatterjee and R. Rajagopal offered valuable help and patronage which gave me time to finish this book along with my journalistic assignments. I am also thankful to Bharat Bhushan, Sankarshan Thakur, Devdan Mitra, Rakesh Joshi, Shubhabrata Bhattacharya, Radhika Ramaseshan and Prakash Patra for their help.

Among friends I wish to particularly thank Nirmal Pathak, Swaraj Thapa, Priya Sahgal, Hartosh Singh Bal, Sheela Bhatt, Askari Zaidi, Sunetra Chowdhary, Rama Laxmi, Bhavdeep Kang, Shikha Parihar, Richa Sharma, Naghma, S.A.H. Rizvi, Avinash Dutt and Farhan Ansari for their useful tips.

To my wife, Dr Farah Kidwai, who has always been a source of inspiration and support, I express my thanks. I must also mention A.A. Kidwai, Dr Aziz Ansari, Ajum Ansari, Dr A.R. Kidwai, Sarah bhabhi and Saima, to whom I am deeply grateful.

A special thanks to Saad–Ghazia, Shahab–Sadia, Saif–Farha, Shams, Umar, Umair, Ayesha, Samad, Suboor, Falah, Abaan, Shad and Safia for keeping me laughing.

Finally thank you Penguin Books, my editor Ranjana Sengupta, and Debasri Rakshit for her meticulous editing, and Prita, Meru and Shantanu for all the encouragement.

New Delhi   Rasheed Kidwai
July 2008

PROLOGUE

The original Mrs Gandhi—Indira—had delivered a second successive election victory for the Congress in 1971 but before that she had to win a war. The reigning Mrs Gandhi—Sonia—has also led the Congress to a consecutive poll success but hasn't had to go so far as to fight an external war, though there have been many domestic battles.

On this count, both Indira and Sonia have won elections back to back. Indira never won a third one running.

Given the culture of worship in the Congress, no one would openly weigh Field Marshal Sonia against Indira but comparisons are inevitable if only because they share the name. And if only because they're both women leading the country's oldest party in circumstances very different but also similar in that each has had to skipper the ship in stormy waters.

Sonia considers Indira to be her role model with whom comparisons are by definition not possible. But her style is also sharply different from that of the late prime minister who was not known to be democratic in the way she ran the party.

Since 1998, when she was a reluctant entrant into politics, Sonia has been anything but a control freak, a term often used for the Congress high command under her mother-in-law. With the exception of J.B. Patnaik in Orissa and Vilasrao Deshmukh/Ashok Chavan in Maharashtra, Congress chief ministers have seldom been shunted out by Sonia.

Even her core team, consisting of Ahmed Patel, Oscar Fernandes, Janardhan Dwivedi, Digvijay Singh and others, has remained intact with minor fluctuations. Unlike in Indira's days, the team of advisers has not grown into a cabal at whose feet the party and the nation have to worship.

Sonia's respect for regional leaders like Sheila Dikshit, Bhoopinder Singh Hooda, Ashok Gehlot and other chief ministers has resulted in the Congress consolidating its gains in Delhi, Haryana, Rajasthan and other states.

Some Congress leaders find Sonia's task of reviving the party more daunting than in the Indira era when there were no powerful regional parties to battle, nor any compulsions of coalition politics.

For most part of her tenure, Indira's Congress had a strong social base of Brahmins, Dalits and minorities and her standing among the scheduled tribes was unchallenged. Once she had established her authority after the Congress split, Indira didn't have to worry about winning elections until she lost her head and declared Emergency.

Sonia, on the contrary, had everything going against her when she took charge with the BJP growing in power. Congress leaders refer to Sonia's own 1998 remark that she was not Jawaharlal Nehru's daughter to illustrate the difficulties she had to face till 2004 when she led the party to power. She had made that statement when Sharad Pawar, P.A. Sangma and Tariq Anwar had raised the issue of her foreign origin.

When power was waiting at the door of 10, Janpath, she made Manmohan Singh the prime minister, a step which might not have been expected of Indira who in her time did not allow what she considered parallel centres of power to develop. Since then, Sonia has tried to stay in the background while Singh ran the country amid loud whispers of conflict that never developed into anything serious.

Having won another election in 2009 with such flourish, there were many in the Congress who thought that under Sonia and Rahul, the party would rediscover its national character by stamping its presence again in Uttar Pradesh and taking its tally beyond 200 Lok Sabha seats. Twelve years ago, when Sonia took the helm, the doubt was if it would push past half that number.

Sonia has done many things differently from her larger-than-life role model. But, since numbers are what decide polls, the winner of Mrs G vs Mrs G can be called with certainty only in 2014 if Sonia delivers a 3–2 score by winning three consecutive elections.

Between 2004 and 2010 the United Progressive Alliance (UPA), which had come into being hurriedly and under extraordinary circumstances following Sonia's act of renunciation, functioned well under Manmohan but the coalition faced innumerable challenges from within and outside. In the larger context, it worked more like a bureaucratic machine than a political conglomerate. There were many lacklustre performances in some of the key portfolios, while ministers frequently differed with each other, sidelined their juniors and cared little for a sense of accountability—a basic feature of parliamentary democracy.

On 30 September 2010 when the Lucknow bench of the Allahabad High Court delivered its landmark judgment on the vexed Babri Masjid/Ramjanmabhoomi dispute, both Sonia and Manmohan dithered instead of assuming a proactive role to pave the way for the construction of a temple and a mosque as suggested by the judges. The Congress's lack of enthusiasm in acting as peacemaker showed Sonia's own assessment of the Ayodhya dispute as the Congress's Achilles heel. India's first prime minister, Jawaharlal Nehru, was quickly dragged into the Ayodhya imbroglio in December 1949 when idols were surreptitiously placed inside the sixteenth century Babri mosque.

Nehru had asked the then Uttar Pradesh chief secretary, Bhagwan Sahay to restore status quo. But the then deputy commissioner of Faizabad, K.K. Nayar wrote lengthy letters ruing that he had failed to find 'any Hindu even among Congressmen' who were ready to support the administration's move for removal of the idols. The ICS officer said that each time he went to the site, he was greeted with the slogan: '*Nyaya anyay karna chhor do, Nayar, bhagwan ka phatak khol do* (Stop talking about justice or injustice, Nayar, open the door towards the deity).'

Decades later, in 1986, when Rajiv Gandhi was prime minister and the Congress was in power in Uttar Pradesh, the fast-paced events leading to the opening of the lock surprised even the BJP, which highlighted the Congress's role in a white paper published after the Babri Masjid was demolished. Through 1986–1989, Rajiv Gandhi, his home minister Buta Singh, and the then Uttar Pradesh chief ministers, Veer Bahadur Singh and N.D. Tiwari kept trying to occupy centrestage in Ayodhya, coming up with different plans. In 1989 the government even allowed the *shilanyas* (foundation ceremony) at the site. Somehow, each of these measures boomeranged.

P.V. Narasimha Rao, who watched this period from close quarters before becoming prime minister and a central figure himself, articulated his dilemma in a book, *Ayodhya: 6 December 1992*, published a year after his death in 2006. Reflecting on how the BJP's 'pseudo religious movement' could not have sustained itself on a purely religious plane, Rao said it needed a political reaction to flourish. 'I cannot escape the uneasy feeling that we Congressmen (while in the Congress) supplied it with just that . . .'

After the Babri demolition, Rao became disillusioned and wrote with an air of dejection that while the Kalyan Singh government and the BJP were largely responsible for the 'wanton vandalism', his Congress colleagues in the ministry, too, had been guided by 'political and vote-earning' considerations. 'They had already made up their mind that one person had to be made historically responsible for the tragedy . . . They got a stick to beat me with. I understood it.'

With such a history, Sonia's/Manmohan's hesitation to act as an arbitrator in Ayodhya was not without reason.

As chairperson of the UPA and head of the Congress parivar, Sonia spent most of her time intervening in crises and engaging in firefighting without disturbing protocol and hierarchy. As head of the National Advisory Council, Sonia was able to push through some subjects that were close to her despite a three-year absence due to the office of profit controversy (Chapter eleven).

The NAC served as a platform to build her legacy as a driver for policymaking in the UPA government. While the Planning Commission deputy chairman and a member of the National Advisory Council (NAC) Montek Singh Ahluwalia disagreed that the Sonia panel worked as a 'super cabinet', all the big ideas came from it rather than 24, Akbar Road, the Congress party headquarters in New Delhi.

For traditional Congressmen, it was disappointing that the NAC instead of the party showcased her as a political leader and her vision for the country. The absence of the Congress party's intellectual capability to influence government and bureaucracy was a clear departure from the past. In its first avatar, 2004–06, the NAC earned credit for pushing the National Rural Employment Guarantee Act, the Right to Information Act and the Domestic Violence Bill which were largely responsible for the UPA retaining power in 2009.

Between 2004 and 2010, 24, Akbar Road, contributed little in terms of either generating new ideas or sending any concrete proposal from the party to the government. Some party leaders wondered if the Congress in power had assumed a negative role with functionaries acting more to kill or blunt any fresh initiative rather than utilizing the talent it has at its command. For the first time since Independence, the grand old party failed to provide what its former president B.P. Sitaramayya had described as 'life-sustaining doctrines pumped through the arteries of government'. Sitaramayya had spelt out the relationship between the Congress party and the government at the Jaipur All India Congress Committee (AICC) session in 1948 saying, 'The Congress is really the philosopher, while the government is the politician. The latter has power and the former has influence.' By 2009–10, Sonia tried to cater to the rural and urban aspirations through blending the experience of NGOs and professionals at the NAC.

However, the NAC itself was not free from its in-house squabbles. The right to food debate saw a sharp division between members of civil society that Sonia had carefully drafted and those economists–experts who believed in 'Manmohanomics'. While Harsh Mander, Farah Naqvi and others pushed to extend the food subsidy not only to the below the poverty line (BPL) families but to some segments above the poverty line, other members opposed it on the grounds that supplying 35 kg of grain per household will not be feasible without imports which they contended may erode the country's overall food security.

Union agriculture minister Sharad Pawar too disagreed with Sonia's ambitious food security plan and even asked Dr Manmohan Singh to reduce his workload. Pawar was opposed to some of the radical provisions of the draft food security bill and reportedly communicated to Manmohan Singh that, if passed, the proposed legislation would affect food procurement and send fiscal discipline haywire. The NAC chief's view was that universal entitlement of food security was not feasible, given the cost of grain subsidies. Moreover, he felt that it was neither necessary nor desirable to extend food subsidy to the billion-plus population. Pawar reportedly cited the Suresh Tendulkar Committee's observation that the number of families below the poverty line (BPL) totalled an estimated 37.2 per cent of the population.

Subsequently, the NAC climbed down from the promised universal Public Distribution System (PDS) to targeted PDS on grounds of non availability of food grains. But noted agriculture economist M.S. Swaminathan, also a member of the NAC, disagreed pointing out that non availability of food grains was not the problem. He sought inclusion of coarse cereals such as jowar, ragi, bajra, etc., so that the food basket was enlarged.

But the babus in the prime minister's office, Krishi Bhawan and the Planning Commission were not impressed. Advocating what they called as minimalistic entitlement under the right to food, the bureaucrats sought to push for cash transfers and continued to raise the spectre of non availability of food grains during droughts when the needy would need it the most. Without mincing words, Swaminathan lamented that there was no political will to eradicate hunger in spite of India being home to the largest number of hungry people in the world—48 per cent of children and 40 per cent of malnourished women. Swaminathan quoted J.R.D. Tata to express his feelings, 'I don't want India to be a super power, I want India to be a happy country.'

A section of the NAC wanted the handing over of food security issues like purchase and storage to the private sector but Swaminathan dubbed it as 'a recipe for national disaster' and asserted, 'It will lead to chaos, it will lead to food riots, it will be the greatest harm done to the people of the country. You can't abdicate the primary responsibility of feeding the people. The private sector has no obligation at all to feed anybody. I think their only interest will be making money. I think it is a wrong policy. I think it is a dangerous policy. It is a socially dangerous policy.'

By November 2010, corruption hit the UPA when union telecom minister A. Raja had to resign, Congress leader Suresh Kalmadi became the guilty man of most wrong doings in the organization of the Commonwealth Games and Ashok Chavan had to resign as chief minister of Maharashtra over his alleged role in the Adarsh scam. The Adarsh society shot into the limelight claiming Chavan's job after three of his relatives were found to be members in the thirty-one-storey building meant for Kargil war widows and heroes. The other members residing in plush Colaba in south Mumbai included politicians, retired army officers and senior bureaucrats and their relatives. They allegedly connived to grab the flats in the building which had come up on one of the most expensive pieces of real estate in the country.

The clean image of the UPA suffered a huge setback after Raja resigned amid allegations of misappropriation of funds during the bidding for the allocation of 2G (second generation) spectrum licences issued to private telecom players at throwaway prices in 2008. The allegation against Raja, who hailed from the UPA ally Dravida Munnettra Kazhagam (DMK), was that he issued telecom licences to eight new operators at throwaway prices. Later, two of these new licensees sold a chunk of their stake to foreign operators and made a neat profit, which accentuated the charges of enriching a select few at the cost of the exchequer. Critics pointed out that had the licence or the spectrum been auctioned to the players the government would have gained substantially, and according to some estimates the gain would have been to the tune of Rs 60,000 crore. The Comptroller and Auditor General (CAG) of India, however, pegged the spectrum scam to Rs 1.76 lakh crore while holding Raja responsible for flouting rules and procedures.

It was not the enormity of the defeat in Bihar but the spotlight on corruption that bothered Sonia Gandhi the most. A day after the Bihar verdict, Sonia was in Anand Bhawan, Allahabad, that had served as the AICC headquarters during the pre-Independence era to mark 125 years of the Indian National Congress. She insisted upon having 'zero tolerance' towards corruption claiming that her party believed in dealing with the menace with a heavy hand. 'Every time any corruption related issue has come to our notice, the Congress-led UPA government has always shown promptness in taking action,' she said adding, 'The Congress has never spared anyone indulging in corrupt practices because we know that corruption is the worst malady facing our nation and is, therefore, also the biggest hurdle in the path of our development.'

For the Congress insiders, Sonia's anxiety was a reflection of her family's difficulties in tiding over the ghost of the Bofors scandal and a series of other similar ones that badly damaged the credibility of the Rajiv Gandhi government. In some ways, Bofors singularly contributed for Rajiv's downfall as it gave an otherwise demoralized and fragmented opposition a sense that together they could humble the Congress which was holding 413 MPs in the 542-member Lok Sabha.

Sonia's own long-term political strategy hinges upon Dr Singh's clean image and good governance plank. By 2014, the Congress, perhaps under a younger leadership, would need to display Dr Singh's tenure as exemplary. On the other hand, a tainted UPA-II may force the party to sit out as it happened during 1996–2003 when the Narasimha Rao regime's numerous acts of omission and commission had a telling affect on the Congress's fortunes.

Politician Sonia is said to be acutely conscious that more than evidence and facts, public perception matters on sensitive issues like corruption in high places. So far, her assessment is that the integrity of the prime minister and the Congress leadership is somewhat intact, but the AICC chief seems to be mindful that public perception is changing and another scandal involving a Congress leader may drastically alter the entire game.

Sonia's discomfort towards corruption was also evident in the manner in which she asked A.K. Antony to man the defence portfolio. In South Block, 'Mr Clean' Antony has a reputation of being status-quoist, a minister who is perpetually wary of catching a cold or clearing any project that may lead to a scandal.

The dual power centre model and coalition dharma also posed its own problems for Sonia. When the UPA was formed in 2004, Sonia had cleverly earmarked a political role for herself as UPA chairperson while the executive role of running the government was assigned to her appointee, Dr Manmohan Singh. But in practice, the Westminster parliamentary democracy model was designed in a manner of functioning as prime ministerial democracy. The prime minister being 'the shining moon among lesser stars' was expected to act swiftly and often secretly as demonstrated by Indira Gandhi on numerous occasions. In the UPA, the decision-making process entails a huge consultation route, calling for meetings between the 'big two' and their set of advisors who often worked at cross-purposes.

For instance, when the enormity of Raja's alleged misdeeds became apparent, the UPA for over six months did virtually nothing. Behind the scenes, an anxious prime minister and his men reportedly tried to gauge DMK supremo M. Karunanidhi's mood. Sonia was brought into the picture when intelligence agencies convinced the prime minister that a major scandal was about to break. The political leadership then reportedly engaged a former chief minister of Punjab to sound out a Governor considered close to the DMK. By the time a reluctant Karunanidhi was made to see reason, the opposition had decided to stall the Parliament session and demand a joint parliamentary probe (JPC).

Apart from the Raja issue, it was an open fact that the prime minister was less than satisfied with some ministers but his mandate is such that Dr Singh does not have the power to sack an erring minister.

The UPA's frequent spat with the Supreme Court was another area of grave concern. Sources close to Sonia wondered why suddenly the apex court had started making stringent and strong remarks against the UPA. Unlike Indira Gandhi's battle against the judiciary over bank nationalization etc., politically, this time around, the Congress was not in a position to strike back.

The grooming of the heir apparent, Rahul Gandhi, is also being done in contrasting fashion. Indira's critics say she had given Sanjay too much power too quickly and, to a lesser extent, to Rajiv too. Rahul's climb has been slow and steady. Before the 2009 elections, he was only an MP with a famous surname who led the party's babalog. He was not made a minister, nor given a disproportionately large role in the party set-up.

Rahul slowly but emphatically proved his worth. The implications of the party's stunning Uttar Pradesh comeback in the 2009 Lok Sabha convinced most in the Congress that the young Gandhi would earn a large reward. But on his part, Rahul kept denying that he was being readied for the prime ministerial role. In the Congress organization, Rahul's presence posed piquant problems for a number of party leaders who had cut their political teeth under Sanjay and Rajiv Gandhi. They lacked rapport with the AICC general secretary. Even an old guard like Pranab Mukherjee went public saying he did not see himself serving under a government that might be headed by Rahul Gandhi.

Rahul's near obsession with inner-party democracy, particularly among the young wings of the party, failed to show any results. Rahul engaged the Foundation for Advanced Management of Elections (FAME), a NGO run by former election commissioner J.M. Lyngdoh and K.J. Rao. Lyngdoh and Rao specialized in conducting 'free and fair' polls. Amid stiff opposition from the Congress, Rahul assigned FAME the task of streamlining the organizational polls in the Indian Youth Congress and the National Students Union of India (NSUI). He also gave an undertaking to the image-conscious Lyngdoh and Rao that no person having a criminal record will be allowed to contest the party elections. More significantly, Rahul agreed that all disputes relating to organizational polls would be settled by FAME and not by the party. This was a drastic measure considering the big wigs always fancied having influence over the NSUI and Youth Congress.

FAME began well by conducting polls for the Youth Congress and NSUI in Punjab, Delhi, Uttrakhand and other states in a rather transparent manner, but senior Congress leaders and regional party satraps were far from pleased. Party leaders who did not come out in the open against FAME lamented the former bureaucrats' tendency to target close relatives of established party leaders. Moreover, the allegation was that these election officials focused on 'free and fair' polls ignoring other critical elements in politics such as caste considerations, the ability to win in assembly Lok Sabha polls and factional balance among regional satraps. For instance, in Chhattisgarh, it debarred Amit Jogi, the son of former state chief minister Ajit Jogi, from contesting as Youth Congress chief on grounds of his 'tainted image'. Amit too did hot help his cause when he got a membership form carrying Rahul, Sonia and Ajit Jogi's photographs.

Working on its limited mandate, FAME also failed to develop a culture of constructive dissent. The losers in the party posts failed to figure anywhere. This was in sharp contrast to established norms in politics. For instance, Hillary Clinton fought a close contest against Barack Obama during the Democratic Party presidential primaries, but when Obama became the forty-fourth President of the United States, he assigned Hillary the most important assignment of the US Secretary of State (equivalent of a foreign minister).

In spite of these problems and the rout in Bihar assembly polls where the Congress nominees forfeited deposits in over 200 out of the 243 seats, Rahul continued to be viewed as a prime ministerial candidate. Even the Chinese political establishment envisaged great interest in him. When Rahul visited China in 2007, the otherwise aloof Chinese went an extra mile to welcome him. The Chinese establishment viewed Rahul as the 'princeling' who is tipped to take up a future leadership position in India. The spotlight on Rahul was so bright that some leading communist leaders succeeded in convincing Rahul, and in turn Sonia, that instead of viewing itself as an Asian counterweight to China, India should cooperate rather than compete with China.

At his 12, Tuglaq Road, residence, Rahul mostly wears kurta–pyjama during his meetings with Congress workers but in the evening, he is often seen in jeans and T-shirts. The visitors at his residence are greeted with a notice board stating two rules:

1. No autograph.
2. Do not touch feet.

Rahul's political ascendancy made the BJP and other opponents remark that Sonia's act of renunciation is a clever ploy to keep the seat warm for Rahul, run the Manmohan Singh regime by 'remote control' and reward loyalty at all levels. Such a theory, however plausible, is seriously flawed. As in any other sphere, politics is too complex a field, filled with too many imponderables at work to be guided by a script. One needs only to take a closer look at Sonia's life to confirm it.

ONE

A LONG JOURNEY FROM ORBASSANO

Sonia was born on 9 December 1946 in Orbassano, in northern Italy. For the family, Sonia, the second daughter, was a little princess, their Cenerentola, or Cinderella. The nickname was not entirely fortuitous. Unlike her sisters, Nadia and Anushka, Sonia always wanted to be different. She was ambitious, though she confided little about her ambitions. As a young girl she was never comfortable in the dusty industrial town on the outskirts of Turin where she grew up. When Sonia lived in Orbassano, the town was a muddle of apartment blocks and houses that had come up in the early 1950s as a result of the post-war boom in northern Italy. It was too undemanding and lower middle class for a Cenerentola.

She was a good student but not an exceptional one, except in her gift for languages. She could converse easily in Spanish and Russian. She would also develop fluency in French. Nowadays she is at ease in Hindi too and reads her speeches from texts in the Devanagari script.

The credit for teaching her Russian goes to her father, Stephano, who had fought in Russia with the Germans. He was captured and detained in the towns of Vladimir and Suzdal as a prisoner of war for several years till three Russian women—Nadia, Anushka and Sonia—helped him escape. A grateful Stephano gave these Russian names to his three daughters. Stephano—or Eugenio, as he liked to be called—

remained steeped in memories of Russia, its language, culture and food till his death in 1988.

Stephano was hard-working and disciplined, qualities he passed on to his family, especially Sonia. As a self-made man who had been through some very tough times, he took pride in providing for his family. He had come to Orbassano from Asiago in the Veneto region as a poor mason and made good in a small construction business through his dedication and fair dealing.

Stephano brought up his daughters in the traditional Catholic way and was wary of foreigners. He was not charmed when Sonia informed him about tying the knot with the Indian prime minister's son. His inflexibility on this count estranged him from Sonia, so much so that he did not attend Sonia's marriage and predicted that it would end shortly. Sonia's maternal uncle, Mario Predebon, gave away the girl in the civil marriage that took place on 25 February 1968.

However, Sonia's defiance did not result in a complete breakdown in father–daughter relations. Stephano became extremely fond of Rajiv when he visited Orbassano, but Rajiv's entry in politics in 1981–82 again made the old man worried. Stephano never visited India, but he was well versed with the political situation here and worried about religious intolerance. His friends in Orbassano claimed that Stephano, who often shared his fear of fanatics harming his daughter, would never have approved of Sonia's entry into politics.

His forceful and rather strict side often placed him at odds with his family, resulting in frequent quarrels between husband and wife. The quarrels drew Sonia closer to her mother, Paola.

By Sonia's own admission, she was a naughty and 'very active' girl in her early life. She would play hopscotch for hours or join the neighbourhood boys in a game of football. She wanted to be a teacher, but Paola wanted her to pick a more paying profession.

Josto Maffeo, one of her early boyfriends, recalls her as one with a fiery temper. He can remember occasions when she hit him with her thick Italian–Russian–German dictionary. Maffeo, a journalist with a Spanish daily, was unwilling to say anything further about Sonia.

This reluctance is in common with others in Orbassano who know the family.

When a group of Indian journalists visited the town in 1998, one neighbour, who claimed to have studied with Sonia, described her as a 'nice person' but one who was aware of her 'social superiority'. According to her, after finishing school, Sonia went to a more fashionable college, the Convent of Maria Ausiliatrice in Giaveno, fifteen kilometres away.

Sister Domenica, who was an assistant when Sonia studied at the convent, remembers her well. According to her, Sonia was lively though not over-exuberant, and she studied just enough to get by. Her colleague, Sister Anna Maria, recalled Sonia's visit during a school reunion. Dinner was being served when she suddenly announced she had to leave. She said that she had a special guest coming to dinner—the son of Indira Gandhi. 'She was always a little manipulative. She should do well in politics,' said Sister Anna Maria, while speaking to *Frontline* correspondent Vaiju Naravane in 1998.

Family friends said that by early 1965 Stephano had made enough money to fund his daughter's education in Cambridge. Locals recall that the real change in the living standard of the Maino family came in the 1980s, a period which also marked the emergence of Rajiv Gandhi on the Indian political scene. Some Italian businessmen attributed Maino's success to the 1980s' boom in the construction industry, but in India exaggerated reports about the Maino family's fortunes were viewed with suspicion.

Nehru–Gandhi family friend Mohammad Yunus, a journalist and administrator, was among the handful of persons from Rajiv Gandhi's side who visited the Maino house, a neat double-storey at Number 14 Via Bellini, in a neighbourhood inhabited mainly by people in the construction trade. He said, 'I can say without fear of contradiction that they are a decent middle-class family. The stories about their fabulous home and millions gained through their India link can be termed as sheer nonsense.'

Sonia's sister Anushka and niece Aruna run an antique shop called Etnica two kilometres away from Orbassano at a commercial complex in Gerbola di Rivolta. The shop contains artefacts from India such as Pichwais, Tanjore paintings, silver pieces from Bikaner and expensive shawls.

Etnica served as the basis of the campaign against Sonia by her detractor Dr Subramanian Swamy, who accused her of smuggling Indian artefacts. He followed up his charges with a slew of letters to the prime minister, the home minister, the Enforcement Directorate, the Central Bureau of Investigation (CBI) and other investigative agencies, besides filing several petitions in the Delhi High Court. The court issued notices to the central government and concerned agencies, and proceedings continue. The Congress is dismissive of the charges, saying they are not worth the paper they are written on. 'You know what Swamy is . . .' commented a party spokesman, referring to Swamy's reputation as a maverick politician who in his career has traversed almost the entire political spectrum, as also his fierce friendships and relentless enmities.

Congress leaders said that Swamy failed to understand two things. First, during the time of Indira Gandhi, Sonia was a member of the prime minister's gift committee and was asked to select gift items to be given to visiting foreign dignitaries. Secondly, Sonia is herself a connoisseur of art having done an art appreciation and restoration course. She is a collector of miniature Tanjore paintings and artefacts from different states. Her friend and interior designer Sunita Kohli said, 'She has taste as also extensive knowledge of Indian arts, crafts and textiles. She is easily able to identify the designs of most Indian weaves.'

Vaiju Naravane admitted that the presence of the shop on the outskirts of Orbassano continued to nibble at her consciousness like a buzzing bee refusing to go away. She found its location incongruous. A shop like this would do well in Rome or Milan. But Orbassano? 'It's like setting up an expensive store selling Swedish furniture on the outskirts of Faizabad!' she said, drawing a comparison with a small, dusty town east of Delhi.

Other aspects of Sonia's past have been questioned too. Her detractors led by Swamy alleged that the Lennox Cook School, where

Sonia studied English in 1965, was a KGB outfit, which closed shop soon after she left Cambridge. The authorities at Cambridge strongly refute the charge. By official accounts, the school was founded in 1961 by John Lennox Cook, a former senior tutor at the Bell School, Cambridge. Cook retired in 1985 after turning the institute into a great success, and it was then taken over by Anglo World Education Ltd, which runs a chain of such schools worldwide.

In Cambridge, Sonia stayed as a paying guest with an English family. She was homesick, and her unfamiliarity with the language didn't help. It was a difficult time for her. As she recounts in *Rajiv*, she used to feel miserable and homesick.

Her search for Italian food led her to Varsity, a Greek restaurant, the next-best option as she failed to find an Italian one, and to her introduction to Rajiv Gandhi. Each evening, noisy groups of students from Cambridge University would gather there over a pint. For Sonia, one of the boys in that large group always stood out. She described him as 'One with big, black eyes and wonderfully innocent and disarming smile'.

Rajiv made the first move using a common friend, Christian, who played the go-between. He was a German who was also doing the language course and, luckily, fluent in Italian. One day at lunchtime, he introduced Rajiv to Sonia, who recalls, 'Our eyes met for the first time directly at a close distance. I could hear my heart pounding. As far as I was concerned, it was love at first sight. He later told me that it was for him too.'

According to Tahir Jahangir who was sitting with Rajiv at the time, when she passed from their table, all conversation halted. 'Soon the conversation resumed but I noticed that Rajiv was lost in thought, and did not participate. He had a dazed expression on his face. He got hold of a paper napkin and a biro and carefully began to write out a poem on the napkin. He then called Charles Antoni, the tall, handsome owner of Varsity, over and asked him to get the best bottle of wine Varsity had. Rajiv then requested Charles to personally go up to the girls, present the bottle of wine, pour it out, and then give the napkin with the poem to the girl who had been introduced as Sonia Maino, and to top it all belt out an Aria!'

When Rajiv Gandhi became prime minister of India, Charles came to India to spend a week. He flew to Delhi at his own expense but when he reached Delhi airport, he was detained. Charles was not carrying a valid Indian visa. When he was asked he said he was not aware that a friend of the Gandhis would require a visa. The airport authorities did not take him seriously but he was allowed to make one telephone call. Within half an hour, half a dozen official Ambassador cars arrived and Charles left the airport for Race Course Road, sipping Thums Up at the back seat of one of the cars! Thereafter, he was looked after by his hosts, spending a magnificent weekend in Tropical Island in the Indian Ocean, and the rest of the week sightseeing in Delhi and Agra.

Life in Cambridge was easy and fun-filled. Rajiv shared an apartment at 28, Derwent Close with Arun Singh, Deep Kaul (son of former diplomat T.N. Kaul), Pakistani national Mehmood and Anderson (who runs a successful publishing business in Amsterdam and London these days). The roommates contributed money to buy a beat-up Beatles Volkswagen. Robin Sarin, Rajiv's contemporary in Cambridge, recalls that the car would often break down and Rajiv would fix it. 'He loved looking inside the engine and seemed to know everything about it,' Sarin remembers, adding that even now it seems like it was just the other day when Rajiv was seen happily moving about in Cambridge.

Sonia's host in Cambridge was from her native country, a fifty-year-old Italian woman called Patina who lived with her boyfriend Saleem, and owned several bed-and-breakfast houses for students. Sonia was put up at Patina's property at 59, Tennyson Row near the station. Sonia also stayed for a short duration at 65, Lensfield Road next to a pub called Spread Eagle.

At Cambridge, Rajiv and Sonia frequently went to movies in the three cinema theatres. The first movie they saw together was Satyajit Ray's *Pather Panchali*. Rajiv often took Sonia out to the river Cam, punting for hours, or to the riverside county famous for its tea. The duo was fond of dancing but shared a dislike for alcoholic beverages. Deeply in love, Rajiv promised to take her to the Taj Mahal but much to his surprise Sonia knew little about the great monument of love. He narrated the history of the Taj, explaining how Emperor Shah Jahan built the incomparable monument to his beloved wife Mumtaz Mahal as a token of their inseparable love.

Funnily, for quite a while, Sonia had only a hazy idea of Rajiv's political link, the primacy that the Gandhis enjoyed in India. Only when a friend of Sonia showed her a photograph of the visiting Indian prime minister, did Sonia realize that the Gandhis were the number one political family in India.

A year later, Rajiv visited the Maino house in Orbassano. The prime minister's son spent the day visiting the Orbassano city centre. Late in the evening when he met Stephano, he came straight to the point by asking for Sonia's hand. Stephano was stunned. Though suspicious of foreigners, Stephano had no doubts about Rajiv's determination to marry his daughter. He made known his apprehensions about his daughter getting used to life in India. He then told Rajiv and Sonia not to meet for a year and then see if they still wanted to spend the rest of their life together.

The year-long forced separation was the most difficult period for both Rajiv and Sonia, but a year later, they were even more deeply in love. A man of his word, Stephano had no choice but to accept the inevitable. The old man's pride, however, came in the way of his attending the marriage.

Indira Gandhi's approach was different. Rajiv wrote regularly to her and told her about Sonia. She agreed to meet her in London where she was going to inaugurate an exhibition on Jawaharlal Nehru. Sonia was extremely nervous. The meeting at India House failed to take place as on the way there Sonia completely lost her confidence. Rajiv and Indira were understanding. The meeting was rescheduled at the residence of the Indian high commissioner. Sensing that Sonia was uncomfortable, Indira spoke to her in French, in which Sonia was much more at ease. Recalling the meeting, Sonia wrote, 'She spoke to me in French, knowing I was more fluent in it than English. She wanted to know about myself, my studies. She told me that I need not be frightened because she herself had been young, extremely shy, and in love, and she understood perfectly.' Small gestures such as this from Indira gave Sonia the confidence that she could be a daughter-in-law in the distinguished family.

Sonia arrived in Delhi on 13 January 1968. She and Rajiv got engaged in a simple ceremony twelve days later. As the prospective 'bahu' (daughter-in-law) of the Nehru–Gandhi family, Indira Gandhi did not want her to stay with them and staying at a hotel was out of the question. Her aide and confidant T.N. Kaul and family friend Mohammad Yunus suggested that Teji Bachchan play host to the bride, and the matter was resolved. The proposal found immediate approval from Rajiv, Sanjay, Amitabh and Ajitabh Bachchan. Amitabh, yet to become a superstar, was Sonia's first friend in India.

The marriage took place on 25 February 1968 on the back lawns of 1 Safdarjung Road after a brief mehendi ceremony at the Bachchans'. The civil marriage was a simple affair. Rajiv wore a cream silk Patiala achkan and chooridars with a pink Bharatpuri turban while Sonia wore a pale pink khadi sari without much jewellery. In keeping with Kashmiri traditions, Sonia wore floral jewellery—jasmine garlands tied on her ankles, wrists and neck. Sanjay, like Rajiv's cousins, wore a pink turban and cream-coloured achkan. There was only light refreshment at the wedding. In the evening, however, there was a lavish dinner at Hyderabad House, off India Gate, where official banquets are held, to which about two hundred and fifty guests were invited. The guests were seated on the floor and served a sumptuous Kashmiri banquet. A day later, Indira hosted a reception at the Ashok Hotel at which choice Parsi, Kashmiri and Italian cuisines were served to the one thousand invitees.

Sonia became pregnant in 1969 but suffered a miscarriage. She held Indira responsible for it, blaming her obsession with fitness and yoga. Sonia, as family sources said, had no problems with learning yoga from Swami Dhirendra Brahmachari and others, but she was not too comfortable with it during her first pregnancy.

The acrimony ended when Rahul was born in June 1970. According to Sonia, during that period Indira became her 'real mother' taking 'exemplary care' of her. Sonia seldom had problems with Indira, despite the latter's imposing personality. As she told Eric Silver of the Guardian News Service in 1986, 'My upbringing is such that I feel my husband is superior and his mother even more superior.' Sonia also told a visiting Italian magazine correspondent that Indira Gandhi was as affectionate as a real mother. 'Living with her was a wonderful experience,' Sonia said, adding that she could never forget Indira's small note to her soon after her marriage when her mother left for Italy. 'I was feeling lonely and depressed. As soon as I returned from the airport, I got her note. It said: "Just to say hello and to tell you that we all love you."'

However, after her mother left soon after the wedding, Sonia felt lonely and depressed. Though she loved Rajiv dearly, there were too many adjustments that she had to make as Indira's daughter-in-law. By Sonia's own admission, she had difficulty coping with the piercing eyes she confronted each time she stepped out of the house. She also had problems in adjusting to Indian conditions. Initially, she did not like Indian food or Indian clothes, but Indira and Rajiv did not force anything on her except for one thing—speaking in Hindi at the dinner table, a custom everyone had to follow. Slowly, Sonia began liking Indian food. Nowadays, pasta, lasagna and spaghetti are rarely cooked at 10 Janpath.

Usha Bhagat, Pupul Jayakar and Mohsina Kidwai, close associates of Indira, recall how the otherwise formidable Indira became dependent on Sonia in all matters pertaining to the household. Bhagat and Jayakar have often spoken of the importance Sonia gave them, telling them that she was blessed with three mothers-in-law who adored her.

On her part, Sonia seemed to have understood her mother-in-law early. Her upbringing in Italy came handy as she was brought up in a close-knit and conservative environment where family values were accorded top priority. Indira was deeply moved by Sonia's simplicity, retiring demeanour and reticent nature. The mother-in-law never found Sonia to be possessive about Rajiv. Sonia helped her in selecting saris, picking gifts for visiting dignitaries and looking after personal guests in the prime minister's residence. Indira was particularly delighted by Sonia's selection of an ankle-length coat made of quilted Rajasthani fabric that the Indian prime minister wore for the opening of the festival of India in London. Indira's friends recall how she praised Sonia for picking a golden sari with a Kashmiri-embroidered border for the opening of the Commonwealth group of ministers' meeting in Delhi.

Commenting on her perception of relations with in-laws, Sonia told interviewer Pushpa Bharti, 'A lot of my friends have problems with their respective mothers-in-law. But I never had any such problem because my upbringing was totally different. Since childhood, I had been told that my husband would be superior to me and my mother-in-law, being his mother, would be so much superior.' Articulating further, Sonia commented, 'A man is the object of his mother's love for 25–26 years. You cannot expect him to switch all his love to you suddenly. It just would not be right. You should also extend some understanding towards your mother-in-law; you cannot expect her to change overnight. If she is possessive about her son, you must give time to adjust. During this period of adjustment, if you stand by her and extend your support, your relationship will never flounder . . . Mummy [Indira] and I were always very close. I was always understanding and she always showered me with love.'

Indira too did not have any problems getting along with Sonia. She repeatedly told close associates like Pupul Jayakar, Mohammad Yunus, Mohsina Kidwai and others how comfortable she was with Sonia. She used to say, 'It is amazing to know how easygoing Sonia is. Somehow she gets to know what I want. The beauty of it is that I do not have to tell her about these things.' She may have been referring to the change in Sonia's style of dress after Rajiv entered politics. Sonia discarded jeans and skirts in 1981, opting for saris and salwar kameez, a gesture that Indira Gandhi appreciated.

Sonia and Sanjay also used to get along very well. Rajiv, Amitabh, Ajitabh, Sonia and Sanjay would go out for drives, movies or have ice cream on the India Gate lawns. When Sonia was pregnant with Rahul, and Rajiv was away on flights, Sanjay was extremely caring, sitting with her at mealtimes and keeping her entertained with his talk.

On 20 June 1975 Sonia Gandhi had her first brush with politics, coming face to face with a crowd of about 100,000 people at Delhi's Boat Club. It was eight days after the famous Allahabad High Court verdict setting aside Indira's election from Rae Bareli. Sanjay, who was chief organizer of the solidarity rally, broached the subject of the entire family attending it. 'We must all be seen together,' he argued. Both Sonia and Rajiv felt awkward but agreed to go along. Sonia wore a khadi sari and stood next to Rajiv, Maneka and Sanjay on the stage, behind Indira. While Maneka was thrilled, enjoying every bit, Sonia could not muster the courage even to wave at the crowd. She was amazed at how Indira could mesmerize a crowd as she recalled the services of the Nehru–Gandhi family and vowed to continue to serve the people till her last breath.

Later, after the lifting of the Emergency and the election defeat in 1977, Rajiv and Sanjay began having bitter fights. Somehow Rajiv was convinced that Sanjay was responsible for the downfall of 'Mummy'. Rajiv had all along disliked Sanjay's extra-constitutional authority. During the Emergency, one day as he was returning from Bombay, he was stopped and diverted because of a VIP movement. The VIP turned out to be his younger brother. Rajiv's companions asked, 'Younger brother is going; elder brother is diverted to a lane. How do you like it?' Rajiv was quick to reply, 'That's politics.'

For many family friends of the Gandhis, in a sense, however, the process of political orientation for Rajiv and Sonia had already begun once they moved to Indira's house. Much as they disliked the world of politics, they were already being sucked into it. According to them it was Sonia's love for Rajiv that brought her to India. It was her love for Rajiv that allowed Rajiv to join politics in 1980 realizing that Rajiv had to fulfil his duties towards his mother. In 1984, it was because of her love for Rajiv that she let him become prime minister much against her wishes because she felt he had a duty to perform. Years later, in 1997–98, she was drawn into politics as she could not see the disintegration of the party Rajiv adored.

The period following the Emergency was extremely tough for the Gandhis. Out of power and facing a battery of allegations, Indira had to move out of her Safdarjung Road residence to a much smaller and modest 12 Willingdon Crescent. It was in this smaller house that Sonia really became close to Indira. Family friend Mohammad Yunus recalled receiving small notes from Indira saying, 'Rajiv and Sonia have been extremely helpful and supportive. God bless them all.' Sonia and Rajiv tried to move in Delhi's social circles to defend their family but wherever they visited, they were faced with hostility.

The hardship ended when Indira stormed back to power in January 1980. Indira was back as prime minister and the family moved to 1 Safdarjung Road. Destiny took a tragic turn on 23 June 1980 when Sanjay, flying a Pitts S-2A two-seater, crashed into a tree barely twenty-five metres from Willingdon Crescent. Sonia and Rajiv were in Italy on a holiday. The then foreign secretary Romesh Bhandari contacted them and industrialist Swraj Paul sent a special plane to fetch them.

In Sanjay, Sonia not only lost a close relative but a friend too. Sonia always viewed Sanjay as a gentle, sensitive family man who had an eye for detail and perfection. According to her, the media's portrayal of him as a haughty and ruthless person was scripted by his political opponents. Even today, Sonia and her family are extremely fond of Sanjay's son Varun. While Varun calls her 'Sonia chachi', Sonia always addresses him as 'Varun darling'.

The sudden and tragic demise of Sanjay had important political repercussions. He was Indira's political heir and indispensable political adviser. Indira suddenly grew old and restless. As Sonia observed, 'For my mother-in-law, it was a devastating blow. She had lost not only a beloved son but her most trusted aide.' Sonia's relationship with her mother-in-law changed as Sanjay's untimely death was followed by some unfortunate partings in the family. The then prime minister was also worked up over the bitterness with Maneka Gandhi that followed. The grandmother missed spending time with toddler Varun.

This was something that often upset Indira so much that she would get up in the middle of the night and start walking in the lawns rather aimlessly.

Pupul Jayakar and Mohsina Kidwai felt that Indira started looking upon Sonia more as a daughter than a daughter-in-law. If Indira had a headache, Sonia would prepare chamomile tea. She would bring a hot tub of water to soak Indira's aching feet each time the prime minister returned from a long tour.

Sonia understood Indira's need for Rajiv. Both Sonia and Rajiv may have never envisaged a political role but they realized that Indira needed her son. Sonia sacrificed her strong views for the love of Rajiv and Indira. In June 1981, Rajiv won the by-election from Amethi, accepting a political commitment that left very little time for his family and passions like flying, pets and photography.

Short of quality time, Rajiv kept writing to Sonia. In one letter he said, 'Like Hindu traditions say, a man is only half a person and his wife makes up for the other half. I feel exactly like that. I know that without you I would find it very difficult . . . even more so now that I am in politics.' Cine actor Amitabh Bachchan, who was a close buddy of Rajiv and enjoyed an excellent rapport with Sonia then, too observed, 'I know that his [Rajiv] family meant a lot to him. He was a devoted husband and a devoted father. One of the biggest regrets that remained with Rajiv was that he was not able to devote enough time to his family. But I think his family understood the enormous task he had taken upon himself. They cooperated. And also when he was with the family, he was hundred per cent with the family.'

Interestingly, the moment Rajiv joined politics, Sonia's sartorial taste transformed. Gone were the days of T-shirts, jeans, long skirts or Western suits. Careful about her appearance in public life, Sonia began wearing chic salwar suits, printed cotton saris, handloom saris, kurtas and other traditional Indian outfits.

Indira was quick to spot the change. One day she asked Sonia if someone had spoken to her about what she should wear. Sonia smiled and said nobody had. Indira went on to add that even if anyone suggested such a thing, she should feel 'free and comfortable' in whatever she wore. Sonia, however, remained firm in voluntarily discarding Western outfits. The mother-in-law told a personal friend, 'It is amazing . . . the ease with which she adapts herself. Look at her! Now she has an aura that was not there before. I suppose that comes when you are no longer just married to an individual but to the family, values, society and country.'

This period also marked Sonia's becoming a little aloof with her circle of friends. She curtailed her outings and dinners with a view to preventing people from approaching her. This was necessary because Rajiv had become general secretary of the AICC and was getting a hang of everything related to politics. Under Indira's close supervision, he was given a suite at 1 Safdarjung Road. Rajiv was provided with a private secretary, V. George, and associates Vijay Dhar and Arun Singh. Dhar's father D.P. Dhar had been in Indira Gandhi's inner circle of advisers. Rajiv's office used to be an alternative durbar where regional satraps, warring ministers, industrialists, scientists and senior bureaucrats made a beeline.

Sonia's move to control access to her was significant because everyone was trying to get close to Rajiv, often with personal and selfish motives. On hindsight, Sonia's apprehensions proved true when Rajiv Gandhi became prime minister and got embroiled in one controversy after another thanks to the naivety of people in his close circle who turned out to be mere fair weather friends.

A TALE OF TWO BAHUS

At first Sanjay's marriage with Maneka in March 1974 did not bring about much change in Indira's household. There were occasional tantrums, but both Indira and Sonia were sympathetic towards Maneka, young as she was. As in a typical Indian family, as the elder bahu, Sonia had a special place. She was responsible for running the kitchen and deciding the menu. Maneka had little interest in the kitchen, so there were no clashes on that count, but she enjoyed helping Indira getting quotations for her speeches. After the Emergency, in 1977, when Indira was out of power and under attack from the Janata government, she managed *Surya* magazine and used it as a tool to run down Indira's opponents. Maneka proved a staunch defender of the family's interests and, through the magazine, gave back as good as Indira received, running a series of exposés that did immense damage to those who were arrayed against Indira.

Occasionally there were big fights inside Indira's house. On one occasion, Maneka got so angry with Sanjay that she removed her wedding ring and threw it at him. Indira lost her temper too, as the ring had belonged to her mother, Kamala Nehru. Sonia picked up the ring and said she would keep it for Priyanka. These days, Priyanka wears it.

The ring, inset with diamonds and other precious stones, twenty-one exquisite saris, two sets of gold jewellery and a khadi sari made of yarn spun by Jawaharlal Nehru in jail were Indira's gifts to Maneka when she married Sanjay.

Another big fight was witnessed by B.K. Nehru when Sanjay threw a fit at Sonia because an egg was not properly fried. According to Nehru, Indira did not reprimand Sanjay, but she appeared acutely embarrassed by Sanjay's conduct. In his memoir *Nice Guys Finish Second*, Nehru described the scene at Indira's 12 Willingdon Crescent house: 'More often than not, there was servant trouble. Sonia was the cook, Maneka merely ate. Indira's two sons and their wives were certainly not on the best terms with each other.'

Journalist and author Khushwant Singh too recalls that Rajiv and Sanjay had their differences. 'Once I happened to be there when Rajiv and Sonia were celebrating one of their children's birthdays. I noticed that the two brothers and their wives occupied different ends of the house and had very little to do with each other.'

Both Rajiv and Sonia had not liked the imposition of the Emergency, but they chose to remain silent. At one party during this time, Sonia met Naveen Patnaik, son of Biju Patnaik, the towering Orissa politician and head of the regional Utkal Congress (currently known as Biju Janata Dal and headed by Naveen) who was jailed in the round-up of Opposition leaders. Sonia had no hesitation in sympathizing with Biju's son: 'It must be terrible for you that your father is in jail. I am sorry about it.'

Friends of Indira said her two bahus were completely different since they came from diverse backgrounds. Sonia had been taught not to raise her voice or show dissent; Maneka was more outspoken. Maneka hardly measured her words before speaking. The Gandhi–Anand households were never at ease except during the Emergency when Maneka's mother, Amteshwar Anand, became a close companion of Indira.

Maneka and Sanjay used to have the usual family arguments over minor things like food, but many times they were witnessed by the entire family. Exaggerated accounts were later given to show Maneka as irresponsible, but sources close to Sonia maintained that at least in the first few years, the family had adjusted and they had a good time.

Maneka had a keen interest in politics, a fact she never tried to hide. Yet over the years, Indira started trusting Sonia more, seeking her advice on everything from the choice of menu to her selection of saris. She also valued Sonia's aloofness towards politics and matters of statecraft.

Sonia got along well with Sanjay except when he appointed her as a director in Maruti Technical Services (MTS), a dubious subsidiary of Maruti. Sonia signed on the dotted line entitling her to a monthly salary, 1 per cent commission on net profits, house and travel expenses, car, driver, etc. However, none of these perks was directly passed on to her. Sonia was unaware of the larger, legal dimensions but when Rajiv came to know that MTS was posing as a consultancy service and had taken ten lakh rupees from Maruti, which was struggling to survive in spite of generous contributions from public sector banks, he was livid. Angrily, he asked Sonia, 'How could you do this?'

A commission of inquiry headed by Justice A.C. Gupta probed the issue and submitted its report in 1978 during the Janata Party regime. The commission concluded, '[I]t is a fact known to all concerned that Shrimati Sonia Gandhi was a foreign national. In view of the provisions of the Foreign Exchange Regulation Act of 1973, which had come into force on 1 January 1974, she could neither hold shares of any Indian company nor hold any office of profit in such company from the date the act came into force without the prior approval of the Reserve Bank of India. Ultimately, she tendered her resignation on 21 January 1975.'

The issue resurfaced when Rajiv took over as prime minister. Rajiv, refuting the charge, made it clear that his wife never drew a monthly salary of Rs 2500 or visited the Maruti office or factory.

After her defeat in the elections of 1977, Indira was forced to vacate the prime minister's house and move to 12 Willingdon Crescent with her daughters-in-law, grandchildren, attendants and dogs. These were difficult times for the family. The family cook died in a road accident in Allahabad and Indira was too scared to pick a new one. According to Pupul Jayakar, Indira feared that her detractors would send a spy masquerading as a cook or use him to poison her and her family.

During these trying times, Sonia took over, cooking for months till a replacement was found. She was seen frequently at Delhi's Khan Market, a shopping area favoured by diplomats and bureaucrats, picking vegetables, meat and grocery items. At the back garden of Willingdon Crescent, Sonia started growing several vegetables like broccoli, palak, bhindi, lauki, dhaniya, mirchi, niboo, etc. She personally chose the seeds and monitored growth. When the fresh vegetables made their way to the dinner table, Sanjay lavishly praised her, describing her as a 'model bahu' of Indira.

Indira, facing challenges from various quarters, also would not leave an opportunity to praise Sonia. This upset Maneka, who was also trying to help out her mother-in-law with the feisty *Surya* magazine, among other things. Maneka wondered why Sonia was treated as special just because she could buy groceries and cook.

Indira's family friends attribute a number of factors to Indira's preference for Sonia over Maneka. 'In many ways, she was much more Indian than an average Indian girl,' Mohsina Kidwai recalled. 'Indiraji always admired her for her good eye for handicrafts, handloom and antiques. She shortlisted and selected menu for dinners. When the Frontier Gandhi, Khan Abdul Ghaffar Khan, visited India in connection with the Gandhi centenary celebrations, Sonia was Indiraji's personal emissary looking after his one meal a day, food, etc.'

Indira's return to Parliament in 1978 from the Chikmagalur parliamentary seat in southern Karnataka—where she won by a massive margin—marked a turning point. Incidentally, the seat was vacated by H.D. Deve Gowda, who later would head a rag-tag coalition as prime minister in 1996–97. The Chikmagalur victory restored the confidence of the family. For both Sonia and Maneka, life at 12 Willingdon Crescent was a lively experience of an Indian joint family with its share of skirmishes and happy moments. Maneka and Sonia temporarily became friends when Maneka was expecting Feroze Varun. The elder sister-in-law took care of her food, giving her vital tips and spending a lot of time with her until the baby was born in March 1980.

Maneka was very fond of 12 Willingdon Crescent. It was here that she began to fully understand Sanjay and what he was trying to accomplish. The man was in a hurry to transform India into a modern nation state. Maneka was convinced that Sanjay was grossly misunderstood. A lot of the mess that was created by Congresswallahs during the Emergency was quietly passed on to Sanjay, she felt. Likewise, the media, suffering from Emergency excesses, held him accountable for crimes that he had not committed, as she expressed repeatedly in interviews.

Maneka's attachment to 12 Willingdon Crescent was so intense that she made an attempt to move in there in 2001 as a minister in the Vajpayee government. The government forced a private trust headed by Sonia in memory of Sanjay to move out of the government premises that it had been occupying for more than a decade. Maneka, who had little or no sympathy for the trust for its open association with Sonia and the Congress, made no efforts to stall the eviction. Instead she made a bid to wangle the ministerial bungalow on grounds of her emotional links with the house. But the house was already taken over by one E. Punnuswamy, a Pattali Makkal Katchi (PMK) MP from Tamil Nadu, who bluntly refused to move out. Maneka was disappointed, especially with the urban development minister, Jagmohan, who ignored her plea. The office-bearers of the Sanjay Gandhi Memorial Trust blamed her for inaction and belittlement of Sanjay's memory. 'As [a] Union minister in [the government], she should have resisted. It was one among a few institutions in memory of Sanjay,' said Captain Parveen Davar, secretary of the trust. Maneka's camp denied the charge, saying she had no sympathy with a trust that had become a dumping ground for out-of-work Congress politicians. The trust was finally shifted to a small room at 24 Akbar Road.

Sonia and Rajiv were away in Italy when Sanjay died in an air crash while practising loops in his Pitts S-2A aircraft over Safdarjung Airport on 23 June 1980. The chartered flight arranged by Swraj Paul to fetch them picked up Maneka's mother, Amteshwar, sister Ambika, and Congress leader V.C. Shukla from London on the way to India. Shukla and Paul kept telling Amteshwar that she should try to keep the two families together and rally round Rajiv. Amteshwar was too grieved to apply her mind to this aspect. However, within days the Anand family, which had risen from being a decidedly middle-class army family to one with political clout during the Sanjay era, began to be viewed with suspicion and distrust. A section of Congress leaders who had suffered during the Sanjay era began a campaign saying that the Anand family wanted Indira to draft Maneka into politics. The whisper campaign had its impact.

In any case, Sanjay's death had changed everything. Indira was a broken person. Sometimes she would hold herself responsible for Sanjay's death; sometimes she would blame the young widow. In her wavering mood, she began putting pressure on Rajiv to give up flying completely, fearing for his life. Rajiv was in no mood to oblige his mother, but he agreed to take leave to be at her side.

Word was soon out that Rajiv would emerge as Sanjay's successor. It came as a rude shock to Maneka, as Indira had promised to make her her personal secretary. Maneka wondered how Indira could draft a political novice like Rajiv. After all, on numerous occasions Indira herself had described Rajiv as an apolitical person.

Indira's close circle, ranging from Pupul Jayakar, Dhirendra Brahmachari and R.K. Dhawan to writer Khushwant Singh, was sharply divided on the issue of Sanjay's successor. Some media persons who had easy access to Indira and Maneka's family began lobbying for a political role for Maneka. Indira was undecided.

Sonia opposed Maneka's entry. Although she was not keen for Rajiv to become a political player, she viewed Maneka as an unpredictable and ambitious person. According to Pupul Jayakar, 'At first Indira understood Maneka's despair. She was anxious to find something that would occupy Maneka's time and in a compassionate gesture to the young widow, suggested to Maneka to become her secretary and travel with her. This upset Sonia. Letters were exchanged between Sonia and Indira, and Indira, realizing the need for Rajiv and family, withdrew the offer.'

Sonia may have blocked Maneka's entry into politics, but she was equally opposed to Rajiv stepping into Sanjay's shoes. At one juncture, she even threatened to walk out of his life if he were to join politics.

Sonia recalls that she 'fought like a tigress' for the sake of Rajiv and the children but most of all for 'our freedom—that simple human right that we had so carefully and consistently preserved'.

Sonia, however, slowly gave in, realizing that both Rajiv and Indira needed each other in the political arena. 'I understood Rajiv's duty to her. At the same time, I was angry and resentful towards a system, which, as I saw it, demanded him as a sacrificial lamb. It would crush and destroy him—of that I was absolutely certain.' For Rajiv, his decision was reminiscent of his mother explaining why she had to become housekeeper to Jawaharlal Nehru: 'It was not really a choice . . . there was nobody else to do that. I felt that there was a void and I could not see anyone else filling it; there was in a sense an inevitability about it.'

Sonia has never clarified why she vehemently opposed Maneka's entry into politics. Sources close to Sonia said she felt Maneka's inexperience and haughty behaviour would become a liability for Indira. Sonia was also said to be extremely wary of the Anand family, particularly of Amteshwar Anand.

The exit of Maneka from the Indira household witnessed many turns and twists, an ideal script for any saas–bahu serial on television. Indira's so-called perfect bahu, who cooked food, bought groceries, helped her choose the right saris, raised children and showed no inclination towards politics and politicking, strangely made no attempt to be a peacemaker. Some of Sonia's friends said that her conduct must also be seen in a human context. After all, she too was a bahu and had to protect her turf. Her assessment of Maneka's potential threat and her personal bias may have prevented her from acting decisively.

Maneka, however, does not hold Sonia responsible. According to her, Indira and other members of the family changed their attitude once Sanjay died: 'I realized that I was nothing but Maneka to them.'

Maneka began working on an independent line in her effort to enter politics. She had the support of some influential friends of Sanjay who had benefited immensely under him, but many backed out when

Maneka told them she was planning to go against Indira. Suddenly Maneka discovered that except for Akbar 'Dumpy' Ahmad, known for his fiery speeches and outspoken behaviour, virtually everyone else had changed loyalties. Dumpy, who loved dogs and the good things in life, stayed on, working round the clock to float the Sanjay Vichar Manch, a quasi-political outfit. Indira was livid and plainly told Maneka to leave Safdarjung Road if she wished to run a political organization.

Although a political novice, Maneka played her cards well, dictating the timing of her exit from the Indira household. At the time, Indira was in London with Sonia while Rajiv was busy learning the ropes of politics and governance from a select band of academicians, bureaucrats and technocrats.

Indira returned from London on the morning of 28 March 1982. Family watchers said the prime minister was in a foul mood, so much so that she did not even return Maneka's greeting. Soon Indira stormed barefoot into Maneka's room in the company of two witnesses, Dhirendra Brahmachari and R.K. Dhawan, ordering her to leave her residence. Maneka first exhibited innocence, wondering why she was being given marching orders. When Indira referred to her Sanjay Vichar Manch speech, Maneka said she had cleared it. This infuriated Indira further. They exchanged heated words, and Indira told her to leave without any belongings.

The debate went on for long and finally at 1 a.m., Maneka began walking out of the house. For the dozens of media persons, including the correspondents of major foreign news agencies like Reuters, AFP and British Broadcasting Corporation (BBC), it was an opportunity of a lifetime. 'There was Indira, shouting, hair dishevelled, and Maneka, sobbing in a low voice. I have watched hundreds of Hindi films and soap operas but nothing like that. It was so real,' said a photographer who captured the entire episode on film.

Indira's two daughters-in-law are still at loggerheads. Sonia refuses to comment on Maneka, but Sanjay's widow is not so diplomatic. She is known to make acerbic remarks about her sister-in-law—on her political style and way of functioning, even personal comments. Speaking on Doordarshan, Maneka said, 'It is true that she is a foreigner. But more than that, she has never done any social work and does not have any training. We are not born politicians, but you learn, study, and most important, you feel that something should be done.'

The rivalry between the two took a piquant turn when Maneka, who had won as an independent from Pilibhit in western Uttar Pradesh, became a minister in the NDA government headed by Atal Bihari Vajpayee in 1999.

In a subsequent reshuffle she was appointed minister for culture, a position which gave her supervision over various family trusts headed by Sonia. Maneka ordered a probe into alleged financial irregularities in some of these trusts and questioned the trust deed of the Indira Gandhi National Centre for the Arts (IGNCA). The pace at which she started looking into these institutions upset many people. In an abrupt move, she was taken out of the ministry and moved to the more innocuous department of statistics. Maneka held Sonia responsible for her exit.

The publication of *Indira: The Life of Indira Nehru Gandhi* by Katherine Frank provided further ground for discord. Maneka alleged that the older bahu of Indira was instrumental in the inclusion of hoary tales involving Sanjay in the book. She claimed that Sonia and the Congress party were trying to project Sanjay in a poor light and show Sonia, Priyanka and Rahul as the true inheritors of the Nehru–Gandhi legacy. Frank had met Sonia while conducting research for the book and acknowledged Sonia's support in terms of granting access to family letters and photographs.

When the book came out, some Congress leaders felt portions of it showed Sanjay and Indira in a negative light, but aide and adviser on literary matters K. Natwar Singh and party spokesman Jaipal Reddy advised Sonia against issuing any statement or demanding a ban. Maneka acted quickly against some statements in the book and won an out-of-court defamation suit in England. Maneka quickly asserted that it was Varun's sense of outrage against Frank that prompted her to file charges against the author.

Maneka is dismissive about her failure to inherit the legacy of the family. According to her, the whole idea of linking the Congress with the Nehru–Gandhi legacy is incorrect. 'The legacy lies in carrying out the ideals set by the family,' she says, asserting that it does not matter to her that it is Sonia who is accruing the political benefits of belonging to the dynasty.

While the young Gandhis were reluctant to attack one another in public, K. Natwar Singh launched a no-holds-barred verbal assault on Maneka. The Sonia camp was quick to remind the nation about the circumstances and the manner in which Maneka made common cause with Indira's detractors, eventually accepting the post of a junior minister in the coalition led by the BJP.

THE PRIME MINISTER'S WIFE

It was the morning of the last day of October 1984. Indira, as was her habit, kissed her grandchildren goodbye before they left for school. But Priyanka could not help notice that grandma had held her longer than usual. Indira then moved to Rahul almost whispering to him not to cry in case something happened to her.

Since June 1984, when the Indian army had stormed the Golden Temple at Amritsar to flush out separatists contemplating an independent Khalistan in Punjab, Indira was somehow convinced that she was going to die, possibly a violent death. She had been speaking to Rahul, who was a young boy of fourteen then, about funeral arrangements and telling him she had lived her life. Rahul was perhaps too young to understand but in him Indira had found a perfect companion to share her inner thoughts. On one occasion, Rahul reported Indira's conversation to father Rajiv. Rajiv could not stop tears coming to his eyes but smiled faintly when Rahul told him that 'dadi' had told him not to weep if such an occasion arose.

On 31 October 1984, Indira's official engagements were to begin with an interview with Peter Ustinov. The cameras were in place when Indira began walking, sporting a bright saffron-coloured sari at 9.12 a.m. As she crossed the wicket gate between 1 Safdarjung Road, her home, to her office at 1 Akbar Road, she acknowledged the greetings of a turbaned security guard. As she smiled back, she saw him train a gun on her. Narain Singh, who was holding an umbrella over Indira, threw the umbrella and started shouting for help. But before he and other guards of the Indo-Tibetan Border Force could reach the spot, the assassins Beant and Satwant Singh had pumped in thirty-six bullets.

Indira had been advised to wear a bulletproof vest and remove Sikh security guards but she had refused to do both. She felt it was unnecessary to wear a heavy bulletproof jacket at home and hated the idea of 'discriminating' among her security guards. In fact, a few weeks ago, Indira had rather proudly pointed at Beant Singh, saying, 'When I have Sikhs like him around me I do not have to fear about anything.' Indira, however, was obsessed with fears of her family being harmed. P.C. Alexander, who served as secretary to her, recalls, 'From June 1984 she lived with a dreadful thought. She kept repeating that there was a plot to kidnap the children. Nothing I said could allay her fears.'

Sonia had just finished washing her hair when she heard gunshots. Initially, she could not figure out what had caused the sound—it felt like a burst of Diwali crackers but with a peculiar difference. She then began sprinting, screaming, crying 'mummy, mummy'. Still wearing a gown, Sonia cradled Indira's head on her lap as the white Ambassador raced the three-kilometre distance to Delhi's premier All India Medical Institute of Medical Sciences (AIIMS). Indira was perhaps dead on arrival but doctors laboured for hours to revive her, giving her uninterrupted blood transfusions.

Rajiv Gandhi was in Bengal on a pre-election tour when an Intelligence Bureau (IB) official broke the news to him. Rajiv froze and instantly asked him about 'mummy's well-being'. The official said he had no idea. Rajiv rushed back to Calcutta, driving a jeep himself. In Calcutta too, everyone from Chief Minister Jyoti Basu to Siddhartha Shankar Ray refused to confirm Indira's death, saying she was being operated upon at AIIMS.

On the flight to Delhi, he entered the cockpit and switched on the pilot's radio set which confirmed Indira's death quoting the BBC. Rajiv went directly from Palam to AIIMS. Sonia burst into tears as soon as she saw Rajiv. Rajiv too broke down but regained composure when P.C. Alexander gently tapped his shoulder. Alexander recalls the poignant moment, 'Anguish was written all over his face. Rajiv gently clasped Sonia's hand and talked to her slowly and intimately. Tears were rolling down her cheeks and she ardently pleaded with him not to agree to be the prime minister. Rajiv was kissing her forehead and trying to convince her he had to accept the office as it was his duty to do so in that hour of grave crisis.' Alexander said he had to make a determined bid to 'tear him away from Sonia'.

President Giani Zail Singh was away in Sana, Yemen, when he received a call from Delhi informing him of the assassination and asking him to return immediately. Zail Singh, whose relationship with Rajiv would deteriorate over the next few years, said he had decided to appoint Rajiv as the next prime minister without consulting anyone. He claimed that he chose Rajiv to honour the wishes of Indira. 'I know her mind and that is what she wanted, though we had not discussed it specifically. I just know her mind.' Explaining his choice later, Zail Singh said, 'He had always had a clean image, his age was in his favour and I thought at the time he was intelligent.' Post-retirement he observed rather sourly, 'I think differently now.'

Rajiv said he had never toyed with the idea of becoming prime minister of India. It did not occur to him till R.K. Dhawan, Balram Jakhar and Alexander collared him at AIIMS. 'I was not happy. I talked with Sonia and she was totally unhappy. However, we discussed it and weighed up all pros and cons and finally we decided to accept it.'

After Indira's assassination, Sonia went into a shell and it took her months to recover. She lost over fifteen pounds in two months and her asthma attacks became more frequent. Rajiv's entry into politics also made an impact on Sonia. She had already given up dressing Western style and had rescinded her Italian citizenship in 1983. She now began accompanying Rajiv on political tours, where she was told to smile, wave and demurely walk behind him. She confined herself to concentrating on Rajiv's parliamentary constituency of Amethi—a dusty principality in the Awadh region of Uttar Pradesh whose only claim to fame is its tag as the seat won by Sanjay, Rajiv and now Sonia—prodding Satish Sharma to take action on the many complaints and requests sent by constituents.

Rajiv was in the habit of sharing everything with Sonia. He would be up late nights, enthusiastically telling her the finer points of Indian history and how advancements in science and technology could transform Indian society. Slowly Sonia started taking an interest, sharing Rajiv's vision of India.

As the prime minister's wife, Sonia's photographs of that time depict her as an inscrutable person, constantly tense, aloof and cold. Rajiv's critics were quick to brand her as the power behind the throne. Someone described her as Noor Jahan of Turin while others likened her to a Sphinx, the mythical Greek monster with a woman's head and lion's body who waited outside Thebes, asking travellers a riddle and killing them when they failed to answer it.

During Rajiv's tenure as prime minister (1984–89), Sonia attempted to keep away from politics and lead a normal life. Her social circle consisted of a small group of European and Indian friends. The highlight of each week was the Sunday brunch, when these friends—mostly businessmen and junior diplomats—would gather at 5 Race Course Road and chatter delightedly in French, Spanish or Italian. Ottavio Quattrocchi was one of the friends present at the Sunday brunch. Another permanent fixture was Nadia, Sonia's sister, who is married to a Spanish diplomat, José Valdemoro, then posted in New Delhi. Some of these Sunday meals were Indian and served in thalis. Often, Sonia exhibited her culinary skills by cooking lasagna and prawns in hot garlic sauce, which became a rage among friends.

When Rajiv was prime minister, there was a strict demarcation between 7 Race Course Road and the adjoining 5 Race Course Road that served as his office and residence respectively. No one—including such close associates as Indian Foreign Service (IFS) officer Mani Shankar Aiyar and senior Indian Administrative Service (IAS) officer Wajahat Habibullah, who were in the Prime Minister's Office (PMO), and close associates like Sam Pitroda and P. Chidambaram—was allowed inside Rajiv's family quarters. Both Mani and Habibullah had studied with Rajiv in Doon School but their proximity-cum-friendship was not enough to have easy access to the Sonia household.

Access was limited to a handful of personal friends like Suman and Manjulika Dubey, Jaya and Amitabh Bachchan, Arun and Nina

Singh, Mohan and Nirmal Thadani, Michael and Usha Albuquerque, Sunita and Ramesh Kohli, Ottavio and Maria Quattrocchi, Satish and Sterre Sharma, and a few others. Dubey, an outstanding journalist, remained a close Rajiv associate all along. His wife, Manjulika, assisted Sonia with her book, *Rajiv*.

Sonia's day started at 6 a.m. with bed tea. The family would be at the breakfast table at 8.30 a.m. Once Rajiv left, Sonia would scan the newspapers, attend to household details. Usually, between 11 a.m. and 12.30 p.m., she would go shopping or to exhibitions. When Rajiv was away, her evening schedule included watching movies on video.

During this phase, each of her gestures came under close public scrutiny. Soon word started going round that Sonia's collection of saris, sandals, shahtoosh and jamewar shawls and artefacts put her in the same league as Imelda Marcos.

Sonia's close friends explain this by saying that her collection of saris consisted largely of gifts received by Indira that were passed on to her. When Sonia took over as the Congress president, she started a practice of donating saris to AICC karamcharis. Sources said she received more than one thousand saris in 1999 as gifts from Tamil Nadu, Karnataka, Kerala, Andhra Pradesh, Pondicherry and other states. Year after year, the collection kept growing.

Sharad Pawar even coined the memorable phrase 'sari diplomacy' in the context of Sonia receiving saris as gifts. Just before raising the banner of revolt against Sonia in May 1999, Pawar alleged that Arjun Singh's wife, Saroj, aka Rani Sahiba, used to pick Chanderi saris for Sonia. 'It helped to strike a rapport,' Pawar said.

Things were moving smoothly for Sonia and Rajiv till 16 April 1987 when a Swedish radio station made a startling disclosure, the reverberations of which haven't died down yet. It broadcast details of bribes that, it alleged, had been paid to Indian politicians to clinch the $600-million Bofors gun deal. The contract was the biggest export order ever won by Sweden, and Martin Ardbo, the ecstatic managing director of Bofors, had even hoisted the Indian flag at the company's works at Karlskoga.

According to noted journalist Vir Sanghvi, here Rajiv's

inexperience showed and he paid a heavy price. An experienced prime minister would have said, 'We will investigate the matter.' But Rajiv went on to claim that not only had bribes not been paid but that no commissions had been given because the deal had no agents. 'This was a silly thing to do because all his critics had to do now was to prove that commissions (not, in themselves, illegal) had been handed out. And sure enough, it turned out that contrary to what it claimed, Bofors had paid commissions,' Sanghvi, who has closely followed the Bofors case, said.

The Opposition's charge that Rajiv or his family took the bribe was more baffling. Bofors was the choice of army headquarters and, more specifically, of the then army chief General K. Sundarji. Not a shred of evidence to link Rajiv to the alleged financial improprieties in the deal was ever produced but the scandal badly damaged Rajiv's credibility and resulted in his downfall.

The Opposition dragged Sonia's name too in the deal, alleging that one of the agents, Ottavio Quattrocchi, was an Italian, a friend of Sonia, who was often seen at the prime minister's residence. One immediate fallout of the broadcast was that Quattrocchi, whose name cropped up in the deal, was dropped from the elite group at the prime minister's residence. With him, European business and diplomatic friends drifted away, and the Sunday brunches with their continental fare and thali lunch vanished.

Suddenly, Rajiv's government was under scrutiny, and Sonia found herself a target. In each deal that the Rajiv government signed, an Italian connection was probed. When Rajiv dropped Arun Singh as defence minister, the gossip mills began working overtime. The two Doon School buddies reportedly fell out over Bofors as Singh favoured cancellation of the deal once the charges of a kickback gained credence, but Rajiv overruled him saying this would lower the country's image among international arms manufacturers.

Sonia and Arun's wife Nina used to be on the best of terms in the 1980s, when Arun used to look after the Amethi parliamentary seat. Nina would accompany Sonia to Amethi to distribute medical supplies and undertake other welfare activities. The women were regularly seen together travelling from village to village. They would listen to the people's grievances and tell them about women's emancipation and family planning. Sonia used to avoid making political speeches, restricting herself to asking them to vote for Rajiv. 'Patiji ko vote dijiye' (vote for my husband) was one of her favourite sentences. She would giggle after finishing it, much to the amusement of the people of Amethi, who were extremely fond of her.

Arun Singh has never spoken about why he fell out with Rajiv. He left Delhi, settled in a remote farmhouse in the Kumaon Hills of Uttaranchal, and staged a comeback many years later, in 2001, to accept a low-profile but important assignment in the defence ministry.

Rajiv later became conscious of the spotlight on Sonia and tried some damage control. He had not realized that except for Lal Bahadur Shastri, previous prime ministers were either widowers or widows. The Indian masses and media were not equipped to deal with a glamour couple like the Kennedys or the Blairs. His projecting himself as a good family man got him the image of a henpecked husband. Even Congress leaders dissatisfied with Rajiv found Sonia a soft target.

Rajiv's lifestyle also came under close scrutiny. His love for designer shoes, fast cars and expensive items became hot subjects of discussions and debate. In New Delhi, for the first time the prime minister was seen driving himself, and this in a swanky Mercedes-Benz gifted by Jordan's King Hussein. Mani Shankar Aiyar, a foreign-service bureaucrat-turned-politician, had another explanation for why people, particularly media persons, considered Rajiv a yuppie. 'Perhaps they do not like to see a man born with a silver spoon in his mouth turn it into gold,' he said.

Rajiv also drew criticism for his cherished annual holidays, when he used to pursue his interest in photography and wildlife. Much before he entered politics, Rajiv and Sonia used to regularly vacation in Italy and India. During Christmas and New Year, the entire family, including Sonia's mother, her sisters and their husbands, used to get together. The practice continued when Rajiv became prime minister. Sonia's mother and sisters went to Kanha National Park in Madhya Pradesh in 1985 with Rajiv, Sonia, Priyanka and Rahul. Next year, it was Ranthambore, where reigning film actress Sridevi performed before a select audience. The media lapped up the event. In a poor country, the chief executive was not expected to have a good time.

Rajiv was unmindful of the criticism. He ignored advice and continued to live his life the way he liked to. In December 1987 the destination was Lakshadweep. The Bofors scandal, meanwhile, was gathering force. By the time Rajiv realized that the tide was turning against him, it was too late.

Rajiv Gandhi's defeat in 1989 was a blessing of sorts for Sonia and the children. As leader of the Opposition, Rajiv had much more time for them. For Sonia, the disappointment of defeat vanished quickly upon seeing Rajiv savour simple, everyday pleasures again. There were uninterrupted meals. 'Sitting . . . in tranquillity, we would occasionally watch a video film together, listen to music,' she said. Rajiv was also not too disheartened by the defeat. He told a music-loving friend from outside the political arena, 'Finally some peace for me. I can now just sit and listen to music with the children. I want to resume my interest in amateur radio.'

However, political developments quickly began drawing Rajiv's full attention. 'He was a changed man,' recalled Ahmad Patel, a party leader from Gujarat close to Rajiv. 'He wanted to identify with the common man. For months, there was no air conditioner at 10 Janpath,' he said. Rajiv then embarked upon a sadbhavna yatra, travelling by train through western Uttar Pradesh to Lucknow braving the heat in ordinary class. The gesture made an impact, and he began drawing huge crowds.

During this period, as Rajiv and Sonia found time to be together, he began sharing his views on political issues with her. Sonia listened attentively and often offered advice. Rajiv admired her photographic memory and her sharp ability to judge those around him.

During the 1991 elections, Rajiv drew up a list of party candidates who needed financial help. When he died in the midst of electioneering, his grieving widow sent funds to them. It was a gesture that touched them deeply. Former AICC spokesman Chandulal Chandrakar, for instance, once refused to obey the party line during the Narasimha

Rao regime when he was expected to distance himself from 10 Janpath. Chandrakar had no regrets. He said that he would never turn against the family, narrating how he got ten lakh rupees when he needed the money most. 'Rajivji had died, and I was in the middle of elections. I had no hope from any quarter till I received a note that said that in accordance with Rajivji's wishes, the money was being given to me,' Chandrakar recalled. Unfortunately, Chandrakar did not live long enough to see the emergence of Sonia as a politician.

Sonia and Rajiv's twenty-third wedding anniversary fell on 25 February 1991. The couple had a quiet dinner in a restaurant in Tehran. A week before that Sonia was in Amethi when Rajiv decided to launch a diplomatic initiative to end the Gulf War. Rajiv was extremely keen to take Sonia along. A special aircraft was sent to fetch her. 'He was extremely edgy as there was some delay in Sonia's arrival. She got only a few hours to pack her bags but managed to accompany Rajiv,' a Rajiv associate said.

Rajiv visited Amethi for the last time in April 1991, and Sonia was with him. Rajiv told his constituents, 'It may not be possible for me to come [again]. But Sonia will be there to look after you.'

The Bofors affair meanwhile meandered through tortuous legal corridors within and outside the country. After eighteen years of legal tussle and a probe that cost Rs 250 crore to prove a Rs 64 crore scandal, the case which unseated Rajiv Gandhi collapsed on 31 May 2005 when the Delhi High Court acquitted the three Hinduja brothers in the Bofors pay-off case and slammed the prosecution for wasting public money. Justice R.S. Sodhi said the prosecution failed to substantiate charges. In Vir Sanghvi's assessment, throughout the Bofors debate, neither the BJP nor the Congress was telling the full story. For the Congress to say, 'Look, the gun has performed so well in Kargil' was to miss the point. Of course, Bofors is a good gun—at that level, they all are—but that does not mean the deal was clean. Equally, for the BJP to act as though the Gandhi family's involvement is a matter of record is to overstate the case.

FOUR

A TUG OF WAR

When P.V. Narasimha Rao took over as prime minister in 1991 at the age of seventy-one, little was known about him in spite of his decades of experience in public life, as chief minister of Andhra Pradesh and Union minister for external affairs, human resource development, and home and finance, among other portfolios. His long stint in Delhi had made him a sort of outsider in his native state of Andhra Pradesh. But in Delhi, he had many friends and admirers. Indira was extremely fond of him, giving him key assignments in spite of the stiff opposition from many towering state leaders like M. Chenna Reddy, Brahmanand Reddy and Vijay Bhaskar Reddy. He was one of the few to have access to her residence. After Indira, Rajiv too found much to admire in him, including his low-key style of functioning and his ability to defuse even the most volatile situation.

Many Congress stalwarts saw him as a harmless sort of person, a stopgap arrangement, and a man who was on the verge of retirement. The reading of Arjun Singh's and Sharad Pawar's camps was that the old man would not survive for long, and they would soon be stepping into his shoes.

For Sonia, Rao was a bit of an unknown quantity. She saw him, as did others, as learned and wise, and a loyal and highly respected senior leader of the party. Their earlier meetings, when he used to come to meet Indira, did not go beyond exchanging namaste. Upon Indira's death, Rajiv had requested Rao and Mohsina Kidwai to lead the funeral procession. Thus, when Sonia learnt that Rao had been chosen to lead the party, she did not oppose his candidature—which could be seen as an approval of his appointment. She was, in any case, hardly in a frame of mind to ponder over such an issue. Sources close to her, however, maintain that she would have expressed reservations had the party picked Sharad Pawar as its leader.

Both Sonia and Rao were reticent persons, and when he took over as prime minister, the two hardly spoke to each other, preferring to deal with Wajahat Habibullah and Ramu Damodaran. Habibullah, an IAS officer of the 1968 batch from the Jammu and Kashmir cadre, was drafted as the chief executive of the Rajiv Gandhi Foundation (RGF), headed by Sonia, while Damodaran was private secretary to Rao. The Narasimha Rao government's decision to loan a senior officer like Habibullah was a departure from government rules and procedures, and it was made as a special gesture towards Sonia, who was heading the foundation.

Between them, Habibullah and Damodaran helped prevent many skirmishes between Rajiv's widow and Rao that were engineered by senior party leaders for their own political ends. However, when Habibullah left for his home cadre as the divisional commissioner of Srinagar in 1994 and subsequently Damodaran was sent to the United Nations, relations between Rao and Sonia began to deteriorate.

Rao had started off on the right foot. Within days of taking over as prime minister, he made a gesture that was appreciated by Sonia. He was appointed as a trustee of the RGF. There was a tussle as to where the first RGF meeting should take place. Sonia was keen to have it at 10 Janpath, but some persons close to Rao raised the issue of protocol. Habibullah and Damodaran saved the situation when the latter communicated Sonia's request to Rao that she was in no mental condition to visit 7 Race Course Road since it used to be Rajiv's office. Sensitive to her feelings, he called up Sonia saying that he would go over to 10 Janpath. However, in Congress circles, the PM's gesture was misconstrued as paying obeisance. The RGF meetings continued at Sonia's residence till another trustee, Dr Shankar Dayal Sharma, became the President. They were then held at Rashtrapati Bhavan.

The first budget of the new government was presented by Dr Manmohan Singh, Rao's surprise choice as finance minister to sort out the country's economic mess. Dr Singh, a brilliant academician and economic guru who had also been governor of the Reserve Bank of India (RBI), embarked on massive economic restructuring. His was a landmark budget that introduced measures to privatize the economy and structural reforms and included, as a special gesture, a Rs 100 crore grant for the RGF. The Opposition quickly made an issue of how a private trust was being given taxpayers' hard-earned money. All hell broke loose. Sonia, Priyanka, Rahul and Amitabh Bachchan, all members of the RGF, were aghast. Some of Rao's ministerial colleagues blamed the prime minister for embarrassing Sonia. The Rao camp retaliated, pointing a finger at the shouting brigade, a band of self-proclaimed Rajiv loyalists, for the fiasco.

The shouting brigade was an influential group of Rajya Sabha members consisting mostly of first-timers who had been hand-picked by Rajiv and comprising Suresh Pachauri, Ratnakar Pandey, S.S. Ahluwalia and Baba Mishra; their only claim to fame was that they had the ability to pounce on anyone who dared to speak against Rajiv or Sonia in 1991. The group had tried hard to prevail upon Sonia to take over the party leadership. At one juncture, Sonia got so tired of their antics and statements that she denied them an audience. Pandey, for instance, kept telling the world that he had taught her Hindi, though Sonia had actually learned the language at the Hindi Institute in Green Park. On another occasion, he said he would offer his skin if Sonia wished to wear shoes made of it. Ahluwalia began embarking on an annual yatra collecting holy water from all the rivers and carrying it to Sriperumbudur. Yet Ahluwalia, known for his sense of timing, eventually gave up on Sonia and joined hands with Narasimha Rao, becoming a junior minister, and then shifted loyalty to join the BJP. By 2002–03, he was the BJP's favourite spokesman to attack Sonia on major television networks!

Whatever the reason for the grant, the move boomeranged. Withdrawing it would only worsen the embarrassment. Rao asked Dr Manmohan Singh to clarify the government's position to Sonia.

Dr Singh called on Sonia, but as he sat facing her, he could not muster the courage to come to the point. He kept speaking in general terms till tea was served. Finally he began slowly, apologizing, saying that he had no intention of embarrassing her or belittling the cherished memory of Rajiv, and then going on to explain the government's dilemma. The grant was withdrawn after Sonia wrote a letter to Rao. It said, 'While we thank you personally and your colleagues for this most generous gesture, it would be best if the government instead identified suitable projects and programmes and fund them directly and thus honour the memory of my husband.'

After the row over the RGF grant settled down, another controversy arose, this time involving Sonia's private secretary, Vincent George. The Congress was to select party nominees for the Rajya Sabha from Karnataka, and some senior party leaders ganged up against Margaret Alva, who was seeking an unprecedented fourth successive term. They propped up George's name, though he actually hails from Kerala. (For the Rajya Sabha seat, the candidate should be a resident of the state from where he is contesting, but it is a convention that is often flouted.) Rao was hesitant to clear George's name, though almost all the party bigwigs, particularly K. Karunakaran and Arjun Singh, were keen that he be nominated. There was no word from Sonia either in favour of or against George. As Rao was leaving for Russia, he called on Sonia to inquire if she wanted George to be in the Upper House. Sonia made it clear that if the party wanted to give a ticket to George, the decision should be based on merit and in keeping with political considerations. Rao understood the point. When the list of candidates was faxed from abroad, George had been denied a ticket. Instead, Margaret Alva's name was on the list.

To many, this issue was a major factor in the distrust that characterized the relationship between 10 Janpath and 7 Race Course Road over the next four years. Sonia's private secretary, it was claimed, became hostile towards Rao. The theory went that George was singularly responsible for widening the wedge between the two, and he had a role to play in the events that finally led to the split of the party.

Disgruntled leaders and party activists unhappy with the Narasimha Rao regime began to be given audience with Sonia. George would call up MPs saying that Sonia was free to meet them between 5 and 7 p.m. on particular days. The message was clear: they were welcome to air their grievances to her. Congressmen readily obliged George, and the queues outside 10 Janpath were never small.

To the outside world, the importance of Vincent George was never fully understood. His role was either exaggerated as that of some kind of super boss or downgraded to that of a petty clerk. The truth was different. For ten long years, between 1991 and 2001, when he was finally sidelined, George had the distinction of having constant access to Sonia. He was in charge of arranging meetings—be they with senior leaders or grass-roots workers, industry and other bigwigs or supporters from the villages—and tracking down party leaders. His supporters even today boast of 'George sahib' being able to find any party leader within half an hour—a distinction that no one in the party could match. He was loyal, hard-working and efficient, and he never exceeded his brief. Unlike R.K. Dhawan and M.L. Fotedar, George was unfortunate not to have been given a political position as a reward for his sincerity.

Narasimha Rao's detractors, including Arjun Singh, K. Karunakaran, M.L. Fotedar, K. Natwar Singh, K.N. Singh and Sheila Dikshit, moved closer to George. An effort was made to keep conveying to Sonia that all was not well under the new government, be it in respect of the Ayodhya dispute, the economic reforms, which were seen in many quarters as being anti-poor, or the tardy probe into the Rajiv Gandhi assassination case. Sonia may have had her own view on all these issues, but George's role was significant. He facilitated the access of a large number of Congress leaders and MPs who wished to drive home the same point to her—that the Congress would lose its character if she did not intervene. The private secretary, it was said, missed no opportunity in forwarding press reports and other titbits to Sonia that Rao was systematically trying to undermine the Nehru–Gandhi legacy.

The prime minister could sense the deterioration in relations with 10 Janpath, but for reasons best known to him, he made no attempt to develop a personal rapport with Sonia, preferring to depend upon the Damodaran–Habibullah channel, which ended by early 1994.

In September 1991, the Election Commission announced by-elections for the Amethi Lok Sabha seat that was represented by Rajiv Gandhi. The shouting brigade, now renamed the Sonia brigade, swung into action. The likes of Ratnakar Pandey, S.S. Ahluwalia and Suresh Pachauri were back in action openly asking the prime minister to call on Sonia and persuade her to contest from Amethi as Rajiv's successor.

There was a renewed 'Sonia lao' (draft Sonia) campaign. This time, Sonia lost patience. Acting on the advice of Rahul and Priyanka, the family decided to go on a tour of Europe and America. The loyalists were stunned, but those who knew her well sympathized with her predicament. Priyanka was most upset with the campaign. One day, she told the RGF trustees, 'What do they [the Congressmen] think? Should we keep sacrificing our lives? We have had enough of politics.'

When Rao heard of Sonia's travel plans, he immediately called on her. The meeting lasted for an hour. Sonia made it clear that she had no intention to contest Amethi. He said that there was a view in the party that Captain Satish Sharma, who used to look after Amethi when Rajiv was prime minister, should be given the party ticket. Sonia's response to this was the same as when the issue of giving a ticket to Vincent George had been raised—that a ticket to Captain Sharma should be given on merit, in keeping with political considerations. Captain Sharma was given the ticket, but the impression that went round was that Sonia had recommended him. Sharma's own statements corroborated this view. Taking a leaf from the Ramayana, he said that like Bharat he was keeping the seat secure for Bhaujai (sister-in-law). He succeeded in convincing the Amethi electorate that his candidature had Sonia's blessings and that she would soon be contesting the polls to look after Amethi.

Sonia exhibited her political colours, perhaps for the first time, when the Babri Masjid was demolished on 6 December 1992. She overruled P. Chidambaram and other members of the RGF by having the foundation issue a hard-hitting statement condemning the act. Chidambaram and others were of the view that the foundation was an apolitical trust; as such, there was no need to make a comment on a political issue. Sonia summarily rejected the argument. She pointed out that Rajiv and other members of the Nehru–Gandhi family were closely identified with the country's secular fabric, and if the RGF failed to express its sense of outrage, she would be betraying their legacy. The statement Sonia issued as chairperson of the foundation indicted the Narasimha Rao government too. The prime minister, also a trustee of the foundation, had to swallow the reprimand.

Sonia's stand on the Babri Masjid demolition rang alarm bells across the political spectrum. Those close to Rao took it as a confirmation that the lady at 10 Janpath was indeed biding time for a more active political role. His detractors were delighted, for they sensed this too. Rao, battling on many fronts, once again made little effort to clarify his government's position to Sonia and the misunderstanding only grew further.

Not everyone in the Narasimha Rao camp was sitting idle. Prior to the Babri demolition, Congressmen, particularly from north India, were upset over talk in party circles that the days of the family were over. Rao was dubbed as Chanakya, the legendary practitioner of statecraft in the Mauryan empire, and a reluctant revolutionary. He was being compared with Jawaharlal Nehru in terms of his scholarship and conduct as a statesman. Like Nehru, he was seen as a man who understood the intricacies of international affairs and was guided by a profound commitment to the task of nation building. If Nehru was the father of the planned economy, Rao was the father of the new economic policy that would put India on par with other developed nations. Some political commentators compared him to Lal Bahadur Shastri in trying to take India on a new path. Like him, however, they said, he was not being allowed to grow, simply because he did not belong to the family.

In 1994, an independent television producer prepared a capsule on the Congress campaign for the assembly elections. The presentation was made to Rao and his close associates, but it was rejected on the grounds that it focussed on the party's glorious past, starting with Nehru and going on to glorify Indira and Rajiv. Hours later the producer was given an audience with Sonia to narrate how he was discouraged from highlighting the family's contribution.

Rao, who was just short of a majority in the Lok Sabha, initially played his cards well. There were unconfirmed reports of the Chanakya trying to get tacit support from the likes of Chandra Shekhar, V.P. Singh, Ramakrishna Hegde—people known for their antipathy to the family—and the Left, promising to end dynasty rule. In private conversations, the prime minister reportedly told Atal Bihari Vajpayee of the BJP, with whom he had an excellent rapport, that the options before the Opposition were limited—back him or bring back the dynasty it always opposed. To many Congress leaders, particularly those from the south, Rao was a symbol of the aspirations of the rank and file. On other occasions, the Narasimha Rao camp tried to play the Brahminical card, emphasizing to leaders like Vajpayee that in the post-Mandal era, he would check the rise of the Bahujan Samaj Party (BSP) and other caste-based political outfits.

Rao's parliamentary affairs minister, a canny politician from the tribal-dominated areas of undivided Madhya Pradesh and a key player in the Sanjay Gandhi era, Vidya Charan Shukla, also added fuel to fire. Shukla, who had deserted Rajiv in the late 1980s, along with V.P. Singh and Arun Nehru, told the Lok Sabha that the controversial Bofors papers were on the way. The anti-Rao group in the Congress ran to 10 Janpath, accusing him of trying to browbeat Sonia. Bofors was a red flag to Sonia. Arjun Singh, Madhavrao Scindia and Natwar Singh wondered why Rao was not disciplining Shukla. 'Do we take it that there is no difference between the Rao regime and V.P. Singh?' they asked. V.P. Singh had been Rajiv's foremost critic on the Bofors issue. Locked up in Swiss vaults, the Bofors papers never came, but Sonia did not take kindly to the oblique threat.

In the beginning, Rao called on Sonia on the eve of every Cabinet reshuffle, but he discontinued the practice after his advisers told him that it was seen as a sign of weakness and projected her as some sort of extra-constitutional authority. In any case, he and Sonia were hardly discussing politics when they met, not to mention ministry formation exercises! The conversation would, after the exchange of pleasantries, invariably revolve around the studies of Rahul and Priyanka, the life and times of Indira and Rajiv, and generalities such as the weather.

Rao's less-than-frequent visits to 10 Janpath became a subject of intense discussion among Congressmen. Many leaders who used to view 10 Janpath as a shortcut to success and patronage started avoiding George and Sonia, preferring to associate themselves with Rao. As a reaction, some Congressmen from Uttar Pradesh, Bihar and Madhya Pradesh increased their visits to 10 Janpath, as they were unable to get into the Narasimha Rao camp.

All through this period, Sonia remained indifferent to politics. She was happy to receive various foreign dignitaries who called on her, oblivious to the rumblings in the ministry of external affairs. Some officials in South Block—which houses the external affairs ministry—raised the issue of protocol, wondering why dignitaries like Yasser Arafat, Nelson Mandela and King Hussein should call on a person who was not holding any public office. Rao overruled such objections. As long as these leaders had no reservations about visiting her, the government should not needlessly raise the issue of protocol. Suddenly, however, in 1995, South Block intervened. Sonia was told that Prince Abdullah of Jordan would not call on her. Instead, she would have to go and meet him. Sonia asked some foreign policy experts if it was unusual for foreign dignitaries to call on her. Almost all of them said that if the dignitary so wished, there was nothing improper in such a meeting. Congressmen felt such a directive could not have come without the knowledge of the PMO, as the ministry and the PMO work in close tandem.

The differences with the Narasimha Rao government notwithstanding, there were no qualms about accepting government generosity to the foundation. There was an unofficial rule that all projects belonging to the RGF should be cleared on a priority basis. Union ministries such as those for social welfare, the environment, rural development, human resource development, as also the department of culture, cleared virtually every RGF project. Sitaram Kesri, who was heading the social welfare ministry under Rao, was a frequent visitor at 10 Janpath. 'Koi khidmat, koi sewa? (Any favour, any service?)' he would intone as he entered. Arjun Singh and later Madhavrao Scindia were ministers for human resource development. They too had given standing instructions to their officials that all RGF projects should be cleared quickly. Similarly, the Congress governments such as those of Digvijay Singh in Madhya Pradesh, Bhajan Lal in Haryana, J.B. Patnaik in Orissa and S.C. Jameer in Nagaland were extremely helpful where the RGF was concerned.

The government patronage of the RGF continued well after Narasimha Rao. The two United Front governments that followed, headed by H.D. Deve Gowda and Inder Kumar Gujral respectively, were also favourable to the RGF, but the foundation began losing support when the Vajpayee government came to power in 1998. According to some close family friends and senior Congress leaders, Sonia's decision to enter politics was greatly influenced by this factor too. She realized that without her active role in politics, the Nehru–Gandhi legacy perpetuated by various trusts would not last long.

Sources close to Rao said that during his tenure as prime minister, he was always willing to oblige her but a section of the party worked overtime to create misunderstanding between the two. They said that Rao was even prepared to accommodate those raising the Sonia bogey, namely, Captain Satish Sharma, Suresh Pachauri and S.S. Ahluwalia, who were drafted in the Union council of ministers. But in the absence of any clear indication from Sonia, Rao was unable to make out who was close to her.

For example, veteran Congress leader Narain Dutt Tiwari, who later headed the breakaway Congress group with Arjun Singh, failed to get into the prime minister's camp as Rao felt that would anger Sonia. In Rao's assessment, 10 Janpath disliked Tiwari on account of his not-so-pleasant relations with Rajiv, who disliked Tiwari's independence and had been miffed with his refusal to withdraw his nomination from the Nainital parliamentary seat in the 1991 general elections. To Rajiv, it was an act of defiance that smacked of rebellion.

Those around Rajiv had convinced him that Tiwari was emerging as a threat and was contemplating a leadership challenge after the 1991 polls.

But after Rajiv's assassination and the elections which Tiwari lost that same year, the four-time Uttar Pradesh chief minister changed tactics, projecting himself as a Rajiv loyalist. He managed to get an appointment with Sonia, during which he emotionally denied that he had had any ambition to challenge Rajiv's leadership. Sonia did not react to Tiwari's new role and listened to him attentively. Word reached Rao that Tiwari was playing games. No concession was granted to Tiwari who was also trying to get into the Congress Working Committee (CWC) as Rao continued to sideline him. The Tiwari camp thereupon began to allege a sinister design in ignoring leaders from Uttar Pradesh. As long as the Congress failed to revive the party in the Hindi heartland, there would be no threat to Rao's leadership, went the argument. Once again, the lack of communication between Sonia and Rao allowed more misunderstandings to crop up. He never bothered to ask Sonia if she had any serious reservation about Tiwari.

The probe into Rajiv's assassination also created distance between Sonia and Rao. Apart from Sonia, Rahul and Priyanka were extremely keen that the guilty should be punished soon, but the court process required time. The Verma Commission of Inquiry gave its report on the lapses that led to Rajiv's assassination, but many recommendations were not followed up. The Jain Commission of Inquiry, headed by a high court judge, Justice (Retd) Milap Chand Jain, probing the conspiracy angle, went on and on, summoning endless witnesses, to the point that the inquiry became absurd. Several conspiracy theories were presented and dismissed. Some blamed the Liberation Tigers of Tamil Eelam (LTTE), others said it was the handiwork of Khalistanis. Another group blamed it on the Israelis and the CIA. However, there was no clarity as to whether the assassination was a group or an individual effort. There were also allegations that a political clique inside India was responsible for the assassination. The media lapped up the various theories propounded in the small conference room in the Vigyan Bhavan annexe till everyone got tired of the speculation.

Priyanka regularly attended the Verma and Jain Commission hearings at Vigyan Bhavan. From the Congress side, Arjun Singh would not miss a chance to attend and sit through the long proceedings. His presence was not without political significance, but the point remained that the Narasimha Rao government itself appeared casual about the trial.

Rao deputed senior minister P. Chidambaram, who was a trustee of the RGF, to monitor the Rajiv assassination probe. Chidambaram was expected to constantly brief Sonia and her children, but this did not work out once developments in Tamil Nadu politics led to his joining the Tamil Maanila Congress (TMC), a breakaway Congress group which parted company with Rao on the eve of the 1996 elections. The TMC went on to join hands with the Dravida Munnetra Kazhagam (DMK) in the state, which was seen as being sympathetic towards the LTTE, a group viewed as responsible for masterminding the assassination. In 2002, the TMC finally returned to the parent organization under Sonia. Paradoxically, Chidambaram, who continued to be a trustee of the RGF, did not return, preferring to run a smaller party whose influence did not cross his Sivaganga parliamentary seat on the southern tip of the country.

From 1991 to 1996, a section of party leaders, particularly those from north India, never missed an opportunity to knock at Sonia's door. They always got a hearing. Sonia seldom spoke, but her willingness to hear out all those unhappy with the prime minister was indication enough to these visitors that she did not approve of his style of functioning.

Arjun Singh was the first to sense that. Having tried other manoeuvres, Singh and a band of Congress leaders zeroed in on a strategy to make Sonia liberate the Congress. Lacing Nehruvian principles of secularism, plurality, non-alignment and left-of-centre economics with realpolitik, Arjun Singh, M.L. Fotedar, Narain Dutt Tiwari and others not only succeeded in creating more distance between Rao and Sonia but also managed to deal a deadly blow to Rao that finally resulted in the defeat of the Congress in the 1996 general elections.

Singh also raised the bogey of the one-man, one-post issue within the Congress. In the Congress there was a tradition from the time of Nehru that the two top posts—those of leader of the party and prime minister—were often clubbed together, making Nehru, Indira and Rajiv all-powerful. Singh's game plan was to force Rao to leave the party post and thereby curtail his powers, but he refused to oblige.

In 1994, Singh tried to force a vote in an AICC session at Surajkund on the one-man, one-post issue, but the Narasimha Rao camp carried the day with a resolution that there should be an exception in the case of the prime minister. The resolution was adopted by voice vote. For the first time, Haryana policemen manned an AICC session, masquerading as Sewa Dal workers. When former hockey Olympian and party MP Aslam Sher Khan and a handful of partymen marched towards the dais to register their protest, they were badly manhandled. In the mêlée that followed, one policeman in Sewa Dal uniform was seen holding a senior leader by the testicles, threatening him with dire consequences! The dissidents were intimidated by the use of brute force and surrendered tamely.

The event took place on the first day of the two-day party session. Arjun Singh was sitting on the podium watching the drama. At the main entrance, about twenty AICC delegates led by Aslam Sher Khan, Ajit Jogi (who later became chief minister of Chhattisgarh), Dileep Singh Bhuria, K.N. Singh, Sheila Dikshit and others sat on a dharna demanding inner-party democracy. Sher Khan was sporting a white skull cap underlining the fact that Muslims were unhappy with Rao over the events leading to the demolition of the Babri Masjid. When the session began to adopt the resolution by voice vote, Sher Khan, Bhuria and Jogi began protesting, marching towards the dais and eliciting the policemen's reaction.

What was Sonia Gandhi's role in these behind-the-scenes manoeuvrings? Was she party to or aware of what happened at the Surajkund AICC meet? According to senior party leaders, she was very much in the know and had sympathy for the dissidents. However, she was unwilling to come out in the open as she had no desire to head a breakaway Congress group. This line of argument was made clear to the dissidents opposed to Rao. More by body language than a specific commitment, she had indicated that she was not happy at the way the Narasimha Rao regime was functioning and that she wanted the dissidents to go on with their campaign.

The Singh–Tiwari faction finally parted ways from Rao. Arjun Singh resigned as Rao's human resource development minister on 25 December 1994. He was in a hurry to do something. As for Tiwari, he was not holding any important post and his supporters were getting restless.

In the Rao–Singh tug of war, Rao gained an upper hand when the dissidents deserted the Singh camp by 1995 and came back to him. He succeeded in securing a majority in Parliament owing to defections from the Janata Dal. Finally the dissidents came out in the open for a final showdown on 19 May 1995 at Talkatora Stadium.

There was high drama throughout the day. The convention began at 9 a.m., and within hours it became clear that the party was heading for a split. The tone and tenor of the speeches were so critical of the prime minister that they would have embarrassed even the BJP and the Left! Rao was accused, among other things, of the Babri demolition, mortgaging the nation's economic sovereignty, compromising on the Nehruvian principle of non-alignment in international affairs and belittling the legacy of Rajiv Gandhi, besides being a covert agent of the right-wing Rashtriya Swayamsevak Sangh (RSS).

By afternoon, the leaders called on Sonia to inform her that tempers were running high and that she should do something. A nervous Sonia could not bring herself to talk to Rao. She instead chose K. Karunakaran to speak to him to prevent a split. Karunakaran, known for his direct manner, called on Rao, but the latter was unwilling to concede much. He had intelligence reports about the language used by his fellow partymen at the convention. 'How do you expect me to make concessions?' Rao asked. Karunakaran dropped Sonia's name, saying that she wanted him to 'do something'. Rao wearily agreed to look into 'some aspects' of Arjun Singh's agenda, but it was a case of too little, too late.

The rebels were running out of patience. In the evening, they gathered again at 10 Janpath and told Sonia about Rao's offer. 'Madam, we will be lynched. Pani sir se uncha ho gaya hai (Things are beyond repair),' they told her. Sonia kept silent. She had to choose between becoming a footnote in history or betraying some loyal soldiers. The hard calculation that followed in her mind was based upon pragmatic considerations. The rebels were politely told to do what they felt like. The unspoken message was, 'I am with you but the time is not most appropriate.'

Sonia has never commented about what actually happened in May 1995. However, when she took over as the Congress chief in 1998, there were numerous instances when she accorded preferential treatment to those who had left the party during the Narasimha Rao regime and ignored those who had actively sided with Rao. The practice continued till 2001 when the 'T' (the breakaway group was called Congress T—the T standing for Tiwari) charge began to bite, and she quietly began distancing herself from them. The T-brand loyalists sulked, but they could not protest too much, as now they had nowhere to go.

All along Sonia has denied the charge that she had any role in the 19 May split. However, although she may not have had a direct hand in the split, there is a general consensus that she encouraged all those who were opposed to Rao. Throughout the Narasimha Rao regime, 10 Janpath served as an alternative power centre or a listening post against him. From 1994 to 1996, senior ministers in Rao's Cabinet even avoided visiting Sonia fearing that it would go against them.

In the intra-party feud between Rao and Singh, therefore, Sonia was far from being neutral. Her supporters said that whenever she made an effort to keep the party united, the Narasimha Rao camp attached 'political motives' to her efforts. 'She was cultivating a band of loyal soldiers in Arjun Singh, Natwar Singh, M.L. Fotedar, Narain Dutt Tiwari, Mohsina Kidwai, Sheila Dikshit and others. Years later, many of these leaders became part of her coterie and AICC office-bearers. In retrospect, I cannot say that her hands were clean,' said a party leader who had stayed on with Rao.

Leaders like Ajit Jogi and Digvijay Singh, who did not go to Arjun Singh's party, said they had tried hard to ascertain Sonia's mindset but could not gauge it. 'Had she told me I would not have stayed for a moment with the Rao Congress,' Jogi said, recalling the day he, along with a handful of MPs, had gone to seek her guidance. 'She heard us out but did not say you go this way or that way. So we stayed on where we were.' Digvijay too got the same impression. 'Diggy Raja' was an important player. Had he sided with Arjun Singh, the breakaway group would have posed a more formidable challenge to Rao.

For many political commentators, Sonia was playing politics without risking anything. In this sense, the breakaway group was taken for a ride. All along they kept thinking that Sonia would bless them. There was talk that Sonia would attend the convention, but she failed to turn up.

Congressmen have a finely honed survival instinct. A majority of them stayed on with Rao as he was the prime minister, but on 14 March 1998, no one sided with Sitaram Kesri when he was unceremoniously thrown out as the Congress president. The crucial difference between Rao of 1995 and Kesri of 1998 was that Rao could dole out goodies as the prime minister, while Kesri had little to offer as the party president.

Subsequent events too substantiated the view that Sonia had some role to play in the intra-party feud. In 1997, she told Kesri to take back the breakaway group led by Arjun Singh and Tiwari. Kesri was reluctant as he was nursing a grudge against Singh, but Sonia forced his hand by asking him the date on which the merger would take place. A sulking Kesri paved the way for rapprochement, but he refused to greet them. It was left to AICC spokesman Vithal Gadgil to announce the homecoming of Singh, Tiwari and others.

It was not as if the Rao camp was not playing politics. When the elections drew closer, his managers did the unthinkable—opening a Pandora's box called the Jain hawala case. It was a desperate act by Rao to win people's support. There were grave charges of corruption against his government and some of his family members. The Muslims were determined to teach him a lesson on account of the Babri Masjid demolition and both the Right and the Left represented by the BJP and the CPM were gunning for him. Acting on the advice of the director of the CBI, Vijay Rama Rao, who hailed from Andhra Pradesh, Rao ordered an inquiry into the alleged pay-offs to a galaxy of political leaders and ministers that included Lal Krishna Advani, Sharad Yadav, Arjun Singh, Narain Dutt Tiwari, P. Shiv Shankar as also his own party leaders, namely, Madhavrao Scindia, Buta Singh, Bhajan Lal, Vidya Charan Shukla, Kamal Nath and Motilal Vora, besides some top bureaucrats. The hawala case was based on diary entries made by two Jain brothers hailing from Madhya Pradesh who had allegedly bribed several top politicians in return for favours. The entries carried the names of these leaders and the amounts, running into several lakhs, paid to them.

The hawala probe sent shock waves across party lines. It was the first time in the history of India that so many political leaders were booked under the Prevention of Corruption Act. There was a violent reaction. Madhavrao Scindia termed it as a political conspiracy, while Arjun Singh and Tiwari, who were out of the Congress, said it was a political vendetta. But the plight of Vidya Charan Shukla and Kamal Nath was unique. They, like many others, had stood by Rao through thick and thin.

The Chanakya was unfazed. 'Let the law take its course,' he said, generously accepting a plea that all those figuring in the scandal be given a chance to put up a proxy candidate, which could be wife, son, or daughter, to contest the elections while they were embroiled in the case. The suggestion was considered ridiculous, but some actually availed it. Some wanted to field their mistresses! This proposal was vetoed by Rao. Scindia left the Congress in a huff, and till his death, in an air crash in September 2001, he continued to have a profound dislike for Narasimha Rao.

The hawala battle lines were quickly drawn. Politicians framed in the scam decided to come together and 'fix' Narasimha Rao. At an informal level, these leaders remained in close touch with each other. 'Anyone but him,' said a top BJP leader while discussing the Madhya Pradesh Lok Sabha scene with a Congress leader in 1996. The Congress leader was in complete agreement. 'Not Rao. Please make sure that even a dozen MPs do not win from our state,' he said, elaborating upon the caste factors and resources that would influence the results.

The Congress tally from undivided Madhya Pradesh (Chhattisgarh wasn't formed then) got stuck at ten out of forty Lok Sabha seats whereas the Narasimha Rao camp was hoping to get about thirty seats. There were similar stories from other states where Congress leaders worked out a tacit understanding with the BJP and regional leaders to defeat the official nominee. At the eleventh hour, Rao realized the futility of raking up the hawala case. After the defeat, Vijay Rama Rao was shunted out from the CBI and Delhi. But the man under whose tenure the CBI was called the 'Congress Bureau of Investigation' was much smarter than people thought him to be. He quickly changed sides and joined the Telugu Desam Party (TDP) to become a minister in the Chandrababu Naidu government. Mercifully, Naidu assigned him road development, keeping him away from home, intelligence or surveillance departments.

Years later, many close aides of Narasimha Rao who had defended the hawala charge sheet admitted it was a Himalayan blunder. The hawala charges did not stick in court as the judges considered the accusations, mainly in the form of diary entries, abbreviated names and incomplete figures of political pay-offs, non-admissible as evidence.

On 24 August 1995 Sonia decided to go public against the Narasimha Rao regime. The occasion was the anniversary of Rajiv's birthday, and the venue was Amethi, where Sonia expressed her deep sense of anguish over the delay in the assassination trial while addressing a large gathering.

'Sonia, save the country,' the crowd chanted as she, her head covered demurely by her sari, slowly climbed the steps to the rostrum closely followed by Priyanka. Sonia was nervous and hesitant, but Priyanka was a picture of confidence, waving back at the multitude below. 'Mummy, look at the crowds, don't you think you should wave back?' she said, tapping her mother's shoulder.

In her seven-minute speech, Rajiv's widow asked Amethi's citizens to share her vedna (pain) at the delay. She said if a probe into the assassination of a former prime minister could take so much time without making much headway, what would be the plight of ordinary citizens seeking justice? 'You people can understand my feelings,' she said in fluent Hindi, thumping the lectern as she complained about the slow progress of the probe. She may have been lamenting the slow pace of the judicial system in the country, but coming from Sonia at a time when the ruling Congress party was torn by factionalism, the criticism was seen as a thinly veiled attack on the prime minister himself.

Her insinuations became a little more obvious when she declared that the principles of former prime ministers—Rajiv, his mother Indira Gandhi and grandfather Jawaharlal Nehru—were being put to the test. 'There is divisiveness all around,' Sonia said in comments that were interpreted as another jab at the Narasimha Rao leadership. Then, apparently referring to the family, Sonia added: 'This is the time when we should follow the example set by those leaders for whom the nation stands above everything else.'

Barring Digvijay Singh, chief minister of Madhya Pradesh, and party MP Suresh Pachauri who defied the informal word to stay away from Amethi, Congressmen did not come out to support Sonia. To Sonia, this came as a rude jolt. The so-called family loyalists opposed to Rao were quick to tell her that they had warned her. They averred that if she stayed out of politics, the nation would forget her and the legacy of the Nehru–Gandhi family. To some, it was an important political lesson for Sonia, who began seeing merit in the argument.

Rao summoned his advisers to review the situation, but he was told not to worry. S.S. Ahluwalia, who was made minister in the government, was asked to snub Arjun Singh, who had said that it was a matter of shame for all Congressmen that Rajiv's widow was forced to make such remarks. Ahluwalia, no longer part of the Sonia brigade, said, 'Why should we put our heads down in shame? It is a matter of shame for those who have left the Congress.'

Sonia's outburst at Amethi in August 1995 would have created far more political turmoil had it not been for developments in Andhra Pradesh, where Chandrababu Naidu scored over mentor and father-in-law N.T. Rama Rao to emerge as a major player in the national political arena. This would not be the only time that he upset Sonia's plans. He continued to do so in the 1998 and 1999 general elections by siding with Vajpayee.

The Congress defeat in the 1996 general elections came as no surprise to Sonia. She had received ample feedback from all over the country that the party would not reach the 200 mark in the elections. Soon after the polls, the breakaway group called on her, asking her to take over and formally declare the Tiwari Congress as the real Congress, but once again, she remained non-committal.

Within days of the election defeat, it became clear that Rao would not be able to run the party. He was all-powerful and important as long as he was the prime minister, but running an organization was altogether a different game. Sonia was watching developments, keeping an eye on both the Narasimha Rao and Sharad Pawar camps. Pawar was developing close links with the newly created United Front. Sonia had no objection to H.D. Deve Gowda, a powerful backward leader in his home state of Karnataka who was propelled on to the national stage by the United Democratic Front's (UDF) need for a consensus candidate, becoming prime minister, as long as Ramakrishna Hegde was kept out. Hegde, who had been a chief minister of Karnataka, had never tried to hide his opposition to dynasty or his antipathy towards the Nehru–Gandhi family. In fact, Hegde was about to leave the Janata Dal—where he didn't get along with Gowda—and join the Congress during the Kesri era, but 10 Janpath vetoed his return. Hegde was perceived as too independent, and his lifelong opposition to dynasty rule became the biggest obstacle to his return to the Congress. Kesri was upset with Sonia for blocking Hegde's return, but he did not go public. 'Kya batain, hum Madam ki ichha ke khilaf nahin ja sakte (I cannot go against the wishes of Madam),' he said.

Sonia refused to have a say in the appointment of Rao's successor, but she was stunned when she heard the news that Kesri would replace Rao. To many in 10 Janpath, it was Rao's way of seeking revenge from the Congress that first promoted him to the prime ministership and later bluntly forced him to resign as the leader of the party. 'There was nothing meritorious in Kesri except that he was an insignificant backward from Bihar where the party was a big zero. Rao thought he would manipulate Kesri, run the party by proxy or destroy the party by putting in an unworthy person,' a member of the CWC said.

Sonia always had a liking for Kesri even though she used to get constant feedback that he was bad-mouthing her. In Sonia's presence, Kesri always flashed his proximity to Indira and projected himself as a loyalist. But Sonia judged Kesri from the feedback she received from Indira, which was not quite favourable. Given a choice, she would have opted for A.K. Antony as Rao's successor, but to many in the Congress the development could have blocked her own prospects. In that sense, Sonia's move to stay away from Rao's successor paid rich dividends. Antony withdrew from the fray against Kesri and reportedly told his associates that he would not be a good Congressman on taking stand on issues such as Bofors.

When Kesri was unceremoniously removed as AICC chief in March 1998, Sonia retained him as a special invitee in the CWC—a courtesy that was not extended to Rao. Unlike Kesri, the Sonia camp always viewed Rao as some sort of threat, as someone capable of staging a comeback. Initially, Sonia was toying with the idea of drafting Rao as a CWC invitee, but she developed cold feet when everyone in the party and in her family cautioned her against it.

Even Rao's Cabinet colleagues, who had stoutly defended him in the Babri case, told Sonia that Muslims would punish the Congress if he were included. Some leaders, projecting themselves as friends of Rao, said the old man was himself not interested. 'If you need his counsel, we will go and get it. He is one of us,' a senior leader said. Sonia continued to send Natwar Singh, Dr Manmohan Singh and Pranab Mukherjee to seek Rao's opinion on major foreign affairs and economic issues. She called on him when he was booked in the

Jharkhand Mukti Morcha (JMM) bribery case, in which the JMM's MPs were apparently 'lured' to vote for the government in a crucial vote of confidence in 1993. Sonia also asked the AICC's legal cell to extend all help in the JMM case. But given the legal cell's calibre, the Chanakya was wise enough to quickly say a polite thank you and opt for a professional set of lawyers.

Relations between Rao and Sonia could never be termed as good. Whenever the two leaders came together, something happened that widened the wedge. In 2001, when Sonia took complete charge of the party after defeating Prasada in the organizational elections, she invited Rao to attend the Bangalore plenary. The former prime minister was seen sitting on the dais going through resolutions, giving suggestions and raising hands whenever any resolution was put to the vote. To partymen, it was a good sign that the man who ran a minority government for five successful years was advising Sonia.

But the warmth between the two vanished fast when he chose to appear before the Constitution Review Panel headed by his old friend, Justice (Retd) M.N. Venkatachaliah. To Sonia, it was a hostile act. According to her, the panel set up by the Vajpayee regime had a hidden agenda to recommend that persons of foreign origins should not be allowed to hold high office—that of the president, prime minister and vice-president, among a few others. She asked close associates why Rao chose to become party to a panel whose sole aim appeared to be to debar her from holding high office. She first thought of asking Pranab Mukherjee, Natwar Singh or Dr Manmohan Singh to meet Rao to inquire what prompted him to go before the panel but decided otherwise. Within days of his appearance, she directed all party chief ministers, CWC members, Congress MLAs, MPs and other functionaries not to appear before the commission. It was a snub to Rao, and a caution to other partymen too.

Rao sensed Sonia's discomfort and decided to clear the confusion. True to his style, the Chanakya did not approach Sonia directly. Instead he told Mukherjee that he had done nothing wrong in appearing before the commission. According to Rao, he went and met Venkatachaliah to clear Indira's name in the context of the annexation of Sikkim. Rao reportedly told the committee that it was entirely wrong to consider that Indira had played havoc with constitutional provisions while inducting Sikkim as an Indian state. Pranab conveyed Rao's feelings to Sonia, who quickly gave him a clean chit saying that she always held him in high regard as Indira had had great respect for him!

Throughout his tenure as the party chief and prime minister, Narasimha Rao avoided a head-on confrontation with Sonia. After he demitted office, he stayed away from internal politics, though his name was dragged in each time there was a leadership tussle in the party. A number of lightweight leaders like Matang Singh, Bhuvnesh Chaturvedi and Maninderjit Singh Bitta who had come into the limelight during Rao's premiership tried to use their connection with him against Sonia. Matang Singh, a contractor from Assam, excelled in politicking and had become a minister in the PMO in 1995. While he was a manipulator par excellence, Rao tried to balance his role by drafting the low-key Chaturvedi, a journalist-turned-politician from Rajasthan. Bitta was head of the Indian Youth Congress (IYC). He specialized in gathering crowds at short notice to hold public demonstrations. In the Sonia Congress, Matang Singh, Chaturvedi and Bitta lost whatever clout they had had. Matang was expelled, Bitta remained a dissident, and Chaturvedi was seldom seen or heard.

But the former prime minister gave no indication that these individuals had his blessings. His apolitical role was more evident when he refused to support his key manager, Jitendra Prasada, who contested against Sonia for the AICC president's post in November 2000.

Prasada, a suave backroom manager for Narasimha Rao from 1991 to 1996, became a victim of palace intrigue when he was forced to take on Sonia in the party polls. Marginalized in the Sonia Congress, Prasada was initially teaming up with Rajesh Pilot to start a low-key rebellion in the guise of inner-party democracy. The real motive of the exercise was to check Arjun Singh and Madhavrao Scindia, who were calling the shots in the Sonia regime. Some disgruntled party leaders from Orissa, the North-East and Uttar Pradesh along with those outside the Congress who felt threatened by the rise of Sonia quickly began supporting the Prasada–Pilot team.

But these equations changed dramatically with the death of Pilot in a road accident in June 2000. Pilot, who was popular with the middle class, had established a good name for his politically correct stances, clean image and efficiency. Hailing from a modest Gujjar family of western Uttar Pradesh, Rajeshwar Prasad, as he was originally called, joined the Indian Air Force and liked flying so much that he changed his name to Rajesh Pilot. The squadron leader-turned-politician regularly won from the Dausa Lok Sabha seat in Rajasthan where he did not have the advantage of state domicile.

In a political career spread over fifteen years, Pilot loved to take on the high and mighty and enjoyed media attention. He was an efficient minister under Rajiv but after the Babri demolition in 1992, he began to score political points against the likes of Arjun Singh, Sharad Pawar, Madhavrao Scindia and Kamal Nath. On 25 February 1993, when the BJP organized a demonstration near Parliament, Pilot, as a junior minister in the internal security ministry, made unprecedented bandobast to thwart any threat to mosques in the area. Coming as it did soon after the Babri demolition, there were apprehensions that the demonstration could turn violent, but the day passed peacefully. Pilot boasted that had he been in charge of security on 6 December 1992, instead of his senior S.B. Chavan, in the internal security ministry, the mosque would not have been demolished.

Pilot then turned on the heat on godman Chandraswami who was perceived to be close to Rao. A tantrik, Chandraswami had powerful friends like international arms dealer Adnan Khashoggi, the Sultan of Brunei, and Margaret Thatcher, and equally well-placed enemies. In 1995, Chandraswami was wanted in connection with a series of cases, but nobody could act against him due to his high connections. Pilot got him arrested. It was more than a coincidence that in the subsequent Cabinet reshuffle, Pilot was shunted out of internal security to look after forests and environment.

On 14 June 2000, as he drove a jeep at breakneck speed from Dausa to Jaipur to catch a flight to Delhi, he overtook his own escort vehicle at a blind spot and collided with a state transport bus. The man who was always in a hurry left behind a thousand and one unfulfilled ambitions. One of them was to take on Sonia in the Congress organizational polls scheduled in November 2000.

In Pilot's absence, all eyes turned to Jitendra Prasada. Prasada, however, lacked the vibrant, clean image that could generate mass support. Jitty Bhai, as Prasada was fondly called, loved his food, drink and poetry. Coming from a distinguished family in the princely state of Shahjahanpur, Prasada's manners were those of a Lucknowi nawab—he had in fact studied at Lucknow's Colvin Taluqdar College which was once exclusively meant for wards of nawabs and court officers, or taluqdars. He took pride in his family's ties with India's most famous poet, Rabindranath Tagore. Prasada cut his political teeth under Rajiv from 1985 to 1989 when he served as Congress general secretary and Rajiv's political secretary. Prasada retained the prize post when Rao became all-important between 1991 and 1996. Under Rao, the Brahmin from Uttar Pradesh had his task cut out for him. He was expected to keep leaders like Arjun Singh, Narain Dutt Tiwari, Mohsina Kidwai and Sheila Dikshit under check. Prasada did that with all the resources at his command, but in the process, the Congress lost its roots in Uttar Pradesh, the state which mattered most in the country's politics due to its sheer size and population. Once the Congress lost its control over those eighty-five parliamentary seats in the 545-member Lok Sabha, it could never get a clear majority to form a government of its own at the national level.

Prasada, however, miscalculated the political situation while taking on Sonia. He had no illusions about his prospects of defeating Sonia in an election that was tilted heavily in her favour. The entire election machinery was in her hands, including that of picking poll observers and returning officers. Prasada believed that Sonia would ask him to withdraw from the fray and reward him with a senior position in the party.

Leaders like Natwar Singh and Ahmad Patel, who were projecting themselves as peacemakers, cemented this line of thinking. But some leaders in the Sonia camp, namely, Arjun Singh and Vincent George, had other plans. These leaders argued that the tag of elected party chief would go a long way in consolidating Sonia's position in the Congress. At the eleventh hour, they forced Prasada's hands, refusing to concede an inch. Prasada had no option but to take on Sonia.

All AICC functionaries were asked to drum up support for Sonia. In Bhopal, Hyderabad, Jaipur and a few other places where Jitty Bhai toured as part of his campaigning, he was greeted with black flags and locked doors at the Pradesh Congress Committee (PCC) offices. A tense Prasada looked for a way out. Meanwhile, the peacemakers shuttled between his house and 10 Janpath, claiming to be working on some formula that was non-existent.

As the date for withdrawal of names drew nearer, Jitty Bhai waited in vain for a call from 10 Janpath offering a face-saving, last-minute withdrawal. Humiliated and marginalized, Jitty Bhai realized that his gambit had failed. Accompanied by a handful of leaders from Uttar Pradesh, Prasada filed his nomination papers and was humbled in the party polls as Sonia went on to get nearly 99 per cent of the votes. The peacemakers and many of those who had encouraged Prasada to teach Sonia a lesson were nowhere in sight. Prasada did not recover from the trauma of defeat. A few months later, he suffered a brain haemorrhage and died. The man who knew so much about palace intrigue became one of its worst victims.

FIVE

EDUCATING SONIA

The Nehru–Gandhis follow several Kashmiri, Parsi and Hindu traditions, but the most peculiar one is the manner in which they educate their wards. After Jawaharlal Nehru, his great-granddaughter Priyanka was the first graduate in the family. Indira was a good student, but she could not complete her formal education. Nehru was acutely conscious of this, so he made a concerted effort to enlighten her on history, culture, literature, science, technology, religion and a range of other subjects. By the time she became prime minister, her level of knowledge was higher than that of the average graduate or even a postgraduate.

While educating her, Nehru may not have envisaged dynasty rule, but he did have an overwhelming desire to train Indira in a different manner. He had scant regard for the existing education system, including that of public schools and convents. In one of his letters, Nehru wrote to Indira what he expected from her. To prepare her for the future, he 'wrote piles and piles of historical and other letters' to her to gently train her mind in 'that wider understanding of life and events that is essential for any big work'.

Unfortunately, Indira could not give her sons the kind of attention her father had given to her. She was preoccupied with managing the Nehru household and her troubled marriage, and consequently her children performed badly in academics. Asked to comment on his stay in Cambridge where he had gone to do a degree in mechanical engineering at Trinity College, Rajiv would laugh and say, 'Oh, I simply flunked!'

After Sanjay's death, Indira began grooming Rajiv for a greater political role. Belatedly, she made conscious efforts to enlighten him on the finer aspects of polity and governance. Since Indira did not have Nehru's skills, she sought the services of experts drawn from various fields to specially train Rajiv.

Rajiv met daily with the likes of missile man A.P.J. Abdul Kalam, scientist Professor Yashpal, agriculture expert M.S. Swaminathan, economist A.M. Khusro and experts drawn from other fields. These interactions were found to be useful by both sides. Rajiv got tremendous insight into issues facing the nation in all spheres, while the experts had the satisfaction of conveying their views to Indira through Rajiv.

Later, Indira drafted Rajiv's cousin Arun Nehru, a high-flying corporate executive known for his aggressive style of functioning, to serve as Rajiv's assistant. Nehru, nicknamed Appu (baby elephant) on account of his weight, had a way of looking at things that was alien to the political culture of the Congress. He believed in winning at all costs. Behind the polished manner and the fondness for the good things of life was a hard taskmaster who intensely disliked failure.

For Rajiv's friends, the two-year learning period was responsible for Rajiv's focus on modernization and many innovative ideas such as a village-based governance system (Panchayati Raj). Rajiv wanted to have a three-tier system so that villagers would not have to travel hundreds of miles to state headquarters for smaller projects like sinking wells. His other pet subject was the thrust on computerization and information technology. Rajiv, much ahead of other politicians in the country, could sense its impending relevance to a country like India. He was laughed at by Sitaram Kesri and others for relying on computerization of votes, but Rajiv ignored the criticism to focus on time-bound technology missions, initiating electoral reforms, lowering the age to vote, introducing an anti-defection law, offering a political solution to insurgency in the North-East and instituting economic reforms. These were seminal ideas which would change the face of

India. Panchayati Raj, for instance, was a giant step forward that brought governance to the grass-roots level in addition to bringing women into the mainstream, as a third of the seats were reserved for them in the village councils. Great strides were made in communications to link up the country through an accessible telephone system, the full impact coming a few years later with the boom in telecommunications in the country.

Observers viewed Rajiv's brush with these ideas as a mixed bag. As a modern man, Rajiv brought in a whiff of fresh air, but his inexperience and excessive reliance on a close circle of friends often compounded the complex problems and the bigger issues involved. Nevertheless, even his worst critics acknowledged that he was maturing into a seasoned politician at the time of his death.

Rajiv's death brought Sonia into sharp public focus. The alacrity with which the CWC offered her the party leadership and a possibility of leading the nation rattled the Indian intelligentsia. People wondered if she was really capable of leading millions. At that juncture, Sonia's grief was far too intense for her to ponder the question, but with the passage of time, she and others began to reconsider her leadership potential.

The change was evident three years after Rajiv's death. When senior Congress leaders considered to be loyal to the 'family' pleaded with her to discipline Narasimha Rao or play an active role in politics, the housewife did air her doubts, wondering aloud how she would overcome linguistic and cultural barriers to enter an arena where anything and everything is under intense public scrutiny. The supporters brushed aside such apprehensions saying one need not be a born leader. Everything can be arranged, you can be groomed easily, they said, and pointed at the Congress's reservoir of talent. 'Your family has favoured so many over the decades. Can they not teach you a few things?' said a leader from Uttar Pradesh.

Acutely aware of her many shortcomings, Sonia began the exercise of educating herself the moment she firmed up her mind to join politics. Some of her critics said that the idea of setting up the RGF, where an array of experts was summoned on a regular basis, was a first step in that direction. Congressmen vehemently deny the charge. According to them, till at least three years after Rajiv's death, Sonia had no plans to enter politics. 'It was when she saw the collapse of the party and the rise of the BJP that she decided to do her bit to save the nation from the clutches of communalism and fascism,' said a senior CWC member, who also insisted that the idea behind the RGF was a much broader one than merely to fill Sonia in on subjects of contemporary importance.

Sonia had watched Indira and Rajiv tackle the most difficult issues facing the nation, but this was not enough, as Sonia used to avoid taking interest in matters of governance unless drawn into discussion by them. Indira respected her sense of aloofness, except in the last six months of her life when she began sharing a lot of things with a bahu who had become like a daughter to her.

In Rajiv's case too, he would seek Sonia's counsel often. It was an open secret that Sonia was party to Rajiv's decision to join politics even though she had strong reservations initially. Congress circles acknowledge that in 1989, when Rajiv suffered defeat in the general elections and there was talk that the former prime minister would buy a one-way ticket to Italy, Sonia strongly favoured that he stay on in politics.

The stamp of the Nehru–Gandhi family legacy was evident when she finally took over as the party chief in 1998. She took many decisions based on what she had learnt from her mother-in-law and her husband. But what was most remarkable was that she consciously avoided making the mistakes that had proved costly to both Indira and Rajiv. Among them was her decision not to disturb chief ministers of the Congress-ruled states. It was a significant departure from the Indira–Rajiv days, when chief ministers were changed as frequently as three to four times in a five-year term.

Sonia's critics said that political compulsions forced her not to act against the chief ministers. Unlike Indira and Rajiv, they said, Sonia was not the prime minister and lacked the mandate to play musical chairs in the states. But Congress chief ministers were delighted to have a party boss who backed them to the hilt. They were given a free hand to do what they liked.

In the first two years, Sonia removed just one chief minister, Janki Ballabh Patnaik. The Orissa chief minister was replaced in 1999 following the murder of Christian missionary Graham Staines. What upset Sonia most was Patnaik's near endorsement of the Hindutva hardliners' justification of 'disciplining Christian missionaries' and the demand for a nationwide debate on religious conversions. She also had a nagging doubt of his loyalty, suspecting him of being hand in glove with Narasimha Rao and others of the old guard.

Patnaik, however, represented a powerful lobby within the Congress. The old guard was not happy at the summary way in which she removed the chief minister. Subsequent events in Orissa politics didn't reflect favourably on her when the new chief minister, Girdhar Gomang, specially chosen by her, failed to provide relief and rehabilitation after a super cyclone caused heavy devastation in coastal Orissa. She corrected the wrong the following year when she made him state party unit chief after the party's crushing defeat in the assembly polls in 2000. The Congress lost the assembly polls bagging just 10 out of 137 assembly seats.

Sonia quickly learnt the lessons from Orissa. She took a principled decision not to disturb chief ministers and directed all AICC general secretaries to keep them in good humour. Dissident activities against Digvijay Singh, Sheila Dikshit, S.M. Krishna, Vilasrao Deshmukh (Deshmukh was finally removed in January 2003 when the state party leaders and alliance partner Nationalist Congress Party [NCP] asked for his exit) and other Congress chief ministers died a natural death when Sonia made it clear that she was in no mood to hear campaigns to remove a chief minister. Her policy of least interference in the day-to-day functioning of fifteen Congress-ruled states made her immensely popular among the chief ministers. This was a clear departure from Indira's and Rajiv's style of functioning, in which the chief minister's office was a game of musical chairs. If Congress chief ministers like Vasantdada Patil of Maharashtra, M. Chenna Reddy of Andhra Pradesh or Veerendra Patil of Karnataka resisted, they were dubbed dissidents and isolated within the party. People like Digvijay

Singh, Ajit Jogi and S.M. Krishna seldom had problems with Delhi under Sonia. As a result these chief ministers always had a good word to say about her, even in their off-the-record conversations. It also put an end to the counterplots, such as those in the Tirupati and Baramati conclaves where senior leaders and chief ministers had met secretly to plot the downfall of Rajiv and Narasimha Rao respectively.

It is said that Sonia is a good judge of people while Rajiv was gullible. Rajiv could be taken in by sweet talk, emotion and—sometimes—good looks, but with Sonia, the case is different. Her intense look and searching eyes can put her interlocutors off balance and help bring out their true character.

When she took over as the Congress chief, there was a certain unease between her and Sharad Pawar. Though Pawar concurred with the party's decision to request Sonia to save the Congress, he later candidly admitted that he was never comfortable with her. Their conversations never lasted long and even that short duration was punctuated by long pauses. After revolting against her on the ground of her foreign origins, Pawar said that Sonia would never openly speak to him, but a CWC member who had tried hard to bring about a rapprochement between Pawar and Sonia said the same thing about him: 'We encouraged him to have an open, heart-to-heart discussion with the Congress president, but he would just not open up.'

Pawar's detractors alleged that the Maratha leader was not speaking freely because he was thinking of toppling her. Pawar had an informal poll survey done, which concluded that if he raised the banner of revolt against Sonia on the ground of her origins, he would be a second Lokmanya Tilak, the freedom fighter from Maharashtra who took the cause of independence to the people. The actual findings of the survey were never made public.

The process of Sonia's hands-on education began when she started interacting with experts on a regular basis during the last days of the Narasimha Rao regime in 1996. To begin with, even those close to her failed to see a pattern in the exercise, but increasingly it became clear that her interactions with the likes of historian Romila Thapar, sociologist Zoya Hasan, jurist P.N. Bhagwati, former IB chief M.K. Narayanan, and political scientist Rajeev Bhargava had a purpose to them.

Others whom she began to consult once Sitaram Kesri emerged as head of the Congress, were economist Y.K. Alagh, pollster Yogendra Yadav, foreign policy expert J.N. Dixit, L.M. Singhvi (Singhvi later joined the BJP but his son, Manu Abhishek Singhvi, joined Sonia's think tank), Natwar Singh and Pranab Mukherjee. She found Mukherjee an interesting talker and told associates that he came across as an authority on a range of subjects. He also had a fund of anecdotes to spice up his analysis of various issues. Sonia loved his accounts of how Indira solved many tricky problems.

While none of these experts was willing to come on record to describe these interactions, many privately said that they were impressed by Sonia's interest, eagerness and attentiveness. One significant aspect was that Sonia hardly gave her view on any issue, whether it was Ayodhya or economic reform. She would jot down points, and at most she would paraphrase a remark to check if she had understood correctly. In that sense, the teachers were unanimous that Sonia was a good student.

Sonia continues the practice of taking copious notes, even in the CWC meetings. For many party leaders, it is a little unsettling. 'It is as if she may confront us at a later date if we change our stand,' a CWC member said.

After March 1998, when she formally took over as the Congress president, the interaction with the intelligentsia became regular and organized. The party drew a list of about fifty experts on subjects ranging from electoral reforms and delimitation exercise of Parliament and assembly constituencies, to foreign policy, Indian history and the history of the Indian National Congress. In addition, Congress leaders like Salman Khurshid, an authority on constitutional law, economic expert Jairam Ramesh, foreign service expert Mani Shankar Aiyar and politician Margaret Alva (who had a lot of hands-on experience in administration and gender-related issues) began giving notes on important issues pertaining to the nation. Each time you met her, you were supposed to make a presentation. Charts, diagrams and paradigms would help. 'If you go with a problem, you should offer a solution too. That is the survival kit in the Congress when you are dealing with the party chief,' said an associate who had served as a close aide to Indira and Rajiv Gandhi.

While Sonia was a good student, there were minor mistakes that seldom went out of 10 Janpath or the party headquarters at 24 Akbar Road. For instance, in 1997–98, the party decided to set up a panel under Ghulam Nabi Azad to celebrate fifty years of independence. In that connection, the birth anniversary of Bhagat Singh was observed, and Sonia was invited to pay floral tribute to the freedom fighter. A note on his life and times was passed on to her. Sonia rehearsed a small speech but did not deliver it. The mystery was soon solved. Apparently, the speech had constantly referred to Bhagat Singh as Sardar Bhagat Singh, and Sonia got confused seeing Bhagat Singh's picture minus turban but wearing his trademark hat. In that brief moment of decision, she decided to avoid making a speech lest it be misunderstood. Privately, party leaders had a good laugh about it.

There was another incident when Madhavrao Scindia introduced an influential caste leader to Sonia. The person concerned was an important leader in Uttar Pradesh who had cut his political teeth in the Samajwadi Party and the BJP. He had a sharp, analytical mind, and he gave her some expert insights into caste equations in Uttar Pradesh. Sonia, however, did not think much of the emphasis on caste in Uttar Pradesh and spoke her mind. She went on to state that as head of the Congress, she wished to downplay caste considerations. The Uttar Pradesh leader quickly got up saying he would come again when the AICC chief had a better idea of how important caste equations were in Uttar Pradesh politics.

There was another significant aspect of Sonia's education that did not go unnoticed. Over days, weeks and months, Sonia developed some grasp of the issues of the day and began giving short speeches. On economic matters, however, she avoided articulating her point of view. While she listened patiently to discussions on the economic problems facing India, she refrained from offering prescriptions. Initially, she seemed favourable to the left-of-centre approach on economic issues, but in 2001 she veered round to supporting reforms to the hilt.

On the economy, Dr Manmohan Singh emerged as her key tutor. He had been supporting the left-of-centre approach but went on to become the architect of the Indian model of fiscal reforms taking the country out of the economic crisis of 1991. His influence on her was so strong that she refused to heed left-wing leaders like A.K. Antony, Mani Shankar Aiyar, Arjun Singh and a number of others favouring a middle path. To many Congress leaders, this was worrying.

Sonia's trust of Dr Singh led to speculation in the Congress that the AICC chief was projecting him as the party's prime ministerial candidate. Sonia had a genuine liking for Dr Singh, who was known for his clean image. For the traditional dhoti-kurta-clad Congressman, however, he represented the elite. When Madhavrao Scindia was alive, his supporters were also wary of Dr Singh, considering him a challenger to the number two slot in the party.

Sonia tried to master Hindi from various sources before taking the plunge into politics. She had begun learning Hindi at home soon after her marriage. Indira had arranged for a tutor from the Hindi Institute at Green Park to teach her to read and write in the Devanagari script, and slowly she developed a liking for the language. Her teacher found her a good learner who seldom missed her homework.

'I had no choice so I learnt it,' Sonia said, pointing at the tradition of speaking only in Hindi at the dinner table since the time of Motilal Nehru. No one, including the head of the family, was permitted to break the tradition. It is one custom that is still practised at 10 Janpath. In the first few months that Sonia began to speak in Hindi, Sanjay would laugh each time she made a mistake, but Indira and Rajiv would quickly reprimand him and help Sonia. Sonia took Sanjay's remarks sportingly. In 1980, a few days before his death, she managed to correct *his* Hindi. Everyone present had a good laugh. Sonia also made it a point to try to speak to all her Indian friends in Hindi. Now she initiates a conversation in Hindi with all those who hail from the Hindi heartland and speaks in English to those who come from across the Vindhyas.

Once she was elected to Parliament, the process of educating Sonia gained momentum with partymen vying to take up the assignment. The party's former chief whip in the Lok Sabha, Professor P.J. Kurian, who had lost the election, took it upon himself to brief Sonia about parliamentary conventions and customs. Also assisting her were Madhavrao Scindia, Shivraj Patil, M.L. Fotedar, Margaret Alva, Prithviraj Chavan, Salman Khurshid, Arjun Singh, P.M. Sayeed, Mani Shankar Aiyar, Girja Vyas and Pawan Bansal.

Sources close to Sonia said that her first few months in Parliament were most testing. There were five hundred pairs of eyes watching her every movement. The press gallery, special gallery, visitor's gallery, diplomatic gallery were all packed too. There were at least a dozen eager beavers among the Congress benches itching to give unsolicited advice. Worse, trusted hands like Vincent George and Pulak Chatterjee, a bright 1974 IAS officer from the Uttar Pradesh cadre, could not be of any help once she was inside the Lok Sabha. As a Sonia aide said, 'Madam is a reticent person and she hated the intense public glare. She did not want to give the impression that Congress leaders were helping her. There used to be intense relief each time Parliament got adjourned.'

Sonia was aware of the prevailing tension in the Congress Parliamentary Party (CPP) but saw little reason to panic. She told her associates that she needed time, recalling how Rajiv could not make a speech during his first year of Parliament (1981–82).

Slowly, she began learning the ropes. She made her first speech as a member of the Lok Sabha on 29 October 1999, though she had spoken there on five occasions before to felicitate the Speaker and Deputy Speaker, second motions of their election and announce her resignation from the Bellary Lok Sabha seat. Sonia had won from both Amethi and Bellary, but according to the law she could keep just one seat. Bellary, an industrial town in Karnataka, gave Sonia a mandate in spite of spirited efforts by the BJP's Sushma Swaraj who had taken pains to learn Kannada. There was constant media speculation that she would humble Sonia. But a day before campaigning ended, Priyanka arrived, and the entire township was out to see and hear her. Sushma did not wait for the verdict. She knew she had lost.

For her speech, Sonia came prepared with reams of paper printed in bold 30-point type with just a couple of sentences written on each sheet. Sonia began speaking amid catcalls, but Speaker G.M.C. Balayogi was extremely considerate. At the back of his mind was his own experience as he too had faced a communication problem when he was appointed Lok Sabha Speaker in 1998. (He was from Andhra Pradesh and not very fluent in Hindi.)

With this presentation, Sonia passed the litmus test. She began by taking a dig at the Vajpayee regime for attributing the ongoing economic reforms to the Congress. Sonia said, 'I congratulate the government for having read the Congress manifesto in great detail.' The House then saw an emotional Sonia criticize the government's handling of the Bofors issue. She was furious because the CBI had just filed a charge sheet naming Rajiv as the prime suspect in the case. She said that the 'government has been selective and its action is purely political vendetta'. While the Bofors investigation must go on, she said, 'What we cannot tolerate, however, is framing of a man who is innocent and who is not here to defend himself.'

The forceful plea did not work as the government expressed its helplessness in removing Rajiv's name from the Bofors charge sheet. The issue continued to agitate Sonia and Congress MPs. However, her speech made an instant impact on the party MPs. The MPs saw a Sonia who was not hesitant to talk about the Bofors investigation, despite its sensitivity. The memories of a smiling and youthful Rajiv resurfaced. They accepted Sonia as their leader in spite of her many shortcomings.

The weaknesses were evident in her role as leader of the Opposition, which initially left a lot to be desired. Congress MPs were used to be being led from the front, but with Sonia around, it was left to Madhavrao Scindia, Priyaranjan Das Munshi, Mani Shankar

Aiyar, Shivraj Patil and Jaipal Reddy to take on the government. Sonia made elaborate arrangements to decide about the issues of the day. She formed a number of party panels such as a political affairs committee, a legislative affairs panel and a research and reference committee, but very soon they began functioning at cross-purposes and relegating the CPP executive into the background. In the course of 2001–02, very many issues came up, such as the Tehelka exposé, in which a website released footage of some defence officials and ruling coalition party functionaries accepting bribes; the Unit Trust of India (UTI) scandal, in which investors saw their savings whittled away; and the failed Agra summit between Prime Minister Vajpayee and President Pervez Musharraf of Pakistan. The Congress, however, failed to exploit them.

The Tehelka exposé in 2001 by itself was calculated to throw the entire political spectrum into an uproar, alleging as it did corruption at high levels in defence deals. The UTI scam too was an emotive issue as it affected the fortunes of millions of small investors. Having acquired the status of leader of the Opposition, Sonia was expected to interact with her political adversaries like Mulayam Singh Yadav, Chandra Shekhar, Sharad Pawar, Mayawati, P.A. Sangma and others. As she was shy and reluctant to approach them directly, there was a lack of coordination and functional relationship within the Opposition ranks. Samajwadi Party leaders Mulayam Singh Yadav and Amar Singh began openly discrediting her over her failure to take the Opposition along. Sonia sought the help of Jaipal Reddy and CPM leaders Harkishen Singh Surjeet and Somnath Chatterjee to deal with Mulayam Singh while the Congress's deputy leader, Madhavrao Scindia, and chief whip Priyaranjan Das Munshi were assigned the task of interacting with Mayawati, Pawar, Ajit Singh, who had inherited his father Charan Singh's farmer constituency, and others.

In the first few months, the system appeared sketchy, and there was constant one-upmanship between the Congress and the Samajwadi Party on issues such as Ayodhya which showed the Opposition in extremely poor light. Sonia tried hard to build bridges with Mulayam Singh through Jaipal Reddy, Lalu Prasad Yadav and Surjeet, but her efforts failed as he always perceived her as a threat. Unlike Pawar or Pramod Mahajan, the BJP's parliamentary affairs minister at the time, Mulayam Singh never underestimated Sonia's strength given her surname. Privately, he consistently maintained that the threat to him in Uttar Pradesh was not so much from the BJP or the BSP but from the Congress. 'The BJP helps us stay in contention. The Congress can eat up our base,' he once told a party MP who favoured a rapprochement with a secular Congress to keep the BJP at bay.

As both the Congress and the Samajwadi Party were vying for the non-BJP secular space, the two parties could not come together. Each time Mulayam Singh or Sonia suffered a poll debacle, there were calls for realignment of secular forces. On his part, Mulayam Singh kept his options open. He sided with the Vajpayee regime supporting the American war against terrorism resulting in the bombing of Afghanistan when the Congress chose to criticize the government. He had a point man in Amar Singh, a former Congressman who excelled in cutting deals and making friends with influential industrial houses. When the BJP formed a formidable alliance with the BSP in Uttar Pradesh in 2002–03, he sought the services of a prominent industrial house to bring the Samajwadi Party and the Congress together.

Among the Opposition leaders, Sonia enjoyed a special rapport with Harkishen Singh Surjeet and Jyoti Basu, the aristocratic CPM leader from West Bengal who holds the distinction of being the country's longest serving chief minister. When Pawar and Sangma raised the foreign origins issue in 1999, Sonia called on Surjeet unannounced. The veteran communist leader was delighted to receive her at his Teen Murti Lane residence. In the absence of an air conditioner, Sonia began sweating profusely. Surjeet said apologetically, 'I have just one air conditioner and that is in my bedroom. You are like my daughter and in case you do not mind, we can sit there.' The two moved there, but the cane chair which Sonia was offered was ripped. Sonia quietly slipped in a cushion and sat over it while Surjeet began recalling how Indira had checkmated the old guard which had mounted a stiff challenge in 1969. The CPM leader said he would give two mantras to her that would keep her afloat in the worst crisis. 'Beti, remember, India is essentially a poor country, so do not get carried away by the propaganda of the benefits of reforms. The Congress has survived because it has always stood by the poor. For the sake of the nation, never ever give up on the pro-poor tilt,' he said. The other mantra was to stay away from communal forces. 'There might be a temptation to get into power. Always resist such a thing. Our experience of 1989 [when the Left supported a non-Congress government headed by V.P. Singh which was also backed by the BJP] has been extremely bitter. So never ever join hands with communal forces. After all, what is India without the poor and secularism?' he asked. Sonia could not have agreed more. To her, the old man's words were indeed guru mantras.

Sonia greatly missed Surjeet between August 2007 and July 2008 when political ties between the ruling UPA and the Left (which supported the Manmohan regime from outside) reached a point of no return, leading to a complete and ugly break up of ties in full public glare. At ninety-two, Surjeet was too old and ailing to intervene between Sonia–Manmohan on the one hand, and his successor Prakash Karat, the aggressive theoretician, on the other, over the Indo-US nuclear deal. Privately, Karat accused her of breach of faith, a charge that is said to have badly hurt Sonia.

Inside Parliament for the first time during 1998–2004, Sonia, lacking in experience and confidence, became a soft target of the treasury benches. But each time she was challenged or humiliated by the ruling coalition, she prepared to get even. According to family sources, Sonia used to tell her children that her political opponents did not know the stuff she was made of. When Prime Minister Vajpayee taunted the Congress on the party's stand on the nuclear deterrent issue, Sonia kept quiet, causing acute embarrassment to her own benches.

Afterwards she summoned experts on strategic studies, defence and nuclear issues, including those who were not part of the Congress think tank, understood the nuances and went back to Parliament to speak on the subject. Her speech included a reminder of the earlier occasion when she had failed to answer the prime minister's query.

Speaking in the Lok Sabha on 12 March 2001, a somewhat more confident Sonia asked Vajpayee, 'Even on the nuclear doctrine, is there a clarity of vision? Last session, the honourable prime minister raised a laugh by challenging me to tell him what the Congress's policy was on the nuclear deterrent. I do not begrudge the prime minister that laugh, for he is, after all, one of the wittiest parliamentarians in the last fifty years! But sir, we regard national security as far too important an issue to be settled by banter on the floor of the House. So let me throw the question back to the prime minister. What is the NDA government's nuclear doctrine? For the last eighteen months, the recommendations of the National Security Advisory Board have been gathering dust. The three little words, "minimum credible deterrent", do not amount to a policy. They have to be fleshed out; they have to be spelt out as a policy. When that is done, as a responsible Opposition we would react to it and if possible, shall lend support. But how can we, sir, lend support now? How can we support a policy that, as far as we know, does not exist?'

By March 2002, Sonia began crossing swords with the prime minister. Her body language too bespoke a more assured person. On 26 March 2002, when the two Houses met for a joint sitting to discuss the controversial Prevention of Terrorism Ordinance, Sonia alleged that Vajpayee was pushing the ordinance under pressure from the Sangh Parivar.

Vajpayee was offended. A belligerent Vajpayee went all out against Sonia, questioning her tone and tenor. Congress MPs were left stunned. They had an idea that the leader of the Opposition and the prime minister had not been on the best of terms for many months, but the verbal assault in the Central Hall of Parliament left many around Sonia speechless. They said there was nothing in her speech that could have warranted such harsh remarks.

Some Congress leaders saw it as Vajpayee's calculated move to go on the offensive. Rattled by the events in Gujarat and Ayodhya, Vajpayee had chosen to assert his supremacy in a televised debate, they said. The prime minister tried to debunk Sonia's premise that he was pushing through the anti-terrorism bill under pressure from the

Sangh Parivar, a view that had gained currency in Delhi's political circles. Vajpayee was also upset that many MPs, particularly those belonging to the Left, had accused him of acting under pressure from the US.

In his short but acrimonious intervention, Vajpayee was quick to point out that it was a Congress prime minister (P.V. Narasimha Rao) who had called off a nuclear test at the last moment under pressure from a foreign power. He also reminded the nation that he had turned down President Clinton's invitation to visit the US at the height of the Kargil conflict in 1999 when the Pakistani prime minister, Nawaz Sharif, had already reached there.

On another occasion, during the motion of thanks to the President's address, Vajpayee had objected to Sonia's description of the Gujarat riots in 2002 as genocide. The prime minister had cautioned her against using strong words, pointing to possible international ramifications.

At the personal level, too, there was little rapport between the leader of the House and the leader of the Opposition. Vajpayee and Sonia seldom exchanged greetings, preferring to deal with each other through bureaucrats and letters.

Congress leaders said that Vajpayee's strategy to pin down Sonia was a result of the growing clout of the main Opposition party, particularly after its victory in three more states. By 2002, the Congress had gained power in fourteen states and Union territories that covered almost more than half the country. These were Madhya Pradesh, Chhattisgarh, Maharashtra, Rajasthan, Delhi, Punjab, Uttaranchal, Kerala, Karnataka, Pondicherry, Nagaland, Arunachal Pradesh, Manipur and Assam. In addition, the Congress swept the Delhi municipal polls in March 2002, winning three-fourths of the seats. In such a scenario, Vajpayee was under pressure to take on the Congress, they said.

The Vajpayee–Sonia showdown had a sideshow too. Veteran leader Arjun Singh rushed to Sonia's rescue when Vajpayee said of the Congress president, 'Who is she to put me in the dock?' Singh's brief point of order may not have been forceful, but in the context of intra-party affairs, it underlined his importance and his equation with 10 Janpath. Arjun was most vocal and in the forefront of the protest when Vajpayee decided to take on Sonia.

Sonia's determination to learn was widely appreciated in the Congress. Party MP Girja Vyas said, 'There is a fighter in her and that is a very good thing.' Sonia created a huge body called the political affairs committee and began chairing meetings each morning when Parliament was in session. Initially, there were too many conflicting views, but soon Sonia picked experts in various fields who would have a final say on the matter. For instance, Dr Manmohan Singh, Pranab Mukherjee and Jairam Ramesh handled economic matters. Foreign policy matters were largely left to K. Natwar Singh and R.L. Bhatia, who was minister of state for external affairs under Narasimha Rao. Mani Shankar Aiyar and Salman Khurshid were also asked to contribute, but if there was a conflict between Natwar Singh and Aiyar, she would back the former.

On secularism, Ayodhya and the saffronization of education, she looked to Arjun Singh and Rajya Sabha party backbenchers Eduardo Faleiro and K.M. Khan, AICC secretary Janardhan Dwivedi and non-political entities like Zoya Hasan and Romila Thapar. Legal aspects were assigned to former law minister H.R. Bhardwaj, Kapil Sibal and Shiv Shankar. Dr Manmohan Singh, Madhavrao Scindia, Priyaranjan Das Munshi and Pulak Chatterjee were pressed into action to deal with the government, and at the informal level, Maharashtra leader Murli Deora, Natwar Singh and Jairam Ramesh were given the task of speaking to friendly persons in the government to break impasses and get things done.

There were reports that Natwar Singh used his old friendship with Brajesh Mishra to ensure that Sonia was given the chance to address the United Nation's General Assembly on AIDS/HIV in June 2001, much to the chagrin of the Union health minister, C.P. Thakur, who was leader of the delegation. Natwar Singh was also credited with arranging meetings with Vice-President Dick Cheney and other higher-ups in the Bush administration during her first visit to the US as leader of the Opposition in 2001. Sonia's elevation was part of a deal in return for her move to drop Vajpayee's name from a memorandum submitted to then President K.R. Narayanan demanding the prime minister's resignation in the wake of the Tehelka exposé.

The US visit was a milestone in Sonia's political career, enhancing her confidence by several notches. She was relieved to note that everyone spoke from a prepared text, as if speaking extempore indicated a lack of seriousness. She interacted freely with one and all, displaying her sense of humour and personal charm. The Indian community in the US was delighted, finding her a quick-witted, intelligent person.

Sonia's successful US visit created a stir in the government and the BJP. There were many red faces including that of BJP MP Dina Nath Mishra, editor of the book *Sonia: 'The Unknown'*, which levelled many non-serious and bizarre charges against her. Ironically, it was Mishra's party that sent Sonia as a representative of one billion persons to the UN AIDS conference in June 2001. She carried the day with dignity, underlining that although in domestic politics her party had differences with the BJP and the NDA, there was complete consensus on issues such as tackling poverty and disease and on stabilizing the population.

Sonia's style of functioning became a subject of intense discussion in Congress circles. Within days of taking over as party president, Sonia made it clear that the party would be given a corporate touch. She appointed Sangma to submit a report on its functioning. The task force report of 1998 had some interesting suggestions, such as a boardroom-type seating arrangement for the CWC members. Sangma was of the view that in the television era, sitting Indian-style on the floor, resting against bolsters and cushions does not project the Congress as a twenty-first-century political party. He was also against the mandatory dress code of khadi and the provision that completely debars Congress activists from dealing in alcohol. Sonia had a good mind to implement these recommendations on grounds of pragmatism, but before she could act, Sangma walked out of the Congress, forcing her to put the path-breaking report in cold storage. A copy of the report is currently lying under a heap in an outhouse of 24 Akbar Road.

In another effort to introduce a corporate culture in the party, in February 2000 Sonia set up departments for science and technology, environment, human rights, Other Backward Castes (OBCs), minorities, policy, planning and coordination, communications, public relations, media and information, foreign affairs, economy, law and so on, creating 144 posts in the AICC to man these, but party leaders entrusted with the task of running these departments largely remained indifferent. Each departmental head insisted upon getting secretarial staff, fax, telephone and a room, but once the infrastructure was provided to them, they hardly attended office.

Having failed to introduce a corporate culture, Sonia tried to streamline the party's style of functioning. It started with an attempt to carry everyone along, holding monthly CWC meetings and allowing free and frank discussions, but slowly the democratization process gave way to the long-ingrained coterie culture. Though Sonia contested the charge, the AICC chief remained dependent on a select band of advisers. In a bid to ward off criticism, she shuffled around with the coterie, but leaders like Arjun Singh, Natwar Singh and private secretary Vincent George continued to have a final say in all decision making.

Party leaders said Sonia may have lacked Rajiv's warmth, but she was not indifferent like Narasimha Rao. She tried to maintain a certain distance, drawing a distinction between her public and personal life. She made it clear, for example, that Sunday would be her day off, unless there was an emergency. For many Congress leaders, including chief ministers, it was a shock of sorts. Digvijay Singh used to visit Delhi on weekends, but his requests for appointments remained unattended on Sunday, and so he began to call on her on Saturday evenings. In party meetings, there was no scope for loose talk and personal attacks. Mobile phones were to be switched off. She insisted on attendance, making it mandatory for all office-bearers to inform her office in advance about their tour programmes.

Sonia usually came prepared to party meetings and expected others to do the same. There was a meeting of the chief ministers of Congress-ruled states where the Delhi chief minister Sheila Dikshit, and her then Maharashtra counterpart, Vilasrao Deshmukh, got to see another side of Sonia. Both chief ministers had come rather unprepared and failed to give convincing replies about schemes for scheduled castes, scheduled tribes and minorities. Sonia was quick to reprimand them. 'You should have come prepared. What is the point of holding such meetings if chief ministers do not come prepared?'

Accountability was another area that gained currency under Sonia. As party president, Sonia gave a free hand to all office-bearers, but if they faltered, she moved swiftly to punish them. Veteran leader Pranab Mukherjee was sacked as AICC general secretary when he mishandled the party affairs in Haryana by aligning with a tottering Bansi Lal government. Lal, who was defence minister in the Indira government during the Emergency (1975–77), was heading a state government in Haryana when many of his party (Haryana Vikas Party) MLAs began to desert him. Though he was a veteran of many political battles, Lal panicked. He tapped some of his old contacts in the Congress to bail him out. The tide, however, had turned against him. The Congress stepped in but could not prevent the fall of his government. Lal's arch-rival, Om Prakash Chautala, formed an alternative government and called for fresh polls. In these, the Congress lost the state where it had a fair chance of winning before the Lal fiasco.

Pranab later had a thousand and one explanations, but the AICC chief was not convinced. In consideration of Mukherjee's seniority, he was allowed to tender his resignation owning 'moral responsibility'. The Haryana episode served as a warning of sorts for Congress bigwigs. They realized that if a leader like Mukherjee could be asked to go, they were also vulnerable.

Ghulam Nabi Azad became another victim of Sonia's accountability mantra. An assertive Sonia suddenly dropped Azad as general secretary on 27 March 2002 and gave him a punishing assignment as chief of the Jammu and Kashmir Congress, a unit that was virtually defunct in the violence-ridden state. Azad had earned the dubious distinction of being a 'rootless wonder' because he had no support base in his home state. He once contested the assembly polls from Kishtwar but lost miserably.

Azad had dominated the AICC for more than a decade. As AICC general secretary, he claimed to have looked after party affairs of twenty-four states. In scattered tenures, he had the distinction of occupying various rooms at 24 Akbar Road. He had first been spotted by Indira, who drafted him in the Youth Congress. He soon came in touch with Sanjay, who took him under his wing. Azad did not look back. He went on to head the Youth Congress and the Sewa Dal and then became party general secretary. The young man turned out to be an excellent weathercock, having a knack of being in the right spot at the right time. When Rajiv began having problems with Vishwanath Pratap Singh, Azad quickly offered his services, resigning from a ministerial assignment to take up party work. When Narasimha Rao faced a challenge from Arjun Singh, Azad decided to take on the thakur. In an incredible admission, Azad claimed that he had spent more than one thousand hours with Rajiv in private, implying that there was none other who could boast of such proximity to Rajiv!

Once Narasimha Rao was shown the door, Azad became a favourite bhatija (nephew) of 'Chacha' Sitaram Kesri. Until Sharad Pawar decided to throw a leadership challenge to the ailing AICC chief. Azad was in a fix as he was deeply indebted to Pawar. The gratitude stemmed from reasons ranging from Pawar ensuring his victory in the 1984 Lok Sabha elections from Vashim in Maharashtra to mobilizing resources for the Rajya Sabha polls. As Azad dithered and pleaded sick, Kesri became restless over his defiance. The cosy relations between chacha and bhatija took a dive. Till his death, Kesri continued to speak ill of him, but Azad was unmindful. He had found a new mentor in Sonia and bridged his differences with Arjun Singh.

Under Sonia, Azad increased his clout considerably. He was put in charge of party affairs in Karnataka and Kerala in 2001. The Congress won elections in both states. His camp began circulating reports that he had a magic touch, that he was a lucky mascot for the party. He was not a ghulam (slave) but azad (independent). Others said he was indispensable. The talk reached Sonia, and she began looking more closely at his style of functioning. Soon after, the general secretary burnt his fingers in Kerala when he failed to strike a balance between

Chief Minister A.K. Antony and his arch-rival K. Karunakaran. When, in February 2002, the party won elections in the Himalayan state of Uttaranchal, Azad made an abortive bid to prop up trade union leader Harish Rawat as the new chief minister of the state. The elected MLAs opted for veteran leader Narain Dutt Tiwari. The MLAs complained to Sonia that Azad was thrusting his choice on them.

Azad ran out of luck in March 2002 and paid the price for the party's drubbing in the Uttar Pradesh assembly polls. He was AICC general secretary in charge of Uttar Pradesh. Sources said Sonia discarded him because of his proximity to Mulayam Singh Yadav. There were allegations backed by statistics that said the Congress performed badly in places where the Samajwadi Party had won comfortably. The insinuation was that he had tried to work out a deal with Mulayam Singh without taking permission from the high command. The Congress forfeited deposits in as many as 325 out of 403 assembly seats. In the Afzalgarh constituency in Bijnore district, the party finished a distant eleventh, much behind many independents and non-serious players!

Azad's exit, however, surprised many in the party. Senior leaders took it as a sign of Sonia acting independently, dumping her reliance on the coterie.

As the Jammu and Kashmir Congress unit chief, Azad faced an uphill task. The Jammu and Kashmir Pradesh Congress Committee (JKPCC) president was expected to revitalize the party and take on the firmly entrenched National Conference. The problem was that he was perceived to be close to the party's chief, Farooq Abdullah, their friendship dating back to his election to the Rajya Sabha five and a half years before, when the National Conference donated its surplus votes to see him through.

However, with a slice of luck, Azad proved his detractors wrong in Jammu and Kashmir. The outcome of the assembly polls in November 2002 surprised everyone, including Azad, as the party did exceedingly well, finishing second behind the National Conference. The arithmetic was such that a Congress government under Azad became a possibility but Sonia, aware of Azad's limitations, accorded primacy to the mandate in the Kashmir valley where a regional party, the

People's Democratic Party (PDP), under a former Congress leader, Mufti Mohammad Sayeed, had been successful. Sonia overruled the twenty-odd Congress MLAs and crowned Sayeed. Incidentally, Sayeed was among the few Congressmen who had left the party after Sonia had taken over as chief in 1998.

Sonia's sensitivity to the feelings of the people in the state earned her respect. Her decision was dubbed statesman-like. Azad did not protest too much realizing that he was getting a berth in the Rajya Sabha and important assignments in the party. Sayeed and the Congress worked out an elaborate arrangement as part of a common minimum programme for the state.

Azad made a comeback of sorts in 2005 when he bagged the job of chief minister of Jammu and Kashmir replacing Sayeed as part of the Congress–PDP arrangement to share the six-year tenure equally. Azad was considered a rank outsider in the state and his wife, Shamim, feared for his life. But Sonia called her and made it clear that Azad would have to take on the assignment. As chief minister, Azad performed reasonably well as the Valley did not see much trouble during this period, even witnessing the return of tourists on a large scale. Kashmir experts, however, saw little wisdom in maintaining the status quo in the number one troubled spot of the subcontinent. While terror modules from across the border reduced their operation, the peace process between India and Pakistan took a backstage. The period between 2005 and 2008 saw a weakened General Pervez Musharraf and Manmohan Singh getting little time to focus on the vexed issues of cross-border terrorism and Kashmir. In fact, in spite of repeated announcements and invitations, both Manmohan and Sonia could not visit Pakistan.

Towards the fag end of Azad's term, however, the sensitive border state went up in flames over allotment of some government land to the Shri Amarnath Board shrine. As both separatists and right-wing nationalists resorted to violence and the National Conference opposed the move, the PDP snapped ties with the Congress. Minutes before facing a trust vote, Azad announced his move to step down. The maverick could do little to poach or win over MLAs sharply divided on communal lines.

The Congress under Sonia gave high priority to some of the thorny issues that had been hanging fire for years. Successive party leaderships had failed to take drastic action on the issue of reservation for women in party posts, allocation of tickets and party funding. In this arena, Sonia deserves credit for displaying leadership qualities while tiding over the storm within the Congress and enforcing measures that she felt were necessary. The regional satraps and vested interests who thought she could be manipulated were in for a shock. Sonia got the Congress the distinction of being the first political party that gave 33 per cent quota to women at all levels of the party hierarchy. Overruling the majority sentiment, she got sweeping amendments through in the Congress constitution.

On the application side, though, there were genuine problems in getting one-third of women nominees at block and district levels of the party. However, she kept a strict vigil, and whenever she got an opportunity, she filled party posts with women nominees. Under Sonia, the Congress became the first national-level party to support a controversial women's reservation bill that sought to reserve one-third of parliamentary and assembly seats for women. The bill failed to get through the Lok Sabha, but it found a powerful advocate in Sonia. In successive Lok Sabhas, Sonia made it a point to embarrass the ruling coalition by raking up the issue of quota for women. In this respect, she won many admirers across party lines.

On 10 June 2001, the Congress under Sonia became the first all-white party. Chanting a new mantra of integrity, accountability and transparency, the country's oldest political party pledged to accept monetary donations only through cheques. As was the 33 per cent quota for women, the sweeping changes in the way the party was funded was a personal triumph for her. She managed to push through the path-breaking reforms in this murky area, overruling sceptics within the CWC who expressed doubts about the feasibility of cheque payments. But the AICC chief remained unfazed. Sonia said the Congress was prepared to clean up the entire system, but it was for the government to take the initiative to bring about electoral reforms. In her view, the Congress is game on state funding of polls, recommended by two all-party parliamentary panels headed by Dinesh Goswami and Indrajit Gupta, both outstanding parliamentarians who are now dead.

On rough calculation, the Congress's annual expenses (without election expenses) run to about Rs 10 crores, which are raised through all sorts of means, including those which cannot be shown in audit. Sonia said she wanted to change all that. In her scheme of things, everyone who was someone in the party would have to pay to fill the coffers. The party decided to raise a Rs 50-crore corpus by 2003 by asking its eleven lakh active workers to pay Rs 100 a year. For PCC delegates, the amount was Rs 300 a year and for members of the AICC it was Rs 600. MPs, MLAs, ministers, chief ministers, as also chairpersons of district boards, autonomous bodies, municipal corporations and other panels had to contribute one month's salary.

Sonia also thought of some novel methods of raising funds. Those seeking party tickets for elections were asked to pay Rs 5000 for assembly seats and Rs 10,000 for Lok Sabha tickets. In case they failed to get the ticket, the money was non-refundable. Likewise, corporate houses and captains of industry were encouraged to make payments by cheque in accordance with existing rules in the Companies Act. The party recommended that the ceiling under Section 293(A) of the Companies Act, 1956 should be enhanced. The various chambers of commerce welcomed the clean-up resolution. Individuals like Ratan Tata, chairman of the Tatas, who have been advocating the need for transparency and accountability, hailed Sonia's move. Sonia appeared pleased and told aides that party funding was one area where she wanted to do a lot.

Another ambition is to make the Congress a party of the best and the brightest. Unless the party provides a conducive atmosphere for the entry of such individuals, the credibility of politicians will not be restored, she feels.

While Sonia succeeded on some fronts, her public image of an apolitical, reluctant politician was a result of her own creation. She took the plunge into politics but remained morbidly afraid of the media. Her party colleagues perpetuated the fear. The AICC chief restricted herself to giving the occasional sound bite to private television networks.

Sonia tried to interact more with the media but her advisers, including senior party functionaries, scuttled the move. These leaders told Sonia that both Indira and Rajiv had suffered from media witch-hunting. For a long time, Sonia firmly believed that the media was nursing a grudge against her. Each day 10 Janpath was flooded with requests for interviews, but she turned them down waiting for a suitable moment.

One such occasion seemed to present itself when the television news channel CNN collaborated with *Time* magazine, and their team decided to fly down to Delhi in 2001. At the last moment, the interview was cancelled as someone advised Sonia to give her first interview to an Indian publication. She short-listed the largely circulated Hindi daily *Punjab Kesri* (recommended by Priyanka Gandhi) and the *Times of India*, but other newspaper barons threw a fit. The Italian media stationed in New Delhi thought meeting Sonia would be easier for them, but they were in for a shock too, for they were curtly told to get in touch with Ajit Jogi and V.N. Gadgil.

A number of well-meaning persons suggested to Sonia that she have a full-time media adviser or consultant who could help her stay in touch with the media. Sonia was keen to have the services of H.Y. Sharda Prasad, former information adviser to Indira, and Suman Dubey, but both politely declined. A number of retired journalists, journalists-turned-politicians and television personalities were keen, but Sonia did not consider them suitable or lobbying and counter-lobbying within the Congress prevented such an appointment. Ultimately, the move was shelved.

Sonia's inexperience too played a role in her mishandling of the media. In 1998, some months after she took over as party president, she decided to meet those covering the Congress individually. The interaction was supposed to be one-on-one and strictly off the record. She insisted on seeing the list of journalists who were to call on her and asked for the resumés of these individuals. To make matters worse, the AICC's media department began calling up scribes asking them to hand over their CVs if they wished to see the AICC chief. The request created a good deal of merriment till Sonia herself withdrew the demand.

Reflecting back, Sonia spoke at length about herself, her days with Indira and other matters of significance while delivering a lecture on 'Living Politics: What India Has Taught Me' at the Nexus Institute, Tilburg, Netherlands, in June 2007. She said that while she formally joined politics in December 1997 she was schooled in the Nehru–Gandhi's family profession right after her marriage to Rajiv Gandhi. 'My first political classroom thus echoed to momentous unfolding events. Two stand out in my memory. The first was the 1971 crisis which transformed Mrs Gandhi into a statesman. Another memory I have of her as a political leader is of her steely determination to raise India out of the cycle of famine and dependency on imports of food grains. She took tough decisions which laid the foundations of the Green Revolution that transformed our economy.'

Sonia's Tilburg speech echoed with perceptive observations. Elaborating the theme of her speech, she said, 'It is appropriate that I speak to the theme of my lecture in this fascinating country, because the story I have to tell is a bit like the works of two of your greatest artists. Like Rembrandt's, it is a story of light and darkness, of mystery and the hidden hand of destiny. Like Van Gogh's, it is also a story of inner struggle and torment, a story of how the experience of loss can impart a deeper meaning to life.'

She said that having been born in Italy, she learnt of the Risorgimento, of Mazzini and Garibaldi and the unification of Italy. But of India, its history and its emergence as a modern nation state, she was taught nothing. 'My discovery of India happened differently,' she said, adding, 'Our world had been overturned with the death of my mother-in-law. As often happens when one loses a loved one, I sought to reach out to her through her writings. I immersed myself in editing two volumes of letters between her and her father. Through most of her youth, while her father was in British jails, their loving and close relationship found expression in this flourishing correspondence, recording a rich and vivid interplay between two lively minds.'

Sonia said that the Nehru–Indira correspondence introduced her to the Indian freedom struggle as it was experienced and acted upon by two people who went on to play important roles in shaping modern India. 'Along with the books of Jawaharlal Nehru, which I had read earlier, they provided a philosophical and historical underpinning to my direct experience of observing my husband as he carried forward their vision for India,' she said.

Elaborating on her personal life, Sonia said her days as daughter-in-law of the prime minister were permeated by the turbulence of politics. 'Looking back, I can say that it was through the private world of family that the public world of politics came alive for me: living in intimate proximity with people for whom larger questions of ideology and belief as well as issues relating to politics and governance were vivid daily realities.' She said there were other aspects of living in a political family that had an impact on her as a young bride. 'I had to accustom myself to the public gaze, which I found intrusive and hard to endure. I had to learn to curb my spontaneity and instinctive bluntness of speech. Most of all, I had to school myself not to react in the face of falsehood and slander. I had to learn to endure them as the rest of the family did,' she said.

In conclusion Sonia said, 'Those of you who are familiar with India will know that we are famously loquacious. Indeed as Nobel Laureate and Nexus lecturer Amartya Sen has remarked in his book *The Argumentative Indian*, what grieves and frustrates an Indian most about the prospect of dying is that he will no longer be able to argue back! Not surprisingly therefore, public life in India is characterized by vigorous debate and vehement contention. The cacophony of politics is the very music of our democracy.'

SIX

SONIA TAKES OVER THE CONGRESS

It was in the third week of December 1997 that Sonia Gandhi first indicated her willingness to take a more active role in politics. She chose Digvijay 'Diggy Raja' Singh, chief minister of Madhya Pradesh, to break the news. He had called on her complaining against the Congress chief Sitaram Kesri. For him and many other party leaders, Kesri was more of a liability than an asset. The old man who avoided contesting direct elections had no charisma, vision or mass appeal. For him, the route to success was simple—plea, petition and manipulation. Behind a simple Gandhian profile, Kesri was a shrewd politician with a knack of being on the winning side. He had cut many deals and annoyed many partymen. Kesri had survived for decades, but once he took over as the Congress chief, his flaws as a leader became glaringly obvious.

Singh did not mince words in saying that under Kesri the Congress was heading towards disaster. As long as Kesri was head of the Congress, the party would not even get hundred seats in the Lok Sabha polls that were announced for January 1998.

Sonia attentively heard Singh's formulation and then casually asked, 'What will happen if I campaign for the Congress?' He could not believe his ears. 'Madam, that would electrify our rank and file. We will sweep the polls!' He could visualize Sonia addressing mammoth public meetings in his state. To him, it was a reminder of the heady days of Rajiv in 1984 that marked Singh's debut in the Lok Sabha. He could hardly forget how Rajiv had made him Congress unit chief of Madhya Pradesh in 1987 although he lacked experience. Rajiv had sounded him for the coveted post, and Singh blurted it out to his mentor Arjun Singh who, in turn, quickly approached Rajiv offering his services for the job! Rajiv summoned Digvijay wondering how Arjun came to know about a private conversation between them. 'It was an important political lesson for me,' he later recalled, admitting that Rajiv's trust in him made him a 10 Janpath loyalist forever.

Digvijay Singh was not alone in labelling Kesri a liability for the Congress or in being a beneficiary of the benevolent acts of the Nehru–Gandhi family. By December 1997, barring a handful of Kesri loyalists, virtually everyone had turned against him. Ahmad Patel, Kamal Nath, Vayalar Ravi, Ashok Gehlot and dozens of Young Turks frequently met Sonia to remind her of her historic responsibilities to save the nation from fascist forces. As a member of the great family, she could not escape her responsibilities, Patel told her. 'Millions of party workers are willing to die for you. How can you allow the collapse of the Congress before your eyes,' Gehlot said, pointing at the large-scale desertions in the party. Aslam Sher Khan, Mani Shankar Aiyar, Suresh Kalmadi, Buta Singh and P.R. Kumarmangalam were some of the prominent leaders who had left the party. Kumarmangalam died soon thereafter, but one by one, Aiyar, Buta and Kalmadi returned to the parent organization once Sonia took over as AICC chief.

The old guard of the Congress was also at work. Fed up with Kesri's antics, manipulations and unpredictable nature, leaders like K. Karunakaran, Arjun Singh, A.K. Antony, Jitendra Prasada, Vijay Bhaskar Reddy, V.N. Gadgil and Madhav Sinh Solanki kept exerting pressure on Sonia to intervene. Arjun Singh and Prasada, who had masterminded the collapse of the I.K. Gujral government on the basis of the Jain Commission report, gently reminded her of the need to reciprocate the feelings of the Congress workers who could not tolerate the presence of two DMK ministers in a government supported by the Congress.

The moral pressure of the Rajiv assassination probe was, in fact, a turning point. It was one issue that could make the family overcome its reluctance to take an active role in politics. Arjun Singh was the first to identify the weak spot months after Rao took over as the prime minister in 1991. He began attending virtually all the sittings of the Verma and Jain Commission hearings, sending details of the proceedings to 10 Janpath. At first they got no response. Rahul and Priyanka were also regularly seen at the Vigyan Bhavan annexe where the hearings were taking place. But Singh's bid to strike rapport with them did not succeed, since the Gandhi children remained aloof from Congress politicians.

The sum and substance of Arjun's campaign was that unless Sonia took a more active political role, the Rajiv assassination probe would not make any headway, and the real culprits of the dastardly act and the key conspirators might even get away. A secondary part of his campaign was that the Rao government had a sinister design in scuttling the probe—a charge that gained momentum when Arjun Singh resigned from the Rao government in December 1994. Many Congress leaders also felt that Sonia was not convinced that the LTTE was solely responsible for Rajiv's assassination. She was of the view that the LTTE may have been a willing agent for other agencies involved in that dastardly act.

Arjun Singh's detractor Jitendra Prasada used the same ploy to get even with Kesri, which resulted in the downfall of the Gujral government. Like Singh, Prasada hired a battery of lawyers to examine the bulky Jain Commission report picking instances that seemed to link the DMK with the LTTE.

Amidst these behind-the-scenes deliberations, Sonia too had begun putting aside her reluctance towards politics. Events in the past few years had altered her thinking. The betrayal of Narasimha Rao, the tardy progress in the Rajiv assassination probe, the ever-declining fortunes of the Congress and all-round attack on the Nehru–Gandhi legacy weighed heavily in favour of testing the uncertain waters of politics. If the Congress were to disintegrate, would not she be held responsible?

In the next forty-eight hours, she tried to probe Rahul's and Priyanka's mind. Predictably, Rahul became agitated. 'Let us not get into the mess,' was his advice. Priyanka, however, was thoughtful. 'Mama, let us see,' was her response. The family met again at dinner that night. Various pros and cons were discussed and Rahul reluctantly gave up. 'Mama, I will leave work and be with you in all public meetings,' he offered. The family then tentatively decided that Sonia would make the announcement around Christmas so that she could campaign for the Congress in the general elections.

It was at this juncture that Sonia is said to have fallen out with Amitabh Bachchan. Bachchan was completely against Sonia entering politics. He described Congress leaders as vultures who wanted to cash in on the Nehru–Gandhi family's appeal to serve their political ends. For the first time in thirty years, he and Sonia were not on the same wavelength. While Sonia saw some merit in what Amitabh was saying, she stayed with her decision.

Meanwhile, blissfully unaware of the developments at 10 Janpath, 'Chacha' Sitaram Kesri was busy trying to build a band of loyalists for himself. Kesri knew that the party MPs were unhappy over the manner in which he had pulled down the United Front governments of H.D. Deve Gowda and I.K. Gujral. His relations with 10 Janpath had taken a beating over his reluctance to bring down Gujral's government over the Jain Commission report. Kesri was bitter that Arjun Singh and Prasada had succeeded in projecting him as a villain in Sonia's eyes. He tried to patch things up and paid several visits to her, but he failed to gauge her mood. 'There was something in her eyes that made me uneasy, but I had no idea that she was going to take the plunge or dump me so unceremoniously,' Kesri later told his friends in the media, blaming Singh and Prasada for spoiling his otherwise 'excellent rapport' with her.

After all, as welfare minister between 1991 and 1996, Kesri had given standing orders to his ministry officials to clear all projects of the RGF on priority basis. With Sonia as head of the RGF, Kesri thought that his gesture would keep him in her good books. Kesri's logic was simple. A lot of money under his ministry earmarked for non-governmental organizations (NGOs) was going unused or disappearing into the hands of unscrupulous elements. Kesri thought he was killing two birds with one stone. 'Sarkari paisa hain. Agar Indira ke parivar ke paas ja raha hai to kya boorai hai (It is government money. Even if it is going to Indira's family, I see no harm),' Kesri told some journalists.

Kesri had severe limitations as the president of the Congress. Leaders from the south and the North-East had a problem communicating with him, and partymen from the north never accepted Kesri as their leader due to caste considerations. After all, the Congress had retained its upper-caste character in Uttar Pradesh, Bihar, Madhya Pradesh, Rajasthan, Punjab and elsewhere. Kesri also made his dislike for the north Indian Brahmins and thakurs obvious. He was open about forging a grand alliance with the likes of Lalu Prasad Yadav, Kanshi Ram and Mulayam Singh Yadav. His views unnerved a large section of upper-caste leaders from the Hindi heartland who were already struggling to survive, losing successive Lok Sabha polls with huge margins. Kesri's promise to 'Mandalize' the Congress made them sit up, as they were now about to lose their position within the organization too.

Kesri, who came from a modest background and had no formal education, also began priding himself as a commoner who was elected by the party rank and file. Though everyone within the Congress and outside it viewed the organizational polls that concluded in Calcutta in September 1997 as farcical, Kesri took the compliment of elected AICC chief too seriously. His commoner reference was viewed as a sign of defiance towards Sonia and the Nehru–Gandhi family. To make matters worse between Kesri and 10 Janpath, a handful of former MPs systematically began passing on bits of information and gossip to Vincent George exaggerating what Kesri was saying about Sonia and her loyalists. One leader from Madhya Pradesh told George, 'He says he will finish off the Nehru–Gandhi family,' and quoted Kesri as saying, 'The days of rajas and maharajas are over. Foreigners must go back. I have fought thousands of angrez and what is a petty Italian!'

The veteran leader was a great storyteller and gossip, with a view on virtually everything. 'Ek baat bata deten hain (Let me tell you a thing),' he would start. The tale he loved to tell was how Rajendra Babu (Dr Rajendra Prasad, the first President) had a great liking for him. Prasad had visited Danapur and spotted the young freedom fighter in him. 'I went to jail several times,' Kesri would recount, exposing his back to show the spots where he received lashes from the 'lal pagris', as the lathi-wielding Raj police in Bihar were called.

Kesri's detractors had a different story, claiming that young Kesri was booked under hoarding charges during the Second World War. Kesri's take on this was that the British used to deliberately come up with charges such as this to malign freedom fighters.

Sometimes Kesri would speak of how Subhash Chandra Bose was greater than Jawaharlal Nehru. 'I was part of the Forward Bloc and Netaji's team in Calcutta,' he would say, closing his eyes. He would ruminate on how India would have been different if Gandhiji had not made a mistake in picking Nehru instead of Bose. The non-violent pacifist would give way to the radical Kesri. 'We have a slave mentality. We have not got freedom after shedding blood. The non-violent method made us impotent. Had Subhash been around, the country would have been different,' Kesri would say, propagating a theory that the Nehru-led, Delhi-centric Congress consciously suppressed leadership from Bengal. 'From Bose to Mamata Banerjee, it is the same story of suppression and injustice,' Kesri would tell a flabbergasted audience that was left wondering how Bose could be compared to Banerjee.

On 28 December 1997, Sonia chose to go public about her intention to join politics. It was a sleepy afternoon when beat regulars gathered at 24 Akbar Road for a routine press conference. Kesri too wanted to share a word with journalists in a post-briefing informal chat.

He reached the party headquarters at 2.30 p.m., but an hour before the scheduled press meet at 4 p.m., a small note from 10 Janpath ruined his mood. Tom Vaddakan, who rose to become AICC's media secretary, ran through a small passage between 10 Janpath and 24 Akbar Road carrying an announcement from Vincent George that said Sonia would campaign for the Congress in the general elections.

Initially Vaddakan was not allowed to pass Sonia's message to Kesri. The guard outside Kesri's room would not let him in. 'It is important and if you do not let me in, you will lose your job,' an irritated Vaddakan said, but the guard was unfazed. 'Sahib does not want to be disturbed,' he said matter-of-factly. Suddenly, Tom saw Harish Khare, a journalist from the *Hindu* who had an appointment with Kesri. 'Sir, please pass this on to him. It is from 10 Janpath and the guard is not letting me in.' Khare took the note and gave it to Kesri.

Kesri's face fell the moment he finished reading it. He struggled to respond, mumbling to himself, 'Sub kuch khatam. Woh aa rahi hai (It is all over. She is coming).' Kesri then broke the news to Khare. Interestingly, Kesri did not address the briefing to make the announcement, notwithstanding his scores of public statements requesting Sonia to help out the party. It was left to V.N. Gadgil to make the announcement to the world.

In a surprising gesture Kesri refrained from hogging the limelight that day. After all, when Madhavrao Scindia and S. Bangarappa, former Karnataka chief minister, returned to the parent organization, Kesri was there to receive them in the AICC portico and escort them to the briefing room before making a formal announcement. Sources close to Kesri later admitted that the old man was keen to welcome Sonia but decided against it. He was reminded of the designs of his detractors like Arjun Singh and Jitendra Prasada who were using 10 Janpath to dislodge him. Kesri also realized that it was not befitting of an elected AICC chief to be seen as playing second fiddle to Sonia.

When the news of Kesri's defiance reached 10 Janpath, Sonia began wondering if she had taken the correct course. She suddenly realized that her entry would not be as smooth as projected by Digvijay Singh, Arjun Singh, Kamal Nath and others. Her mind raced back to a statement made by a close family friend who had vehemently opposed her decision to enter public life. 'I have been a Congress MP. I know the party too well. It is a snake-pit. You will soon realize that the most trusted persons can turn against you.' The prediction turned out to be true on several occasions. In Sonia's own words, 'I have no regret that I joined politics. But yes, it pained me when I saw people who had repeatedly requested me to take the plunge, level baseless allegations against me and leave the party.' The reference was to P.A. Sangma, Tariq Anwar and Sharad Pawar who revolted and left the party in May 1999.

Sonia shrugged off the idea of withdrawing her move. She foresaw a dismal future for the Congress if she did not join the party. The AICC treasurer, Ahmad Patel, helped her articulate these ideas in a presentation produced with the aid of a professional agency. It said that the Congress would disintegrate into several factions and the BJP would gain strength and undermine the country's secular fabric. The inference was clear: join the Congress and you will have millions of party workers willing to die for the honour of the family.

Sonia was not unaware of the points made by the presentation. As the slides played out the scenario, Sonia firmed up her mind. 'I am a fighter, and I will overcome the handicaps,' she told herself. In the back of her mind was the sequence of events that resulted in the fall of the Gujral government over the Jain Commission report. Years later, Sonia told some family friends that destiny ensured a political role for her. 'I was dead opposed to it. In fact, in 1991 I was shocked and considered Congressmen extremely insensitive when the CWC passed a resolution asking me to take over as the party chief. Seven years after, I just could not resist,' she admitted.

The choice of 28 December 1997 was not without significance. It was the 112th anniversary of the Indian National Congress. The general elections had been announced and the Congress state election committees, central election committee and other important bodies that allot tickets to aspirants were to meet on 3 and 4 January 1998. As the Congress president, Kesri had a final say, but Sonia's arrival spoilt everything. In the meetings that took place, Kesri was reduced to a puppet. Each day, general secretary Oscar Fernandes would bring a file from 10 Janpath that was reportedly sent by Vincent George, and

Kesri was expected to clear all the names. Kesri suspected that Arjun Singh was acting in concert with George and that the duo was keeping Sonia in the dark, but the old man could never muster the courage to complain against George, though he met Sonia a number of times. Each time he said that proper persons were not getting party tickets, Sonia would say, 'Kesriji, please consult Arjun Singhji and Madhavrao!'

The New Year brought chaos. The Kesri camp was busy projecting it as the 'year of Kesri' while Sonia's managers were finalizing venues for her debut and consulting astrologers. On 11 January 1998, Sriperumbudur became the venue of her first public meeting. Requests from prospective candidates pleading that Sonia should touch their constituency flooded 10 Janpath. She was seen as their passport to success.

Vincent George suddenly became extremely busy. Helping him were dozens of loyal workers who were experts in a range of subjects, Congress history and culture among them. It was an elite band of experts that used to help Rajiv. A place's historical importance, link to Indira and Rajiv, and caste and religious considerations were some of the factors that were taken into account in chalking out Sonia's itinerary. After all, she was 'Indira II' in the making. She first needed to regain the confidence of the traditional vote bank—the poor, tribals and weaker sections, the Muslims and other minorities.

As Congressmen made a beeline for 10 Janpath, there was a sharp decline in the number of visitors at Kesri's 7 Purana Qila Road residence. Only the usual hangers-on remained. Each day Kesri was confronted with more bad news. For among the points Sonia made in her speeches was that all was not well with the Congress. She made it clear that she would not confine herself to campaigning for the party but would continue to play an active role in politics even after the elections.

For the first time in the history of the Congress, the party president was kept away from campaigning. None of the states, including his own state Bihar, sought Kesri's services. The old man tried to visit Jalandhar, but the aircraft had to turn around while flying over Ambala as Kesri developed a breathing problem in the unpressurized cabin.

Azad later said that he remained extremely tense till the aircraft landed at Palam. 'I was seriously worried about Chacha's health. He appeared in acute pain, almost choking.'

The outcome of the elections to the twelfth Lok Sabha came as a shock to the Congress. In the back-breaking campaign that saw Sonia address 130-odd meetings, the Congress's final tally read 142. Besides handing over the family borough of Amethi to the BJP, she could not save two of her most trusted lieutenants, Arjun Singh and Narain Dutt Tiwari, who lost in Hoshangabad (Madhya Pradesh) and Nainital (then in Uttar Pradesh). But her managers quickly put the blame on Kesri, who had not stepped out of his house. They said that owing to organizational weaknesses, the party failed to cash in on Sonia's charisma. She accepted the argument and agreed to take direct control of the party, insisting, however, that Kesri step down gracefully and invite her to take over. Chacha was in no mood to oblige her.

Restless CWC members began holding conclaves to work out plans on how to install Sonia. The task was left to Kesri's two favourite 'nephews'—Ahmad Patel and Azad—to sound him out about retiring gracefully. But Kesri laughed off the proposal. 'You have been sent by Arjun Singh and George. It cannot be Soniaji's words. If she wants me out, let her say so,' Chacha said.

Sharad Pawar too joined the 'Kesri hatao' campaign. He was getting feedback from Mumbai and the corporate world that said that as long as Kesri was head of the party, the industrial houses would not support it. Pawar teamed up with Prasada and A.K. Antony, and later Pranab Mukherjee joined in. Every week the senior leaders would meet in small groups to review the situation. Invariably Pawar would favour a 'surgical operation', but Mukherjee and Antony would seek more time.

Sensing trouble, the Kesri camp launched a counter-offensive. The first casualties were the CWC meetings that had to be convened by the party chief. Kesri was advised not to call the CWC as it might ask him to step down. Kesri was convinced that the party constitution gave him ultimate powers and that as long as he was the elected chief, nobody would dare to remove him.

The CWC finally met on 5 March 1998 to assess the party's poor performance in the general elections. The outcome of the meeting was significant on two counts. First, it asked Sonia to play a more direct and meaningful role and requested her to help the party elect the new leader of the CPP, a post that Kesri occupied. Kesri was upset with Mukherjee and Pawar, and he later told Tariq Anwar, 'If Sharad thinks he can become CPP leader, tell him to forget it. Soniaji will never let it happen.' Kesri was proved right for soon after Sonia took over she got herself elected as the CPP leader though she was not an MP. The CPP constitution was amended to state that any party leader was free to get elected to its parliamentary body even if he/she was not a member of either House!

After the Ahmad–Azad mission failed, three senior leaders, Dr Manmohan Singh, Pranab Mukherjee and A.K. Antony, approached Kesri. The trio acknowledged Kesri's services but told him that a change of guard was in the interest of the party. Antony said Sonia was willing to take over. Surrounded by senior colleagues, Kesri was at a loss for words. He said, 'If you wise persons feel that I am coming in the way of reviving the party, I will step down. But I will have a word with Madam.' The leaders thought their mission was successful, but Kesri cleverly used the opportunity to buy more time. He began sounding out CWC members, and much to his dismay, he realized that except for Tariq Anwar, all of them had switched sides.

Kesri then called on Sonia declaring that he was willing to step down as the party chief if she was going to take over from him. Much to his horror, Sonia gently asked him, 'When?' The old man was crestfallen. He could not take on Sonia. After all, it was Indira Gandhi who had made him AICC treasurer. The bravado of being elected AICC chief was nowhere in sight. Kesri promised to hold a press conference to make the formal announcement. For once, he kept his word and did not share his intention even with his close associates. These included some prominent journalists who were his political advisers.

On 9 March, Kesri announced his resignation, but within minutes he changed his mind. Kesri claimed that he had merely stated his intention to step down, though all the major newspapers quoted him as saying that he had resigned. Chacha's coterie chided him for handing over power to Sonia on a platter. Kesri rephrased his comments claiming that he would place his resignation before the AICC general body meeting, which has over thousand delegates, so as to seek their approval. 'They have elected me, and I will seek their permission,' he told the press. But nobody took the statement seriously. Azad, Patel, Arjun Singh and other CWC members quickly called on Sonia, taking credit for the success.

Over the next few days, Kesri went on giving interviews that he had not resigned and that the leadership issue would be settled by the AICC. Number 10 Janpath summoned loyal CWC members seeking an explanation. 'Oh, Chacha is upset over adverse publicity. He is a rustic fellow,' a CWC member told Sonia, as he boasted that he would set everything in order. 'I have consulted astrologers who say 14 March is an auspicious day to take over,' he said, but Sonia only nodded warily.

Antony, Mukherjee and Dr Singh again called on Kesri, but the old man was in a bad mood this time. 'You wanted me to resign. I have done it,' he said bluntly, even refusing to offer a cup of tea to them. Pranab cleared his throat and asked, 'When should the CWC meet?' That remark infuriated Kesri who shot back, 'It is up to me to decide.' The trio faithfully reported the incident to Sonia.

George spoke to Prasada wondering why Kesri was creating hurdles in Sonia's way. Prasada assured him that Chacha would be 'fixed soon'. A day before the coup, on 14 March, he hosted a lunch at which all CWC members except for the Orissa chief minister, J.B. Patnaik, and his Mizo counterpart, Lalthanhawla, were present. Thirteen CWC members gathered at Pranab's house at 9.30 a.m. to draft a strongly worded resolution that asked Kesri to immediately convene a CWC meet to end the uncertainty in the wake of his decision to resign as the party chief. It said that Kesri's gesture had bewildered party workers all over the country and he should step down in Sonia's favour. Pranab discovered a provision in the Congress constitution that supposedly empowered the CWC to take drastic action under very special circumstances. Party leaders later admitted that the provision did not specifically say it had powers to remove an elected party president.

The manoeuvring reached its nadir on the fateful day. As soon as the CWC met at 11 a.m., Kesri began protesting over the minutes of the meeting. He became hysterical when Pranab thanked him for his services as the party chief and moved a resolution asking Sonia to take over. Chacha adjourned the meeting within eight minutes and retired to his office adjacent to the hall where the CWC was meeting at 24 Akbar Road. No amount of persuasion from Dr Singh, Mukherjee, Antony and Patel changed his mind. Those in favour of change had anticipated it all. At 11.20 a.m. Prasada, the vice-president of the party, took the chair, signalling Pranab to move the resolution formally to invite Sonia to take over. The lone Kesri loyalist, Tariq Anwar, followed his leader, refusing to be party to 'the unconstitutional and unprecedented measures' that were being adopted by the CWC. He staged a walkout.

The remaining CWC members then rushed to 10 Janpath. At about noon, the committee formally handed over the chair to Sonia. Kesri's nameplate was quickly removed and thrown into the dustbin and a sparkling black-and-white plaque bearing Sonia's name was fixed outside the Congress president's office well ahead of her arrival at the party headquarters. Sonia came to Akbar Road at 5.30 p.m. to chair the CWC meet and take over as the party chief. She looked bright and confident for the occasion, but she was not pleased about the circumstances in which she was taking over. 'It would have been a lot better if everything had gone smoothly,' she told a party functionary, while admitting that Kesri would not have vacated the seat voluntarily.

As soon as the CWC meeting was over, she called on Kesri, describing him as a 'great leader'. Kesri was once again in a dilemma. 'It was gracious of her to have visited me when friends and colleagues deserted me. However, I failed to communicate the sense of betrayal. I was her host and she was my guest,' he said. Sonia also announced that Kesri's team of office-bearers would remain unchanged.

Kesri died a disturbed and disillusioned man. He could not

reconcile himself to his unceremonious ouster. Left without friends, in his last days, Kesri tried to jump on to Mamata Banerjee's bandwagon, but the Trinamul chief had little to offer. Disappointed, Kesri began lauding Feroze Varun, Sanjay and Maneka's son, as a potential challenger to Sonia, Rahul and Priyanka, but before he could mobilize support for the young Gandhi, he fell in the bathroom. The seemingly small injury led to complications, for which he had to be hospitalized. There was much that he wanted to say, but he suffered an asthma attack and then slid into coma. In the public eye, he died a loyalist, carrying his secrets with him.

SEVEN

THE REBELS

Everyone was growing restless, anxious to catch up with India's World Cup cricket opener against South Africa in England. The 15 May 1999 CWC meeting was supposed to be a brief one, where everyone was in a hurry to finalize the list of candidates for the Goa assembly polls and discuss the Rajiv assassination case as well as poll alliances, so that cricket enthusiasts could return to their television sets as early as possible. At this point, Sharad Pawar, sitting on spotless white sheets, smiled, and P.A. Sangma stood up. The rebellion in the Congress had begun, signalled by the mighty Maratha, executed by the diminutive samurai with a swish of his razor-sharp tongue, and watched by Sonia and the rest of her stunned council.

As recounted by those present at the meeting, Sangma slowly built a case for how the BJP campaign against Sonia's foreign origins was seeping deep down to even remote villages. Then came the unkindest cut. 'We know very little about you, about your parents,' Sangma told her. Those present claim that Sonia was shocked by Sangma's bluntness. He had, after all, been drafted into the CWC as her nominee. The third signatory, Sitaram Kesri's protégé Tariq Anwar, too, had survived in the CWC even after his mentor's departure, courtesy of Sonia.

Then the man she had made leader of the Opposition (until Sonia herself became a Lok Sabha member in September 1999) picked up from where Sangma left off. With opening remarks as deceptive as the smile signal, Pawar said Sonia Gandhi had done a great job as the party chief. 'You brought unity in the party and revamped the organization. However, the Congress has not succeeded in answering the BJP's campaign about your foreign origins. Let us take a serious note of it.'

The lady from Orbassano was confronting a crisis that was much more grave than the one her husband had faced a decade ago when he faced corruption charges in the Bofors gun deal or the ones her mother-in-law faced, in 1969, when she had to witness a split in the Congress, and in 1977, when she had to face a humiliating electoral defeat. Suddenly the reality dawned upon Sonia: she continued to be a loner in what she had thought to be her own 'parivar'.

Sangma went on, 'When people ask us why the Congress has failed to get a qualified Indian among [India's] 980 million citizens as its prime ministerial candidate, we have no answer. I think they are right,' he said.

Perhaps Amitabh Bachchan had been right about Congressmen merely using the Nehru–Gandhi family to stay in power, Sonia wondered. After all, it was these leaders who had pleaded with her to take the reins of the Congress and 'liberate' the party from Sitaram Kesri.

After Sangma had finished his speech, Rajesh Pilot tried to see some merit in what Pawar and Sangma had said. Pilot, however, did not join the rebels' rank, favouring the newly elected MPs to address the leadership issue. At that juncture, R.K. Dhawan lost his cool. He rubbished the Sharad–Sangma theory and said, 'Bhai, you seem to be taking up the BJP–RSS agenda.'

Dhawan had barely finished when the CWC members saw Sonia get up and begin walking out of the room. As Ghulam Nabi Azad, Ahmad Patel, Mohsina Kidwai, K. Karunakaran, Vijay Bhaskar Reddy, Jitendra Prasada and Sitaram Kesri looked on uncomfortably, not knowing what to do, Arjun Singh suddenly got up and ran behind her, not waiting to even put on his shoes. Sonia kept walking, her footsteps loud in the silence. Suddenly she turned around to see Singh, barefoot, hands folded. He did not say anything—he did not need to.

The folded hands conveyed both a request for her to stay on and remorse, his own and that of a large section of party workers.

Singh's gesture was a measure of the stakes involved. It was he who had masterminded the 'draft Sonia campaign'. If she were to walk out of the party, it would be the end of all his dreams, ranging from his desire to see the Congress staging a comeback in national politics to his personal ambition for high office.

A CWC member said the incident was a chilling reminder of 1977, when Indira received a letter with a similar message—challenging Indira's authority as she had lost the confidence of the party and the people—from Jagjivan Ram at a CWC meeting. 'Sonia Gandhi considers her mother-in-law to be her role model. She now has to fight and prove herself like Indira Gandhi,' he added. Sonia, however, had no illusions about herself. When some CWC members approached her, asking her to fight back like Indira Gandhi, Sonia retorted in uncharacteristic manner, 'I am not the daughter of Jawaharlal Nehru!'

Ironically, it was Sonia herself who had raised the issue of the BJP's campaign against her foreign origins, asserting she would fight till the end. Sitting next to Pawar, Dhawan told her comfortingly: 'Madam, you are not alone in this battle. We are all with you.'

Once Sonia walked away, the CWC meeting ended on an abrupt note with Arjun Singh drafting a resolution that attacked the BJP's campaign against Sonia. Pawar and Sangma were unfazed. While leaving, they told Pranab Mukherjee that it was their last CWC meeting.

Just after the meeting, when Mukherjee, Scindia and others were pretending to concentrate on the list of nominees for Goa, Sonia received the letter from the trio that read like a charge sheet against her. Sonia did not bother to read it. Vincent George called up senior leaders including Arjun Singh, Pranab Mukherjee and Dr Manmohan Singh to formulate a response.

Arjun Singh took charge to deal with the crisis. The veteran warhorse quickly branded Pawar, Sangma and Anwar present-day

'Mir Jafars' for their 'betrayal'. He told party leaders that Pawar had lived up to his reputation for ruthlessness by attacking Sonia when she was most vulnerable. It was Singh, as vice-president of the party, who had used his influence to convince a reluctant Rajiv to bring back Pawar in the Congress in 1985.

Pawar's critics point out that shortly after Rajiv's death, he was one of the signatories to the long list of Congress leaders demanding Sonia Gandhi take charge of the party. She had then flatly refused to do so. Again, in 1997, when the Congress plotters quietly staged a coup and Sonia Gandhi took over from Kesri, Pawar was an active player.

In fact, a few days before taking on Sonia on the foreigner issue, Pawar was given the key responsibility of acquiring signatures from probable allies soon after the fall of the Vajpayee government. The letter had made it clear that Sonia would be the prime ministerial candidate. Pawar was also entrusted with the crucial job of stitching up alliances in other states. He was in Chennai only a few days before the rebellion for talks with the All India Anna Dravida Munnetra Kazhagam (AIADMK) chief, Jayalalitha. He was to be in Chennai the day after the CWC meet.

To many, the revolt had been brewing for some months. Beneath the professional veneer, Pawar and Sonia Gandhi never seemed to get along with each other. She preferred to maintain a distance, keeping in mind Rajiv's opinion that Pawar was a good leader but not one to be trusted.

Pawar was not new either to performing sudden somersaults or going against someone whom he had supported. Early in his career, in 1978, he had brought down a Congress government in Maharashtra headed by Vasantdada Patil. According to V.N. Gadgil, Pawar defended Patil in the assembly during the no-confidence motion and, after finishing the speech, went straight to the governor withdrawing support for Patil.

Pawar told his confidants in February 1999 that the Congress was now revolving around 20 Canning Lane, where Arjun Singh then lived. But Singh was not his target. It appeared later to Sonia that

Pawar was unwilling to play Singh's role as the second-in-command. In May 1999, Pawar was fifty-eight and knew fully well that if Sonia took charge, his prospects of securing the prime job in the country would disappear.

In Pawar's scheme of things, revolt against Sonia was based upon a scenario that no political party or group would get a majority in the thirteenth Lok Sabha. Former Prime Minister Chandra Shekhar, Samajwadi Party leader Mulayam Singh Yadav and Samata Party leader George Fernandes were said to be his close associates who convinced him to make a bid for the prime minister's post. The logic was simple—as long as Sonia was Congress chief, regional satraps like Chandrababu Naidu, Mayawati, Mulayam Singh Yadav, Mamata Banerjee and Jayalalitha would not back her for the top job. Pawar, on the other hand, was confident of running a coalition. The 1999 general elections gave a clear mandate to the BJP and its allies. What was worse for Pawar was that in his home turf of Maharashtra, he finished behind the Congress in the state assembly polls—the Congress got seventy-six seats while Pawar's group bagged fifty-eight.

When Sonia reached home after leaving the CWC meet, she could only think of calling Priyanka. They did not speak much, but Priyanka realized that she was deeply upset. Rahul too was in Delhi, and the three got together. Rahul was furious and told Sonia to leave politics for good. Priyanka too favoured Rahul's line. Priyanka picked up a pen and drafted a letter. Sonia and Rahul made a few amendments. The letter was addressed to Pranab Mukherjee, who was the general secretary and had chaired the CWC meeting in Sonia's absence.

On 16 May, the party leadership decided to convene an emergency CWC meeting at 4 p.m. to discuss the Pawar–Sangma–Anwar letter. Pawar, however, informed CWC member Oscar Fernandes that he would not attend the meeting. In case a decision was taken against the observations made in the letter, he should be considered a dissenter, Pawar added. Sangma would not be present either, as he was en route to the US where his son was getting a degree. Anwar came up with the curious excuse that he would not attend the meeting unless Pawar and Sangma were present. The loyalists, however, were unwilling to make any concessions. They pointed at emergency provisions of the party constitution that made it clear that the CWC can be convened at any time with all those present in the capital.

As partymen raised slogans hailing Sonia and condemning Pawar—'Sangma, Tariq aur Pawar, inko maro jute char' (beat up Sangma, Tariq and Pawar with shoes)—a sombre Congress president arrived to attend the meeting. However, she excused herself soon after saying she would prefer to stay away as she would be the subject of the meeting.

Soon after her departure, Vincent George arrived carrying her resignation letter. The letter was dated 15 May, the day the trio fired the salvo. The big news was out. Sonia had quit as Congress president, fifteen months after she took over.

The letter said:

At this morning's meeting of Congress Working Committee, certain of my colleagues expressed views to the effect that my having been born elsewhere is a liability to the Congress party. I am pained by their lack of confidence in my ability to act in the best interest of the party and the country.

In these circumstances, my sense of loyalty to the party and duty to my country compelled me to tender my resignation from the post of party president.

Though born in a foreign land, I chose India as my country. I am Indian and shall remain so till my last breath.

India is my motherland, dearer to me than my own life. I came into the service of Congress party, knowing that it is the only party capable of providing India with a stable, secular, progressive and independent government. That belief remains unshakeable.

I came into the service of the party not for a position or power but because the party faced a challenge to its very existence and I could not stand idly by. I do not intend to do so now.

I have been privileged to receive the love and affection of ordinary Congressmen and women from all over the country and I will continue to serve the party as a loyal and active member to the best of my ability.

Signed,

Sonia Gandhi

The CWC unanimously rejected her resignation. When CWC members called on her to plead that she review the decision, she said she was deeply upset by the staggering display of xenophobia surrounding her origins. She said she had decided to step down as soon as she received the trio's letter on Saturday. Sources close to her said that the AICC chief was deeply upset over the fact that no one tried to cut short Sangma and Pawar when they spoke so harshly. 'It was the silence of the lambs in the CWC that upset her most,' said a close aide.

Family friends said Sonia was pained at the growing attacks on Christians since she took over as party chief. In fact, she had wondered in conversations with several people, including Sangma, if there was a link between her political role and the onslaught. She had also been disturbed by the BJP's consistent attacks on her origins, but she appeared determined to fight as long as the party was behind her.

What she did not expect was a personal attack by her own partymen. For many days to come, Sonia kept asking them where she went wrong and why senior leaders like Pawar and Sangma took such an extreme step. 'She did not want the issue of her foreign origins to come in the way of Congress prospects,' a party leader said.

The timing of Pawar's revolt crippled the Congress. Dates for the general elections were going to be announced and the party was facing assembly polls in Goa. Even senior leaders were groping in the dark on the daunting issue of succession if they failed to persuade Sonia to return. The campaign for the general elections was about to take off and the CWC was unwilling to choose a new leader midstream who could not only hold the party together but also run a credible campaign. In their heart of hearts, every CWC member knew that the Congress did not have such a leader, much less one who could run a victorious campaign.

Theoretically, the Congress leadership had a number of options. It could expel the rebels, a line of action pushed by Arjun Singh. The trio's demand could be rejected through a vote in the CWC, loaded with Sonia loyalists, and then action taken. The rebels could be persuaded to withdraw the letter and leave the leadership issue to newly elected MPs. As a last resort, Sonia could voluntarily make an offer not to hold any public office.

But these options existed only on paper. Most Congressmen were unanimous that no leader other than Sonia could keep them united and win them votes. The rebels had no place in the party; they would have to go.

In the absence of Sonia, the CWC summarily expelled the Sonia-challengers from the primary membership of the party for six years by a majority vote, setting the stage for a split. Significantly, the CWC's decision was not unanimous, with senior leader A.K. Antony registering a note of dissent. Emphasizing the need for unity, Antony objected on procedural grounds, saying the party should first slap a show-cause notice on the dissidents and suspend them before taking any extreme step.

Only Antony could afford to suggest this. The loyalists could not dub him as a rebel given his high standing and clean image in the party. In his brief intervention, Antony said, 'Let us first suspend them. Give them a chance to explain their conduct.' But he was overruled by other CWC members, especially hawks like Arjun Singh, Vijay Bhaskar Reddy and Pranab Mukherjee, who chaired the meeting.

Afterwards, Sitaram Kesri, Rajesh Pilot, Jitendra Prasada and Ahmad Patel said they too favoured a step-by-step approach to deal with the rebels. But they did not say this in the meeting, tamely abiding by the majority view in keeping with the mood of party workers who wanted stringent action.

There were dramatic scenes at the Congress headquarters where an agitated crowd manhandled Kesri, tearing his clothes and damaging his car before the CWC meeting. The veteran leader had to return home to change his clothes. Kesri, who was a special invitee to the CWC, was targeted because of his proximity to Tariq Anwar. Prasada and Pilot were also roughed up over their alleged sympathy for the dissidents. Sonia was quick to disapprove of the action. She called up Kesri and apologized on behalf of the party workers and instructed the Congress general secretaries to restrain supporters.

The CWC members had met several times during the day before formally gathering to iron out their differences on how to tackle the rebels. Antony, Ahmad and Pilot argued that the party should follow procedure as laid down in the party constitution. Mukherjee, Reddy and Singh countered that the CWC had the powers to waive these rules. 'It is in keeping with the party constitution and precedents,' Mukherjee said.

Justifying the expulsions, Mukherjee said Pawar, Sangma and Anwar had violated party discipline by not abiding by the majority decision of Sunday's CWC meeting that rejected their demand. The trio wanted the election manifesto to include a clause that the party would bring in a constitutional amendment to bar Indians of foreign origins from occupying high office. Mukherjee said the issue had no political logic. 'Who should be the prime minister is an issue which should be decided by the voters who elect the MPs,' he added. The CWC members alleged the rebels had deliberately taken up an issue that was raked up by the BJP. 'They have joined hands with the communal and fascist forces,' they said.

The AICC general secretary, Oscar Fernandes, immediately conveyed the CWC decision to Sonia, but she remained unmoved. The leaders then decided to convene an emergency session of the AICC to ratify the CWC's decision and exert pressure on Sonia to rescind her resignation.

Once again Arjun Singh and Vincent George took charge. Akbar Road was flooded with Congressmen of all hues and shades shouting 'Sonia lao, desh bachao'. First the chief ministers of Congress-ruled states called on her. Digvijay Singh said they would all resign en masse. 'We have become chief ministers thanks to you. What is the point in continuing if you are not around?' Then came the chiefs of the state units. Thousands of ordinary party workers got access to 10 Janpath. Some women broke down asking Sonia to reconsider. An elderly Muslim asked Sonia if she had thought about the plight of minorities in a BJP-run government. 'You do not want to fight for us?' he asked.

The road outside 10 Janpath was blocked for days. There were dozens of stalls of state leaders sitting on dharna throughout the day and night, refusing to go unless Sonia reconsidered. When Rahul was returning from a visit with a friend, he was mobbed by partymen requesting him to persuade Sonia to withdraw her resignation. A rethink began between Rahul and Priyanka—perhaps it was wrong to doubt the sincerity of ordinary party workers. The trio of Pawar–Sangma–Anwar might only represent a small minority.

Sonia's critics were also taken aback by the sudden burst of emotion and solidarity. Pawar was quick to realize that his plan had boomeranged. Sonia was getting a renewed mandate from partymen. Instead of weakening her, their onslaught had made her stronger. Pawar's private secretary was seen hovering around 10 Janpath. Each day the news was depressing for Pawar. While it is true some sections of the crowd were mobilized, a large number of them were there out of genuine admiration and respect for Sonia.

CWC members met Sonia individually every day to plead with her. Office-bearers of front organizations of the party issued appeals. The loyalists began regrouping in a bid to crush the Pawar-led revolt. The first priority was to prevent any kind of split. Two CWC members, Rajesh Pilot and Jitendra Prasada, who were seen to be soft on the trio, were quick to issue statements assuring full support to Sonia. Sensing the mood in the party, others like J.B. Patnaik, Santosh Mohan Dev and Sitaram Kesri, who were perceived as being close to Pawar, snapped all ties with his group.

Sonia may have rejected the CWC's plea to take back her resignation, but Priyanka and Rahul now felt that she should persevere. Sonia too was convinced that she should stay on. Ambika Soni, Ahmad Patel and Natwar Singh told her that her exit would strengthen Pawar. 'Do you want to do that?' asked one leader. Family friends said the Priyanka factor too forced Sonia to reconsider. In Sonia's assessment, her exit in 1999 would have adversely affected the prospects of Rahul or Priyanka taking up politics.

As the days passed, Congressmen became more confident that Sonia would stay on. Ajit Jogi, who was Congress spokesman, pointed out that Sonia had not resigned as chairperson of the CPP. She had also agreed to campaign for the party in the Goa assembly polls scheduled for June 1999.

A triumphant Pranab Mukherjee announced Sonia Gandhi's return at a hastily summoned press conference, saying: 'We told Soniaji that she was indispensable and she has withdrawn her resignation.' He quickly lit his pipe—always a reliable barometer of his mood—as a sign that everything was back to normal in the party. Thus, Sonia agreed to preside over the AICC session that was initially called to deal with the crisis triggered by her resignation. Party leaders said Sonia decided to take back her resignation the night before the AICC session because she was told by leaders that they were expecting trouble if she did not preside over the meeting. In a show of helplessness and loyalty, senior CWC members admitted they had even failed to resolve elementary issues such as who should hoist the flag and who should preside over the AICC in her absence.

The drama had indeed about ended when the CWC met in the evening and passed a resolution requesting her to withdraw her resignation. As if on cue, Sonia responded positively to the appeal. Party leaders said once they got the feeling that she was willing to attend the AICC meeting, they stepped up pressure on her to announce the decision immediately.

A week later she returned to the helm, giving her followers renewed hope and to her detractors another chance to dub her as power-hungry and manipulative. The BJP said it was the 'end of Sonia Gandhi's theatricals', while expelled leader Sharad Pawar said, 'It was only expected. The resignation and withdrawal were aimed at diverting attention from basic issues raised by us. The entire show seen in the past few days seems to have been stage-managed.'

Having regained control over the party and reconciled to the idea of staying in politics, Sonia decided to go on the offensive. She dared her opponents to take the issue of her foreign origins to the people and made it clear that she was in the race for the prime ministership. 'The people of India will give a fitting reply to those questioning my patriotism . . . As far as the issue of prime ministership is concerned, the Congress Parliamentary Party will decide it,' she said. Since Sonia continued to be chairperson of the CPP, her statement left no room for doubt on the issue.

Sonia took up the challenge of her adversaries and declared she was as much an Indian as anyone else. 'Meri hindustaniat par shak karne walon ko main jawab nahin doongee. Is desh ki janata degi. Munh tod jawab degi,' she said. She told Congress delegates: 'Yeh desh mere jivan ke pal pal mein shamil raha. Main suhagin yahan bani, maa yahan bani, main widhwa apki ankhon ke samne hui. Is desh ki sabse mahan putri Indiraji ne apni saans meri bahon mein todi.' In essence, those who doubted her patriotism would get a befitting reply not only from her but also from the people. India was an ineluctable part of her life; she was married here, became a mother here and was widowed here. Indira died in her arms.

The impact of the speech was instant. Many AICC delegates were seen wiping tears. Sonia herself sought to explain the circumstances leading to her resignation by accusing Pawar and other expelled leaders of being hand in glove with the BJP and wondering how they could raise the issue of her origins when they themselves had come with folded hands to ask her to take over the Congress leadership. 'Now the same set of people is trying to sow the seeds of doubt in the minds of my countrymen. They have joined hands with the forces against which I came to fight,' she said.

The Congress chief said she had quit a week ago with a 'heavy heart', but had decided to come back because 'the party has given me new assurance and hope'. After refusing to enter politics for seven years, she had not come to grab power, but to 'save the party from disintegration and the country from being overrun by communal forces'. That fight, she asserted, would continue. 'I will not let you down. What has happened in the past nine days should give us inspiration for a new beginning,' she said.

In an echo of Congress chief Dev Kanta Borooah's famous Emergency-era slogan of 'Indira is India, India is Indira', the thundering cry at Talkatora Stadium was: 'Sonia is the Congress, the Congress is Sonia.'

The party may not have emerged stronger from the resignation drama but Sonia certainly had. The party was now more subservient to her than before. Indira had drawn fawning loyalty by dint of her proven ability to deliver power. Sonia did it with no track record and the mere offer of half a hope. That showed much about the state of her partymen. 'Can you imagine this session without Sonia Gandhi?' remarked one of them, as the helmswoman arrived to thunderous ovation. 'There would not have been one. No Sonia, no session, no Sonia, no party.'

And if Sonia unleashed the whip briefly, it was only to ensure there was no detritus of dissent staining her crown any more. 'Those who want to walk with me should do so with their heads and their hearts,' she said, very much the headmistress at an assembly of spanked schoolboys. 'Those who have even an iota of uncertainty are free to chart their own course.'

She left none in doubt that she was, in the fashion of her illustrious mother-in-law, demanding blind personal loyalty and would settle for nothing less. 'I want a Congress that would be prepared to go along with me and be prepared to die for the principles I have decided to follow.'

Well aware that there still were elements in the CWC quibbling about her Italian lineage, Sonia moved quick and hard to terminate the debate with her blunt take-it-or-leave-it approach. The party took it without demur.

The issue of her foreign origins was closed within the Congress. Sonia probably should thank Sharad Pawar for putting an end to what was hitherto a difficult-to-address whisper campaign. He opened the lid on it; Sonia grabbed the chance to shut it tight.

From Talkatora onwards, the re-empowered leader stamped her authority harder and controlled dissent more harshly. The CWC collectively turned more loyal, its members vying with one another to be counted among her supporters.

The AICC session was no more than the inauguration of the new Congress durbar, purged of the black sheep. Arrayed in the new durbar were the courtiers paying obeisance to the new empress. If only she would deliver them an empire.

EIGHT

GENERAL ELECTIONS 2004: THE EMERGENCE OF 'GANDHI' SONIA

The announcement of the general elections 2004 could not have come at a worse time for Sonia Gandhi. Only three months ago the Congress had received a severe drubbing in the state assembly polls of Madhya Pradesh, Rajasthan and Chhattisgarh. The party, led by Sonia Gandhi, was ill-prepared on several counts. For the first time since 1998 when Sonia formally took over as the party president, Congressmen had begun to doubt her ability to lead the party. On the other hand, Atal Bihari Vajpayee's ratings were at an all-time high. The Congress faced a severe resource crunch and there were desertions all round. And the BJP's strategy to court Muslims threatened to make a further dent in the support base of the Congress. The BJP had even succeeded in getting the support of Syed Ahmad Bukhari, the imam of the Jama Masjid, and one of the most vocal and rabid voices of the country's 150-million-strong minority community.

The BJP and its NDA allies launched a high-profile media campaign, claiming that India was shining under Vajpayee's term in office. The 'India Shining' campaign was a major media blitz involving huge advertisements and television capsules. It showcased improved India–Pakistan relations, the buoyant economy, and the mega projects launched, such as the Golden Quadrilateral highway project, to emphasize the point that the NDA should be given another term to make India a 'superpower'. While Vajpayee became a mascot for the BJP-led NDA, his deputy, L.K. Advani, embarked upon a nationwide yatra.

Sonia could sense the growing disquiet. Some of the early poll forecasts gave the Congress only a very small number of seats. The situation was getting increasingly desperate. But true to her style of functioning, Sonia showed no signs of panic. The AICC chief instructed party leaders to avoid mentioning her as the potential prime ministerial candidate. The move instantly drew flak from political commentators like Shekhar Gupta, editor-in-chief of the *Indian Express*, who felt that a 'Vajpayee versus a question mark' contest would only give the BJP an added advantage.

Sonia, however, had her own calculations. The move helped her win allies such as Sharad Pawar, M. Karunanidhi, Lalu Prasad Yadav and others. Some of these leaders, like Pawar, were bitterly opposed to backing her as prime minister. Throughout the election campaign, the Congress and its allies unanimously held the position that the newly elected members of the fourteenth Lok Sabha would decide on the prime ministerial candidate.

Sonia's campaign lacked the BJP's fanfare. But what it lacked in flair she made up for by sheer hard work. She began to work sixteen hours a day, seven days a week, dividing time uniformly between being out in the field and strategy sessions. A team consisting of Jairam Ramesh, Salman Khurshid, Janardhan Dwivedi and others was set up at 99 South Avenue, a small flat that had earlier served as the venue for the meetings of the Congress's think tank, and which now became the party's nerve centre where party bigwigs and strategists spent as many as twenty hours a day.

The traditional modes of managing elections were scrapped in favour of a more corporate style, and professional advertising and marketing agencies such as Leo Burnett and Perfect Relations were hired. The Congress managers realized that there was no way they could match the high-decibel BJP campaign, given the party's paltry Rs 20-crore budget. The party, instead of going for a mega campaign, focussed on a regional strategy with a motto 'think global, act local'. According to Jairam Ramesh, over a period of three months from March 2004, 3000 insertions appeared in the press. Of these, 80 per cent were in the regional media.

The Congress turned the tables with this simple strategy. The alliance gave them arithmetic while the campaign got them chemistry. Ad agency Leo Burnett focussed on the theme of 'aam aadmi' (common man) to do all the talking. The Congress campaign, closely supervised by Sonia personally, targeted the audience with issues like farmers' suicides, the riots in Gujarat, the UTI scam, the scam involving the procurement of caskets for Kargil martyrs (dubbed 'coffin gate' by the media), growing unemployment, etc. Burnett CEO Arvind Sharma and executive director Jayshree Sunder conducted both quantitative and qualitative researches that showed that prior to May 2004, the common man was feeling left out of the sense of well-being that the BJP was projecting. The general feeling of the respondents from across the country was that their life had not changed over the last six years that the BJP had been in power.

According to ad guru Suhel Seth, Sonia understood the spirit of consumers. That was why the masses bought 'brand Sonia'. She became a brand of the masses. During her campaign, she asked the masses to introspect and ask themselves whether they were feeling good or if their India was really shining. And it is this line of reasoning that she pursued with vigour.

As poll dates were announced, Sonia began holding massive road-shows that started from western and then move to eastern Uttar Pradesh. By the time Sonia reached Vijayawada in Andhra Pradesh, she was convinced that the country was craving for a change. She clocked over 70,000 kilometres during the campaign, criss-crossing the length and breadth of the country without much support from the second line of Congress leaders.

Sonia's role as campaigner needs to be seen in the context of the lack of support from other notables in the party. Going by the candidates' demand, apart from Sonia, Priyanka and Rahul, the most popular campaigners were cine stars Govinda, Sunil Dutt and Dilip

Kumar. Almost the entire CWC remained confined to Delhi. Manmohan Singh, who went on to become prime minister, travelled little. His meetings were called off in Indore and elsewhere as the good doctor did not have a mass following. Kamal Nath remained in Chhindwara where he was contesting. Digvijay Singh fought a losing battle in Rajgarh while Arjun Singh toured reluctantly to a few places, failing to get even a single seat for his supporters. Ambika Soni, Ahmad Patel, Mohsina Kidwai, Motilal Vora, R.K. Dhawan, Oscar Fernandes and several 'senior leaders' stayed in Delhi or paid the odd visit to the states they were in charge of as party general secretaries. Most were seen in Sonia's company when she toured their states, waving to voters, who often asked about their identity. This was in sharp contrast to the BJP's well-oiled machinery that included seasoned campaigners like Atal Bihari Vajpayee, L.K. Advani, Arun Jaitley, Pramod Mahajan, Sushma Swaraj and Narendra Modi.

Sonia's speechwriters worked well too, focusing on the NDA's failures, particularly its inability to accelerate rural development and poverty alleviation programmes. For days, the Congress think tank searched for a catchy slogan to counter the BJP's 'India Shining' campaign, finally settling for 'Congress ka haath, Garib ke saath' (The Congress 'hand'—its party symbol—is with the poor). Rahul, who left a lucrative career with a global consultancy firm to enter politics, made a crucial intervention. He, along with Jairam and Dwivedi, argued with the rest of the CWC to drop 'garib' for 'aam aadmi'.

While Sonia was confident of scoring over Vajpayee, the pollsters were completely off the mark. Five major national news networks and scores of newspapers and magazines came up with their opinion and exit polls predicting the NDA's victory. One exit poll gave the Congress and its allies as low a tally as 92 to 102 sets. The highest estimate gave it 190 to 205 seats, which proved closer to the eventual number of 216. When the results came out on 13 May 2004 they were as stunned as everybody else by the outcome.

The month-long electioneering ended on 10 May, but for Sonia Gandhi and her close advisers it was the beginning of another gruelling round of discussions and stocktaking. The channel surfing became more intense and analysing newspaper reports became a major obsession at 10 Janpath and 99 South Avenue. Every day, leaders like Ambika Soni, Ahmad Patel, Oscar Fernandes and others would meet at 11 a.m. at the South Avenue flat, tally their feedback with that of newspapers and television channels and prepare a capsule. The capsule would then be taken to 10 Janpath where Rahul and Priyanka would join Sonia for another 'in-depth' analysis. There were several occasions when Rahul and Priyanka disagreed with the findings, saying that in their view, a particular constituency was a 'no-hope'.

A Congress leader, for example, boasted that the party nominee from Sultanpur, Captain Satish Sharma, would win 'hands down'. Rahul and Priyanka, who had campaigned extensively in the constituency, looked up and said spontaneously, 'Don't think so.' Sonia avoided saying much but whenever she found that her advisers were presenting a rather rosy picture, she would cut in, remarking that according to her assessment, the situation was not that good.

Congressmen were both surprised and elated to see a 'new Sonia'—confident and often blunt. She had been on the road since 4 January and the months spent campaigning had clearly added a lot to her experience. Often, while watching the news channels, she would react instantly. For instance, when a leading television channel gave Telugu Desam leader Chandrababu Naidu nearly half of the parliamentary seats in Andhra Pradesh, she reacted saying, 'That cannot be true.'

On 11 May, counting began in Andhra Pradesh and thanks to the electronic voting machine, the broad trends were out by 10 a.m. Sonia and her children were glued to the television, sipping tea as they watched news presenters and experts giving their comments. By 8.15 a.m., the Congress's success story had begun. A small crowd of partymen from the Delhi Pradesh Congress Committee (DPCC) had gathered outside 10 Janpath. The DPCC general secretary, Shamim Ahmad, could not resist announcing, 'Aaj Andhra Pradesh, kal saara desh (Today it's Andhra, tomorrow it will be the entire country).'

On 12 May, a day after voters in Andhra Pradesh had given a decisive verdict to the Congress in the state assembly, and the rest of the nation waited with bated breath for the outcome of Election 2004, 10 Janpath had a visitor.

Anil Ambani of Reliance, the gigantic private sector company, called on Sonia Gandhi. The meeting was dubbed a 'courtesy call' but Ambani's presence at 10 Janpath created a stir a kilometre away at the BJP's national headquarters at 11 Ashoka Road. Party general secretaries, busy discussing next day's likely scenario, did not take the news very well.

A top BJP functionary known for his proximity to the then undivided industrial house could not help commenting, 'The Ambanis' gut feeling seldom goes wrong.' His remark was quickly rubbished as party functionaries tried to concentrate on their strategy to tap new allies just in case Prime Minister Atal Bihari Vajpayee fell short of securing a clear-cut majority.

Shamim's prophecy came true two days after he had made it. By 10.30 a.m. on 13 May, the verdict was out. Millions of rupees spent on a sleek campaign, the plank of 'India Shining', the Atal Bihari Vajpayee factor—all had come unstuck. On television screens, it was the media-shy Sonia Gandhi, virtually written off from all quarters, one saw.

Watching the results on television, Prime Minister Vajpayee fell silent. He looked hard at his party managers who had advised him to opt for early polls, almost six months before the scheduled time, convincing him that he, riding on a 50 per cent-plus approval rating, was pitted against a 'question mark'. The Opposition, Messrs Pramod Mahajan, Arjun Jaitley, Sushma Swaraj and Venkaiah Naidu had repeatedly told him, was so nondescript and demoralized that it had not mustered the courage to name an alternative prime ministerial candidate.

On 13 May, Sonia remained glued to the television, taking down notes, expressing delight when party nominees were declared victorious. She seldom displayed any emotion to her party colleagues other than smiling broadly. However, when Priyanka Gandhi reached her residence, Sonia cried to her, 'We have done it.' Priyanka held her tight and almost spontaneously the two turned to a portrait of Rajiv.

Among several other important factors, the voters across the country gave a verdict rejecting the skewed growth benefiting a minuscule information technology-savvy Indians while the majority of people coped with difficult economic circumstances. On her part, Sonia Gandhi had gone about stitching alliances astutely, calling on Sharad Pawar at his residence, waiting to receive M. Karunanidhi in the portico when he came to meet her, and according the highest respect to the then CPM general secretary Harkishen Singh Surjeet.

Soon after the verdict in favour of the Congress was out, the allies queued up to give their letter of support to 'Prime Minister Sonia Gandhi'. It took four days to work out all arrangements before the Congress chief finally received an invitation from the President to visit him to explore avenues of government formation.

But the final masterstroke was still to be delivered. It is one that will be debated for a long time to come. Sonia was all set to become prime minister till she opened her cards.

The AICC chief first sounded doubtful on 17 May when she publicly told her allies that she did not want to be the prime minister. Sonia had herself typed a letter addressed to her party MPs and allies but could not hand it over as the entire CPP of over 200 MPs (both Lok Sabha and Rajya Sabha) trooped to 10 Janpath. Once inside, the MPs sensed that something was amiss as Sonia failed to make an appearance even after they had waited for over three hours. Disturbed by the no-show, and having a foreboding of something unpleasant about to happen, they even declined the soft drinks offered, despite it being 44 degrees Celsius in the shade. Manmohan Singh and Pranab Mukherjee arrived soon after to announce that Sonia would call on President Kalam the following day. The announcement cheered party MPs, who thought that Sonia had agreed to take up the job.

However, on the afternoon of 18 May, Sonia called Manmohan Singh and conveyed her refusal, asking him to inform the allies. Some party leaders close to her had feared all along that a drastic measure was lurking behind Sonia's impassive calm. But even Sonia's supposedly closest advisers, namely, Ambika Soni and Ahmad Patel, had no clue about what was going on in their leader's mind. Oblivious of the deliberations between Sonia and Manmohan, Ambika Soni, along with Pranab Mukherjee and a few others, kept waiting to have a word with Sonia. As time passed, Pranab began to lose patience and Ambika started pacing up and down in Sonia's private assistant Madhavan's room. Finally, when Manmohan Singh broke the news to her, Ambika remonstrated with Sonia. Sonia, however, remained unmoved.

Extraordinary scenes began unfolding at 10 Janpath. As a 'loyal' AICC general secretary tried to reason, tears falling incessantly, Sonia turned her face away, saying that if they tried to dissuade her, she would quit as AICC chief.

Why did Sonia opt out of the race? Was she reluctant from day one? Was she unsure of leading a coalition which included unpredictable allies like Lalu Prasad Yadav and Ram Vilas Paswan? A closer scrutiny shows that none of these factors influenced her while declining the country's most sought-after job. Sonia's refusal was a product of exceptional realpolitik. At the same time, it carried the mark of a deeply ethical mind.

Sonia hated the idea of being challenged by a section of her countrymen, however small a minority, that was uncomfortable at the prospect of her becoming the prime minister of India. Sonia said she had no problems taking on people like Sushma Swaraj and Uma Bharti of the BJP, who had been vociferous against her becoming prime minister, but she had 'no strength' to be the 'cause' of a likely civil strife.

Congress leaders said in retrospect that they and the allies made a 'blunder' in trying to assure her that those raking up her foreign origin would be given a befitting answer. Sonia dreaded the possibility of Congress workers battling Sangh activists. She was horrified at the prospect of someone, driven by xenophobia, trying to set himself / herself on fire. She was convinced that the office of prime minister was not worth that. In her view, the country needed drinking water, schools, basic health services, small-scale industries, social security— not a debate centred on her origins. She said her association with the Nehru–Gandhi family had taught her one overriding principle: country first.

Sonia with her mother-in-law, Indira Gandhi, with whom she had a warm relationship.

Sonia and Rajiv Gandhi with Pope John Paul II during the Pope's visit to India in 1986. Sonia had a conservative Catholic upbringing.

Sonia with Prime Minister Narasimha Rao in 1991. He was chosen to lead
the Congress party after Rajiv Gandhi's death.

Maneka and Sanjay Gandhi.
Sanjay died in an air crash
on 23 June 1980.
(PANA-INDIA)

Sonia with her children, Priyanka and Rahul, at Teen Murti Bhavan in 1996.

Sonia (right) with Hillary Clinton (third from right) at Mother Teresa's funeral in Kolkata in 1997. Priyanka Gandhi is seated behind Sonia.

Sonia as president of the Congress Party in 2000, a year that tested her as leader.

Sonia at a meeting in Guwahati with chief ministers of Congress-ruled states in April 2002. With her is the author, Rasheed Kidwai (right) and Kamal Nath, AICC General Secretary (left).
(Courtesy: *The Sentinel*, Assam)

At a press conference held at 10 Janpath on 23 March 2006, Sonia announces her resignation from the Lok Sabha following the 'office of profit' controversy. Rahul Gandhi stands beside her; Priyanka watches from behind the door. (Photo: Rajesh Kumar/ABP)

Congress President Sonia Gandhi receiving Prime Minister Manmohan Singh at 10 Janpath for a Congress Working Committtee meeting in 2008. (Photo: Rajesh Kumar/ABP)

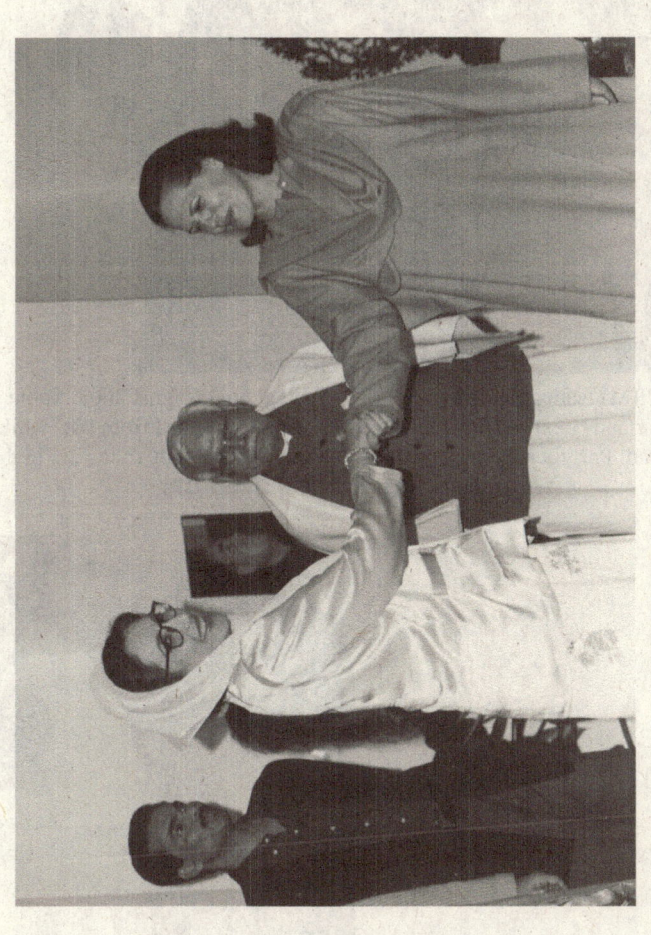

A meeting between Sonia Gandhi and the late Benazir Bhutto in 2001 in New Delhi. Natwar Singh, who later became external affairs minister in the UPA government, looks on. (Photo:, Rajesh Kumar/ABP)

At CPI(M) leader Harkishen Surjeet's funeral on 3 August 2008, Sonia Gandhi stands next to UP Chief Minister Mayawati (third from left) while Samajwadi Party leaders Amar Singh and Mulayam Singh Yadav are in the foreground. (Ramakant Kushawa/ABP)

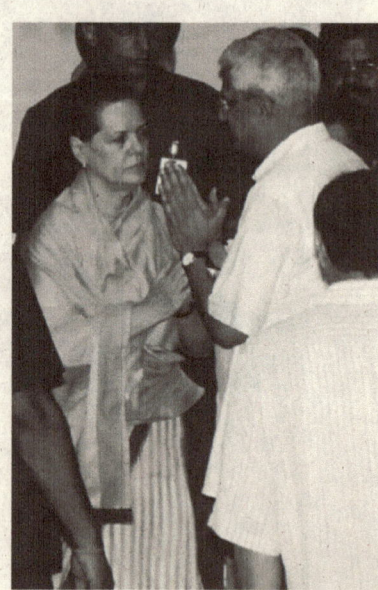

Sonia Gandhi and CPI(M) leader Prakash Karat exchange greetings at Harkishen Singh Surjeet's funeral. (Photo: Ramakant Kushawa/ABP)

Oscar Fernandes, an AICC functionary who became a minister in the Manmohan Singh government, said that on several other occasions too, Sonia had shown a similar sense of tyag (sacrifice). During 2003, when the party was in the Opposition, the AICC office-bearers chalked out a nationwide action that envisaged a one-day token strike across the country comprising a rail roko–rasta roko (block railways, block roadways) programme. Sonia heard them attentively even as Ambika Soni excitedly told her that such a stir would neutralize media criticism that the Congress as an Opposition lacked 'teeth'. At the end of it, Sonia asked the party general secretaries one simple question: 'Who will be responsible if one patient dies failing to reach the hospital?' There was silence, recalled Fernandes, as the office-bearers searched for a suitable answer. 'We had none. The agitation plan was dropped.'

There was another significant signal that most political commentators and 10 Janpath watchers completely missed. In April 1999 when the Vajpayee regime had been voted out, Sonia was tipped to replace him as prime minister but could not due to the opposition from the Samajwadi Party and a few others. In an interview to Vir Sanghvi for NDTV in October 2006, Sonia disclosed that her decision to refuse the prime ministership in 2004 was not a sudden one. Even way back in 1999, when it seemed like the Congress might form the government, the prime ministerial candidate was Dr Manmohan Singh. 'I let Manmohan Singh know in 1999 that he, not I, would be prime minister,' she said. Confirming that she met then President K.R. Narayanan to inform him that Manmohan Singh would lead her party's government, if it came to power, Sonia Gandhi said, 'Yes, that's true. In fact I went first on my own and then with Dr Manmohan Singh.'

However, that time around too, letters from allies were collected on the basis of her being the prime ministerial nominee.

What could be the rationale of projecting Sonia as the possible prime minister and keeping her antipathy for the high office a secret? Why did she not decline the post earlier to counter the BJP's campaign? Sonia has the answer. If she had made public her unwillingness then, the party might have lost motivation. It could also have encouraged factionalism. The Congress president held her silence until the moment came. Having achieved the task of keeping the Congress and its allies united, and believing that she had fulfilled her Panchmarhi pledge to 'restore the [party's] past glory' and make the Congress a party of the 'best and the brightest', Sonia moved on to her original plan: to shun power and ensure smooth succession. Had she announced the decision on 13 May, the fragile unity of what is now called the United Progressive Alliance (UPA), packed with ambitious leaders and whimsical allies, perhaps could not have been achieved.

Sonia remained reluctant throughout and announced her decision after a round of consultations with her children and two apolitical friends. Sources said the decision was not influenced by any of them. The children and family friends backed Sonia's stand, respecting her strong sentiments. Congress sources said Rahul and Priyanka did initially try to influence her, pointing at party workers' sentiments, but gave in seeing she was adamant. Priyanka said Sonia Gandhi never wanted to be the prime minister. Rahul endorsed her decision saying that during the campaign he had called his mother from Amethi to ask if she would be the prime minister. 'No,' she had said, pointing out that her sole aim was to drive out 'communal forces'.

Convinced that a 'greedy' Sonia would grab power at any cost, the RSS had gone on the offensive, saying it would be a 'disgrace' to the nation if an 'Italian leader' was foisted as its prime minister and people would not accept such a decision quietly. 'It will be a disgrace to the nation if the Congress party together with retrograde communist parties tries to foist an Italian leader as prime minister on the country. All self-respecting and freedom-loving people of this country will be greatly hurt if any such mishap occurs,' RSS spokesman Ram Madhav said. After 18 May 2004, the RSS had little to say.

Some former Union ministers belonging to the BJP–NDA claimed that Sonia's renunciation had more to do with practical problems than a genuine sense of sacrifice. In their zeal to dent Sonia's popularity, they even dragged in President A.P.J. Abdul Kalam's name, suggesting that he had pointed out some 'flaws' in Sonia's citizenship. Two newspapers carried the report. The President's office issued a strong denial followed by telephone calls to the newspapers concerned and former Union ministers.

Those who know Sonia well were not surprised by her action. Sonia Gandhi's favourite phrase is: 'They do not know the stuff I am made of.' Pitted against heavy odds, Sonia has had to prove herself again and again. Several evenings, after a long day, she would sit with Priyanka or Rahul to reflect. Each time she sounded disheartened, Priyanka would tell her, 'Mama, the more they attack you, the worse they will get it,' referring to the rivals' criticism of her and the party. Sonia would smile and start playing with her grandchildren.

Circumstances, those who know her say, have trained Sonia in such a way that she is capable of taking tough decisions with ease. There are several pointers in that direction. She had hated the idea of Rajiv Gandhi joining politics, after Sanjay's death, but conceded, realizing that he had to fulfil his duty towards his mother. In 1984, she let him become prime minister, much against her wishes, to enable him to fulfil his duty towards the country. In 1991, she declined to lead the party as she felt she was not cut out for politics. Seven years later, she was drawn into it due to a host of factors such as the likely disintegration of the party. On 18 May 2004, she listened to her conscience when she asked herself if the office of prime minister was worth alienating a section of her countrymen for.

Sonia tried to convince her party MPs and addressed them in the majestic Central Hall of Parliament. Amid chaotic scenes and emotional outbursts, Sonia made a brief speech, explaining why she was 'humbly declining' the post. She said:

Throughout these past six years that I have been in politics, one thing has been clear to me. And that is, as I have often stated, that the post of prime minister is not my aim. I was always certain that if ever I found myself in the position that I am in today, I would follow my own inner voice. Today, that voice tells me I must humbly decline this post. You have unanimously elected me your leader. In doing so, you have reposed your faith in me. It is this faith that has placed me under tremendous pressure to reconsider my decision. Yet I must abide by the principles which have guided me all along. Power in itself has never attracted me, nor has position been my goal. My aim has always been to defend the secular foundation of our nation and the poor of our country—the creed sacred to Indiraji and Rajivji. We have moved forward a significant step towards this goal. We have waged a successful battle. But we have not won the war. That is a long and arduous struggle, and I will continue it with full determination. But I appeal to you to understand the force of my conviction. I request you to accept my decision and to recognize that I will not reverse it. Our foremost responsibility at this critical time is to provide India with a secular government that is strong and stable. Friends, you have given me your generous support, you have struggled against all odds with me. As one of you and as president of the Congress party, I pledge myself to work with you and for the country. My resolve will in fact be all the more firm, to fight for our principles, for our vision, and for our ideals.

Initial shock and anger within the party gave way to respect and genuine admiration. Quickly, the party began to refer to its president as 'Gandhi Sonia', giving her the status the Mahatma enjoyed of the Supreme Leader. There was more to follow. In an unprecedented move, Congress MPs and functionaries collectively amended Section 5(c) of the CPP constitution, making Sonia the chairperson of the CPP and handing her sweeping powers to appoint or sack the prime minister. Under the amendments carried out unanimously, the chairperson of the CPP who would be elected by MPs would nominate two leaders of the party—one for each House. 'The chairperson shall have the authority to name the leader of the CPP to head the government, if necessary,' party spokesman S. Jaipal Reddy said. For a change, there was nobody crying foul or suspecting a sinister design. Sonia had convinced Congress leaders that their welfare apart, she had no other motive.

The gesture won acclaim everywhere. On 20 May, in an editorial, the *Guardian*, London, described her as the 'soul of the party' and wrote: 'The public loves political theatre and Mrs Gandhi is being lauded for an act of renunciation said to be in the true Indian tradition—even if it cannot quite compare with Buddha's resolve to withdraw from the world to seek enlightenment.'

The word from Pakistan was more worthy of note. The *Dawn* said that for Pakistanis events in New Delhi were thoroughly amazing. Columnist Ayaz Amir could not help asking his countrymen to introspect. On 21 May, he wrote:

Consider her measured words, no empty rhetoric (Ms Bhutto please note), no verbosity. Compare this with the desire for eternal power evident in Islamabad and it is tempting to conclude that the Pakistani political class and leadership are simply incapable of getting it right about the country's affairs. Like all his military predecessors Gen. Musharraf thinks he is saving Pakistan. A bit of Sonian renunciation, or call it Sonian wisdom, should do him a world of good.

The day after the renunciation, Sonia began her day with yoga, had breakfast and scanned the papers as an enthusiastic Rahul read out the eulogistic editorials and headlines. Visitors began to trickle in. Sharad Pawar, who was the first to have raised the banner of revolt over her foreign origin in May 1999, greeted her saying he admired her guts and conviction. Sonia smiled without reacting. Pawar joined the government, ultimately settling for the agriculture and food portfolio under Manmohan Singh. Congress leaders did not miss the irony. 'Here is a man who acted the spoiler. And see how he is going to benefit from her at the fag end of his life,' said an MP from Maharashtra.

Sonia's choice of Manmohan Singh as prime minister was flawless. To the outside world, Manmohan Singh has an image of an economic theoretician, a man known for his integrity and poise. Within the Congress, he is a popular figure not because he was good at economics but for never playing 'politics' within the party. Manmohan Singh has consciously stayed away from factional politics. He has always remained by Sonia's side, yet nobody has ever dubbed him part of any 'coterie'.

Only after his elevation to the prime ministership did Congressmen understand why Sonia always kept Manmohan Singh by her side. Manmohan Singh was made chairman of the strategy committee, ahead of a group of thoroughbred politicians like Pranab Mukherjee and Arjun Singh. In the Rajya Sabha, too, Sonia had made it a point to appoint him leader of the Opposition. Sometimes, backbenchers used to wonder why Sonia had promoted a rather 'apolitical' person in a House where the then ruling NDA was in a minority. On his part, Manmohan Singh did not let Sonia down. The two functioned as a team. They enjoyed instant rapport and understood each other well. Both are reticent, hate media attention and avoid the old political culture of flattery and false promises.

Denying that she is now 'the power behind the throne', Sonia says she enjoys a relationship of mutual trust with the prime minister. Explaining her alleged differences with him over the proposed hike in petrol prices, she says, 'I think there was a miscommunication about the exact figure, I mean it was no problem at all . . . we are not competitors.'

NINE

A TIGHTROPE WALK: THE PARTY, THE GOVERNMENT AND THE UPA

A new Sonia Gandhi emerged with the victory in the 2004 general elections and the renunciation. Her body language underwent a remarkable transformation. Those accompanying her mentioned having problems keeping pace with her longer, faster strides. 'Politician' Sonia began to understand Congressmen's obsession with power politics. Each time a low- or middle-rung party worker called on her, she wasted little time exchanging pleasantries or talking about the weather. Her standard responses, 'let us see' and 'okay', forestalled further discussion. In the CPP office, Sonia set a record of sorts by seeing twenty-five party leaders (mostly former MPs) in about twenty minutes.

Sonia's popularity and stature may have soared but not everybody in the Congress was convinced about the course being smooth from here on. The Congress has dreaded the existence of two power centres since the tussle between those loyal to P.V. Narasimha Rao and an apolitical 10 Janpath during the 1991–96 Congress government that led to a split and defeat of the party in the subsequent elections of 1996 and 1998. The optimists were confident that Sonia's popularity would reflect in Rahul's success. But the pessimists were not so sure. If Sonia had been prime minister, his progress would have been smoother, they argued.

Sonia Gandhi's refusal to accept the prime minister's post reopened the issue of dual power centres in the country's oldest political organization. Before Independence, the real source of power lay in the party—but the Congress was a movement rather than a political outfit at the time. After 1947 when the Congress became a ruling political party, matters came to a head between the party leadership and the government led by Pandit Jawaharlal Nehru when the then Congress chief Acharya Kripalani tried to force Nehru to consult party stalwarts before taking crucial administrative decisions.

Nehru, thanks to his pre-eminent status, snubbed Kripalani's plans to 'guide and advise' the government. On his part, Kripalani failed to realize that the top party leadership had moved into government with the formation of the Nehru-led regime in 1947 and only second-tier leaders were left to run the Congress. The tail could not wag the dog. Subsequently, Nehru took on Purushottam Das Tandon, a man known for his soft Hindutva views who became Congress chief in 1952. During this round of confrontation, Nehru humbled Tandon by getting the entire CWC to hand in its resignation and made sure that Tandon would not dare take him on again.

When Indira took over, she had to take on a considerably more powerful Congress syndicate, which initially regarded the new prime minister as a helpless woman who would bow to them. She was appointed premier by party bosses K. Kamaraj and S. Nijalingappa after Lal Bahadur Shastri died in office. However, the syndicate erred in judging Indira. Not only did the new prime minister take on the leaders, she ensured there would be no place in the party for them. Indira proved to be a strong prime minister and ever since, the party president has always played second fiddle to the person occupying the top seat, with the government setting the agenda for the party to follow.

While the tussle between government and party was settled in favour of the former during the tenures of Jawaharlal Nehru and Indira Gandhi, both of whom were powerful prime ministers, it fell to Sonia to reverse the equation. Her prime ministerial nominee would be less powerful than her, no matter how competent he was. As Congress president and its star campaigner, Sonia had far greater power and political legitimacy than the prime minister she would pick.

It has been a Congress convention that the party chief is also the CPP leader. But after Sonia refused to become prime minister, she could not have become CPP leader since the President can invite only the latter to form the government.

Astute party managers like Pranab Mukherjee were quick to offer a remedy and ensure that Sonia Gandhi's authority over the parliamentary wing of her party continued undiluted even though Manmohan Singh was elected CPP leader. The CPP constitution was amended before Singh was elected to create the post of a chairperson more powerful than the CPP leader. Sonia was elected to this post, with the constitutional amendments ensuring that Singh would take over as prime minister essentially as the CPP chairperson's nominee. The amendment is intended to ensure that dual power centres do not emerge in the party.

Before electing Singh CPP leader, the parliamentary party at its meeting adopted two amendments to the parliamentary party constitution. The first amendment paved the way for Singh's elevation to the post of prime minister and the other ensured Sonia's supremacy in the parliamentary party. Under the provisions of the CPP constitution, the CPP leader's post was the highest. As such, Singh would have nominated the leader of the Lok Sabha (he belongs to the Rajya Sabha) and the deputy leaders and chief whips in both Houses. But, as the then party chief spokesman S. Jaipal Reddy later said, Clause 5 of the CPP constitution was amended to create the chairperson's post. Sonia was unanimously elected CPP chairperson, after Pranab Mukherjee proposed her name and K. Karunakaran seconded it.

The CPP leader has always been directly elected by the parliamentary party; the constitutional amendment ensured that the CPP would also elect the chairperson. Under sub-clause 'C', added to the constitution by way of amendment, the chairperson and not the CPP leader would nominate the party leaders in both Houses as well as the deputy leaders and chief whips. The amended clause now reads: 'The chairperson shall have the authority to name the leader of (the) Congress parliamentary party to head the government, if necessary.'

On the basis of this amendment, Sonia proposed Singh's name as CPP leader and cleared the way for his appointment as prime minister. By ensuring that Singh becomes prime minister as a Sonia nominee, the amendment was aimed at pre-empting rival power centres from emerging in the Congress's organizational wing and its parliamentary party.

Sonia assured Congress members that she would be by their side and dutifully discharge her responsibilities as MP, CPP chairperson and party chief. Singh said he was aware of his limitations but would try to carry out his allotted role. He added that he would continue to need Sonia's guidance and leadership.

Sonia then went on to pick a bureaucrat—not a political person—Pulak Chatterjee, a low-key IAS officer of the 1974 batch, to act as the interface between her and the prime minister on all executive and administrative matters. Informed sources said the choice fell on Chatterjee after Ambika Soni, Ahmad Patel and Jairam Ramesh were ruled out, fearing that a political office could create more problems than solve them. Chatterjee became secretary to the prime minister. He was earlier secretary to Sonia between 1999 and 2004 when she was leader of the Opposition. Prior to that, his services were 'loaned' to the RGF.

While Chatterjee consciously kept himself away from politics, he was a familiar figure even for district Congress workers across the country. In room number 44, Parliament House, which served as the office of the leader of the Opposition, he could always be seen working on his laptop or taking a small break to light his pipe. Congress workers and MPs calling on Sonia through personal aides S.V. Pillai and Vincent George never lost sight of Chatterjee. Ever in search of 'persons close to Madam', they made it a point to exchange pleasantries with him and slip their cards. He never disappointed them, getting up from his chair to shake hands with the high and mighty as well as with lower-rung workers. But if any leader tried to get 'over-familiar', Chatterjee could act the stern bureaucrat.

Chatterjee's choice is a reflection of Sonia's and Manmohan's reluctance to draft a career politician for the crucial assignment. They appear to have been influenced by past experience when the office of the political secretary to the prime minister got highly politicized and, in fact, between 1991 and 1996, served as a trouble spot, when P.V. Narasimha Rao drafted Jitendra Prasada as his political secretary with the objective of carrying the party along. The choice also reflected their preferred style of functioning. Both Sonia and Manmohan are reticent and hate the media glare. Given Chatterjee's style of functioning and experience, he is tailor-made to surmount difficulties and avert any controversy between the two power centres at 10 Janpath and the PMO.

This was not the only headache that Sonia had. It is an open secret that there is no dearth of Congress leaders jealous of the good doctor's success. These politicians loathed the idea of an 'apolitical', 'junior' entity like Manmohan, who had joined the Congress only in 1991, becoming prime minister while they, despite being part of the Congress for decades, were forced to serve under him.

Old warhorse Arjun Singh braced for another round of power play in the company of his old foe Sharad Pawar. The veterans, who have crossed swords several times in the 1980s and 1990s, first got down to corner a niche for themselves in the coalition. Pawar forged a 'strategic alliance' with the likes of Lalu Prasad Yadav while Arjun courted the Left parties who support the UPA from outside.

Health may be failing Arjun and Pawar but their sharp political instincts remained intact as they made a determined bid to bounce back to the centre stage of politics. The duo had begun their political career in the 1960s as part of the Youth Congress under D. Tiwari. Both went on to lead revolts in the party—Pawar against Sonia in 1999 on the foreign origin issue and Arjun, in his zeal to flaunt his loyalty to 10 Janpath, against Rao in 1995. While Pawar went his way, Arjun suffered marginalization in his home state of Madhya Pradesh and successive defeats in the Lok Sabha polls of 1996, 1998 and 1999.

He was thus compelled to get a Rajya Sabha nomination, courtesy Sonia.

For many Congress leaders, Pawar's and Arjun's positioning was a reminder of 1991–96 when Prime Minister Narasimha Rao spent most of his time quelling dissent in the party while 10 Janpath maintained a studied silence. This time round too, Prime Minister Manmohan Singh faced a degree of discomfort from both leaders' camps but there was one significant change. If during 1991–96 Sonia maintained an aloof, apolitical profile, in 2004, she had emerged the supreme leader of the Congress and, more important, protector of Manmohan who was her nominee.

From the very beginning, party MPs were firmly told to allow a free hand to Manmohan. The scope for manoeuvring was thus limited to Cabinet meetings. After a few skirmishes where some senior ministers reportedly tried to be one up on Manmohan, Sonia summoned the seniors individually and asked them to stick to the subjects relating to their respective ministries.

At the same time, Sonia was aware that Arjun was required to keep a check on Pawar. There were several other checks and balances that remain hidden from the public eye, which demonstrated Sonia's political acumen and finesse in handling even the most wily and astute players.

But the period between 2004 and 2006 was not easy for Sonia who worked overtime to ensure the smooth functioning of the UPA. Paradoxically, much of the problems came from within the Congress, be it the controversial issue of Arjun Singh announcing a quota for OBCs in higher educational institutions like the IITs, AIIMS and IIMs or the Volcker Report that forced external affairs minister and Sonia loyalist K. Natwar Singh to unceremoniously step down from the Cabinet.

On the thorny issue of quotas for OBCs in higher education, Arjun played his cards deftly, leaving his swelling list of detractors little chance to 'fix' him. Apparently, it was a piece of A3-size paper that created much havoc in Delhi and in the rest of the country, effectively sealing the fate of millions of the 'best and brightest'.

Tucked under the glass on the table of Pulak Chatterjee was a paper divided into several columns listing the UPA government's common minimum programme (CMP) commitments, the name of the parent ministry against each item, legislative and administrative action taken and the response from each department.

When the government's report card was getting ready to mark two years of the Manmohan Singh regime in March 2006, a note signed by Chatterjee made its way to human resource development minister Arjun Singh. For Arjun, a word from Chatterjee was a word from Sonia, expressing her desire for quick implementation.

Arjun seized on this 'routine' missive to start a controversy that subsequently reached dangerous proportions. Sources close to him said he was drawing strength from Chatterjee's note and arguing that he was merely fulfilling his duty. Manmohan and Sonia maintained a studied silence throughout the long and agonizing quota agitation which led to violence and strikes across the country.

At the height of the controversy, Arjun held his nerve as he was aware that he would not become a casualty of the reservation battle because Sonia was not in a position to oppose the concept for political exigencies. The minister rejected calls to re-examine the proposals. 'We are a democracy and not a banana republic. You cannot hijack the process and browbeat me. There is no need for desperation and anger. Their [the students'] issues can be resolved with patience,' he said. Exuding defiance, he took a potshot at the Knowledge Commission, formed by the prime minister, most of whose members have rejected quotas. Arjun said: 'With all due respect to the great Knowledge Commission, I must point out to them that they are not above the Constitution.' The dig was specially directed at Satyam Gangaram Pitroda, popularly known as Sam Pitroda, father of the telecommunication revolution in India.

After Arjun's show of strength, came the Paul Volcker Report which made public a list of corporations and politicians across the world who benefited from an elaborate scam devised by Iraqi dictator Saddam Hussein to make money for his regime and presumably himself from the United Nations' Oil For Food Programme. The Volcker

Committee—set up by the United Nations to inquire into the Oil For Food Programme—named K. Natwar Singh, the Congress party and several Indian companies as beneficiaries of the scandal.

Natwar Singh resigned from the Manmohan Singh Cabinet on 6 December 2005, but not before an ugly show of defiance that embarrassed the party high command. Natwar's unceremonious exit gave rise to the 'T for trouble' theory in the Congress. The reference was to members of the erstwhile Congress T (Tiwari) which had left the parent organization during the Narasimha Rao regime. The 'T' gang included influential and senior members like Natwar Singh, Arjun Singh, Sheila Dikshit, M.L. Fotedar and others. The slur was that much of the UPA's problems were coming from 'loyalists' like Natwar and Arjun.

The 'loyalists' protested in whispers, wondering if loyalty was no longer valued in Sonia Gandhi's Congress. The Natwar Singh saga raised the curtains on a sideshow where party leaders were openly heard complaining how 'loyalists' of the Nehru–Gandhi family have been falling by the wayside for one reason or another.

Besides Natwar, Sheila Dikshit, Arjun Singh, Ghulam Nabi Azad, R.K. Dhawan, M.L. Fotedar and N.D. Tiwari are some of the other 'loyalists' who have been 'sidelined'. Sheila may have been able to retain the Delhi chief minister's chair but it is an open secret that her ties with 10 Janpath are no longer what they used to be. Arjun was once seen as an indispensable member of the 'coterie' but increasingly the human resource development minister had little say in crucial matters of party or government. The unofficial 'number two slot' in the Manmohan Singh government belonged to external affairs minister Pranab Mukherjee and, to a lesser extent, to finance minister P. Chidambaram.

It is an open secret that Azad was more than reluctant to leave Delhi for Srinagar. But as the date for the transfer of power in the border state inched closer, the Union minister for urban development and parliamentary affairs realized he had no option. The seasoned politician bit the bait without making a fuss.

Old family retainers R.K. Dhawan, M.L. Fotedar and V. George too have lost their once-feared clout. Uttarakhand chief minister Narain Dutt Tiwari had a reputation of being a 'politician among politicians' but by the time the state assembly polls were held in February 2007, Tiwari was busy attempting to leave Dehradun for the Raj Bhavan in Mumbai, Jaipur, Hyderabad or Bangalore. The old man did not campaign for the Congress, nursing a cataract operation that he had undergone weeks before the polls. The Uttarakhand assembly results were on predictable lines with the Congress losing the hill state tamely.

In Punjab too, Captain Amrinder Singh sulked and waged a lonely battle to stay in power. The blue blood in the former maharaja of Patiala prevented him paying court to and frequently submitting himself before the 'Delhi durbar'. The Congress did not deny Amrinder's brother-in-law (their wives are sisters) Natwar Singh's allegation that the then chief minister of Punjab did not get an audience with the Congress president for over thirteen months!

Sources close to Sonia, however, denied that she ever played favourites. As leader of the Congress, she does not distinguish between one leader and another on the basis of the past, they said. The sources said she had delayed her entry into politics, refusing to give in to the pressure to take the plunge in 1995 when the 'loyalists' led by Arjun Singh and N.D. Tiwari had split from Rao, because she did not want to be seen as a factional leader. By 1998, when she finally took over, they had returned to the parent party.

The 'loyalists' were, however, obsessed with the past, recalling the days when P.V. Narasimha Rao was calling the shots and the queues outside 10 Janpath were getting shorter. At that time, Natwar, Sheila, Arjun, P. Shiv Shankar and others had raised the banner of revolt against him, alleging that the Congress prime minister was drifting away from Nehruvian secularism. These 'loyalists' claim to have resisted temptation to stick to the time-tested principles of the Congress.

But as one loyalist after the other got the stick, a story from the lore of Laila–Majnu began doing the rounds in the Congress. Laila, having heard that her beloved was wandering in the streets of Baghdad hungry, sent her chambermaid with milk for him. A greedy beggar, his eyes on the milk, started shouting 'hai Laila', pretending to be Majnu. On hearing that Majnu's condition had deteriorated further, Laila sent out her maid again, substituting milk with blood. This time, the beggar pointed to the real Majnu and said: 'Hum to doodh wale Majnu hain, khoon wala woh raha (I am the Majnu for the milk, the one for the blood is there).' Their lips were sealed but the 'loyalists' kept hoping the milk of Sonia's kindness would flow before the blood.

However, Sonia was unforgiving towards Natwar Singh in the wake of the Volcker controversy. As she told Vir Sanghvi, 'As it became clearer that it was true that my colleague had misused the name of the party in some ways, I felt extremely betrayed . . . He was a colleague in whom I had placed trust and I felt very terribly betrayed.'

Sonia's trust in Natwar was evident when she took him along to visit the two ancient Russian towns of Vladimir and Suzdal in June 2005, searching in vain for the prison houses where her father, Stephano, had been jailed during the Second World War. Sonia was in Russia on a personal invitation of then president Valdimir Putin. Sonia was hugely charmed by both cities: Vladimir, the ancient capital of Russia with its huge, gold-domed churches, drawing its name from the great king Vladimir, who brought Christianity to Russia; and Suzdal, which played a key role in the formation of the Russian state in the eleventh and twelfth centuries.

The prison house structures no longer exist. Instead of a prison house, a church stood displaying the names of those who had spent days and nights behind dark cells. Outside the church, Sonia stood in silence for a few minutes after reading the names of the prisoners. As President Putin and Natwar Singh stood at a distance, Sonia let out a secret. Her father had walked all the way to Rome from here after escaping from the prison, covering a distance of over 5000 miles in adverse weather conditions. It took both Putin and Natwar some time to get the import of her remark. Sonia was indeed the daughter of a man of extraordinary character and determination.

At the functional level, while the good doctor and Sonia solved nightmarish protocol problems, Manmohan faced serious and often embarrassing situations. In a parliamentary democracy, the prime minister draws power primarily from his ability to hire and fire members of his council of ministers. Manmohan lacked that mandate. Firstly, he was confronted with heads of alliance parties like Pawar, Lalu, D. Maran and Ram Vilas Paswan as senior ministers, with their lieutenants such as Praful Patel and Raghuvansh Prasad Singh holding key portfolios.

At a political level, these individuals ensured that the prime minister had no powers to assess their performance or intervene in key policy matters, senior appointments, etc. Worse, there were numerous instances of these individuals functioning as per their whims and fancies. In one instance, a minister sat over a decision to import wheat for over six months leading to prices spiralling. By the time the course correction was made the Congress had lost the assembly polls in Uttarakhand and Punjab on the Opposition's plank of price rise. Manmohan had little choice but to watch helplessly.

In another instance, a minister of state refused to clear a project that the prime minister was extremely keen to launch. Repeated attempts were made by the PMO to make the minister see reason. But he did not budge. Often, the minister was heard flaunting his proximity to a senior AICC functionary and claiming that he could not be 'harmed'. This led to Manmohan detractors privately describing the prime minister as 'super-cabinet secretary' who had freedom to address issues ranging from administrative reforms to the pension bill.

This was not it. From among the Congress ministers, P. Chidambaram, Kamal Nath, Arjun Singh, Natwar Singh (till he was minister), Shivraj Patil to some extent and Pranab Mukherjee functioned rather independently. Ministers went public defending or opposing creation of special economic zones (SEZs), and farm sector reforms, and confronting the RBI governor on the issue of foreign banks being permitted to open more branches and ATMs.

In September 2006, whispers gained momentum that senior minister Pranab Mukherjee was nursing an ambition to become deputy prime minister in recognition of his 'Mr Indispensable' tag in the UPA. Pranab denied having desired it but the damage was done.

At a conclave of chief ministers of states ruled by the Congress, an unusually belligerent Sonia Gandhi snatched a question thrown at Manmohan Singh to squash rumours of a move to appoint a deputy prime minister. 'There is not going to be a deputy prime minister and I am saying so categorically,' the Congress president said in a steely voice, before the prime minister, sitting next to her, could reply. Her message went out loud and clear to the who's who of the Congress present in Nainital for the party's chief ministers' conference. Only one big leader was absent: Defence Minister Pranab Mukherjee, who was away attending the UN General Assembly.

Amid these sensitive issues, a minister of state further queered the pitch by leaking Sonia Gandhi's letters to select media on key economic issues. The minister, who doubled up as a wordsmith, survived in spite of leaving many red faces in the government. The problem with the Congress is that at the organizational level it lacks a cohesive economic policy. The party is packed with votaries of a mixed economy. Each time the leadership has tried to familiarize party leaders with the concept of economic restructuring, the latter have made little attempt to understand key concepts. At one stage (before becoming prime minister) Manmohan Singh had even begun avoiding the party fora to explain economic issues on the grounds that it made no sense to them; worse, nobody was prepared to discuss it in a threadbare manner.

Sonia's 'letter diplomacy' too came under scrutiny. A section of the Congress wondered about the merit of her practice, saying that if the idea was to pay service to public anger, as in the case of FDI in the retail sector, it raised questions on whether it was her writ that was supreme in the UPA government. The first letter written by Sonia was about price rise. The prime minister and the finance minister were virtually humiliated at a CWC meeting and the news leaked to the media. Then the government announced some policy measures. The second letter was about the prices of diesel and petrol. Within days, cuts were announced by the government. The third outburst was about farmers' plight under the SEZ policy over the government's inability to come up with a comprehensive rehabilitation policy. This communication came despite the fact that in one of its last acts before Sonia Gandhi quit its chairmanship, the NAC had written to the government with a draft policy. Apparently, neither the Centre nor any Congress-led state government issued any substantive directives to fulfil some of the demands made by the farmers. This was followed by another letter on FDI in retail. Interestingly, Sonia's letter did not oppose it on principle.

According to a Right to Information (RTI) application, Sonia had written ninety-eight letters to Manmohan in the first four years and in 90 per cent of the cases, her words were immediately acted upon. In the seven months after the UPA came to power in May 2004, Sonia Gandhi sent twenty-five letters to Manmohan Singh. The number rose to thirty-four in 2005, fell marginally to twenty-five in 2006 but slumped to a mere eight letters in 2007. In the first six months of 2008, she had sent just six letters to the PMO.

The letters addressed issues ranging from the National Rural Employment Guarantee Programme (NREGA), Ganga Action Plan, Action for Disaster Management, financial implications of recommendations of Budget 2005–06, to the National Rehabilitation Policy, Wal-Mart's proposed entry into India and the Communal Crimes Bill, 2008.

These letters provided the Opposition with a tool with which to hit at the government. BJP spokesman Prakash Jadvekar alleged that it was a way to show Dr Singh his place. His theory was that the letters had very little to do with the subjects they addressed; they were basically shock absorbers. There were other purposes to be achieved by the letters—to express resentment against certain actions of the government which cannot be voiced publicly. 'The whole thing is a charade—more political than real—and designed to fool the people. But Sonia should realize that one cannot fool all the people all the time,' he said.

There were some inherent structural problems too. During Atal Bihari Vajpayee's tenure as prime minister, his principal secretary

Brajesh Mishra doubled up as National Security Adviser enjoying tremendous clout and proximity to the political master. During this period, directors of internal and external intelligence agencies, namely, the Intelligence Bureau (IB) and the Research and Analysis Wing (RAW), stopped the time-tested practice of briefing the prime minister directly on a daily basis. Instead, they reported to Mishra who in turned briefed Vajpayee.

When the UPA came to power, the practice continued. The heads of IB and RAW continued to report to seasoned diplomat J.N. Dixit who enjoyed the complete confidence of the prime minister. Dixit died on 3 January 2005 and was replaced by former IB chief M.K. Narayanan. Strange as it may seem, Narayanan was in a limbo for nearly a decade after he retired from service in 1992. Though with his extreme faith in the Almighty—he makes an annual pilgrimage to Sabarimala and worships at Guruvayur more frequently—he did not bear a grudge against those responsible for it, there was no dearth of M.K. baiters in Raisina Hills. In whispers, his proximity to 10 Janpath was exaggerated and his 'cop-like' approach towards political and diplomatic initiatives with Pakistan, China, Nepal and domestic issues like Kashmir and Naxalite violence were intensely discussed.

Faced with pronounced behind-the-scene challenges, Manmohan responded cautiously and often swallowed pride when disgruntled Congressmen made provocative remarks. Unlike Rao who allowed minor misunderstandings with 10 Janpath to be blown out of proportion, Manmohan went out of the way to ensure that these provocations died a premature or natural death.

At work, Manmohan introduced a new culture. On the face of it, politicians appeared to be in charge of big portfolios but in reality their influence was on the wane. Slowly, highly skilled professionals who shared Manmohan's vision replaced politicians when it came to the day-to-day working of ministries. While ministers like Arjun Singh, A.R. Antulay and Meira Kumar indulged in rhetoric on sensitive issues, Manmohan went around hand-picking lieutenants and associates numbering around twenty technocrats/professionals who called the shots on all key policy issues. Apart from Montek Singh Ahluwalia who emerged as the third most powerful person in the UPA after the prime minister and Sonia, Team Manmohan included highly skilled members of the Planning Commission and the NAC, heads of the finance commission and the scientific advisory council, and the interlocutors for behind-the-scenes talks with the US, Pakistan and China.

However, by the time the Manmohan regime entered its third year in office, it was beset with serious problems and issues that offered no easy solutions. The year 2008 has been particularly bad, notwithstanding its success with the nuclear deal. The performance or rather the lack of it in the Union home ministry and the precarious internal security situation has given both Sonia and Manmohan a bad name. This has also given the Opposition an issue with which it can go to the masses by playing on their perceived lack of security under the regime. Shivraj Patil has been under fire from every direction for bungling in Jammu and Kashmir, his inept handling of terrorist strikes and Maoist attacks, and for the attacks on Christians in Orissa by right-wing fundamentalists. Each time a bomb went off, killing people by the dozen, television images of a nattily dressed Patil infuriated every concerned citizen of the country. His perfunctory expressions of pain and anguish at loss of human lives and his sense of bafflement at those asking for his head have made him an object of ridicule.

When on 13 September a series of explosions ripped through crowded markets in Delhi, killing over twenty people and injuring hundreds, Patil was at a CWC meeting in a cream-coloured bandhgala. By the time he reached home and picked up a fresh bandhgala—a black one—the news of the blast was all over TV screens. He duly went on a round of the sites affected before returning home and changing into a spotless white suit to accompany Sonia Gandhi to a city hospital. As the media went to town savaging Patil for his obsession with sartorial elegance at a time of grave national crisis, BJP spokesperson Ravi Shankar Prasad had one telling question for Patil:

'What is more important, the lives of people or your sartorial elegance?'

Even Congress leaders sympathetic to Patil feel that Sonia and Manmohan had erred badly in handing him a portfolio traditionally reserved for the 'number two' in the government. The home ministry is after all the most prized ministry under a parliamentary democracy and Patil is a lame-duck politician who had even failed to win his Lok Sabha seat from Latur. In the aftermath of the Delhi blasts, Patil went on a rare show of aggressive intent with a police shootout in a sensitive area in the capital where claims were made about the masterminds being arrested. However, his ineptitude came through even in this as increasingly there are media speculations that the 'encounter' was stage-managed only to silence the Opposition's cry for action. This unexpected show of 'action' on his part has, feel many Congress sympathizers, only ended up alienating the Muslim community.

As a tsunami of crises enveloped the government, the prime mister seems to be giving the impression of simply limping from one crisis to the next. The unrelenting rise in prices is driving the 'aam aadmi'— the Congress plank in the previous elections—to despair and bodes ill for the party in the forthcoming elections. While the common man is grappling with rising prices, with terrorists striking almost at will, with Bihar reeling under a flood of immense proportions, and with parts of the country going up in flames every other day, the government's drive and enthusiasm in getting the nuclear deal through came across as strangely misplaced. After all, to the man on the streets, prices and security are issues of greater importance than the nuclear deal whose benefits are still too esoteric for the 'aam aadmi' to be gung-ho about.

Sonia and Manmohan will have to do a lot of fire-fighting if they are to stand a good chance at the hustings. Manmohan's titanic battle with CPM General Secretary Prakash Karat and the Congress move to ally with the Samajwadi Party over the smooth passage of an Indo– US civil and nuclear deal saw the emergence of a 'politician' Manmohan and a 'pragmatic' Sonia which showed yet another fascinating side of these 'reluctant' politicians. Now, if only the duo bring the drive and energy they displayed on the nuclear issue to address more basic daily issues, Congress workers would feel a little more secure about their electoral prospects.

TEN

ENTER RAHUL GANDHI

By January 2004, Rahul had begun to take a greater interest in the forthcoming elections, becoming visible in almost all the strategy meets. His management background and political instincts gave Sonia a much-needed boost. For instance, it was Rahul who prevailed upon Sonia to go 'all-out' on her 'road shows'. Rahul's argument was simple. Go to the masses, mingle with them and see what they think of you. The public meetings or political rallies mostly consisting of hired crowds are of little benefit, Rahul argued.

Sources close to Sonia said Rahul was fielded from Amethi after the Congress managers conducted a secret in-house survey. The little-known survey conducted in 134 Lok Sabha constituencies across the country had tried to gauge Sonia's popularity versus Vajpayee's. The findings showed that pitted against Atal Behari Vajpayee (A), Sonia Gandhi (S) was lagging. If S were clubbed with Priyanka Gandhi (P), the duo would still be short of matching A, but if S plus P plus Rahul (R) took the field, they would neutralize the rival's advantage.

Rahul's entry enthused the party's ranks and file, giving rise to a demand for Priyanka as well. Sonia and the Congress managers kept Priyanka tantalizingly close, putting her in charge of Sonia'a campaign at Rae Bareli and feeding stories to the media that Priyanka would campaign across the country, which she never did. When the four-phase elections were about to conclude and party workers started losing patience, they were told that Priyanka could not campaign in spite of her 'best intentions' as she had to attend to her two young children.

Incidentally, the timing of Rahul's entry into politics coincided with Sanjay–Maneka Gandhi's son Varun joining the BJP. The race began though in a contrasting style and on opposite sides of the political spectrum.

Varun, several years younger to Rahul, seemed in a great hurry to outshine and outscore his more illustrious cousin. The youngster, who studied at the School of Oriental and African Studies (SOAS), London, and fancied himself to be a painter and poet, joined the BJP to enter the Lok Sabha and place himself at par with Rahul, as the parliamentary forum would help everyone judge and evaluate the two Gandhis. However, in May 2004, he was still short of twenty-five, the minimum age of contesting polls, so the BJP used him as a campaigner promising to get him in Lok Sabha in a subsequent by-election.

Varun claimed that he was 'exercized' over the prospects of joining the 'right-wing BJP' but he was left with no choice. Coming from the Nehru–Gandhi family, he loathed the idea of joining any regional or casteist party. He said while joining a national party like the BJP, he made it clear that he would never speak against the family or rake up communal issues. Varun created a flutter when he entered Gujarat and criticized chief minister Narendra Modi's failure to prevent the 2002 carnage.

But closer to the 2009 general election, Varun was a changed man. Campaigning in his parliamentary seat Pilibhit, Varun upset many including those in the BJP for making some remarks that reeked of communal overtones. These remarks also prompted the Election Commission and district administration to clap a show-cause on him. In one instance, Varun was heard saying, 'This is not a hand [Congress symbol], it is the power of the lotus [BJP symbol]. It will cut the head of ... Jai Shri Ram.' At another election meeting, he said, 'If anyone raises a finger towards Hindus or if someone thinks that Hindus are weak and leaderless, if someone thinks that these leaders lick our boots for votes, if anyone raises a finger towards Hindus, then I swear on the Gita that I will cut that hand.'

The Congress, headed by Varun's aunt Sonia Gandhi, was quick to condemn the remarks as 'unethical and against the law'. 'It is condemnable ... that he [Varun] is associated with a party which has this [anti-minority] ideology and culture,' Congress spokesman Abhishek Singhvi told reporters.

Both Priyanka and Rahul quickly distanced themselves from Varun's remarks and even chided him in open. Priyanka observed, 'What Varun had said clearly goes against the principles of the Gandhi family. It is really sad to see him saying all these things on television,' she said while advising her cousin to 'read the Gita and try to understand it properly'.

Rahul was more restrained while making comments on Varun, telling reporters that he would never allow 'hatred and anger' to prevail over him. 'I have been taught since I have been small that hatred and anger can blind you. I do get angry. But I try to sort of lose that emotion. That is what I have been told and that is how I have been brought up,' Rahul said while addressing a press conference in Puducherry on 24 March 2009. When reporters sought his comments on Varun's speech in Pilibhit, Rahul said, 'These are his views. I have my views. My views are you should not carry hatred and anger with you. I was surprised by Varun's views. But life is full of surprises.'

As the Congress MP from Amethi, Rahul continued to work on a larger canvass. He chose to visit war-torn Kabul as his first official visit abroad in 2005. Nattily dressed in a beige suit, Rahul boarded the PM's aircraft and sat alone in the flight, exchanging pleasantries with the crew and occasional words with Natwar Singh and national security advisor M.K. Narayanan. 'He was quite dignified and already knew enough about Afghanistan,' said an MEA official. For most of the visit, Rahul stood on the sidelines, until, eventually, the sidelines became the focus of attention. He stood with the rest of the Indian delegation while Dr Singh and Hamid Karzai addressed a joint press conference, helping Narayanan and Sanjay Baru, the PM's media advisor, as they struggled with their wireless headphones. He was also seen sms-ing feverishly throughout most of the PM's official engagements.

However, later that night he had a post-dinner conversation with Mustafa Zahir, the grandson of former King Zahir Shah, quizzing the latter about Afghanistan's history and Indo-Afghan relations. As the two talked under the chinar trees on the lawns of the Presidential palace, a diplomat remarked that 'the parrots on the trees come from India'. But more than the birds, Rahul was more interested in Track Two diplomacy. His crash course in international relations also involved a trip to Germany in August 2005. Playing favourites, the prime minister gave him a leave of absence from Parliament to attend an international conference on governance.

Next, Rahul was part of an official delegation to Brazil to learn about Brazil's response to the AIDS epidemic (2005). The Sao Paulo visit was part of an initiative by the Joint United Nations Programme on HIV and AIDS (UNAIDS) that sponsors visits by parliamentarians to other countries in order to promote exchanges of experiences in the area of HIV and AIDS. In May 2005, he addressed the World Economic Forum at Zermatt, Switzerland. He was chosen as one of the 238 Young Global Leaders—a group of men and women under the age of forty selected from a pool of 8,000 candidates from around the world to speak on 'towards a better world in the year 2020'. From the industry, Kumar Mangalam Birla, Sulajja F. Motwani, Malvinder Mohan Singh and Rajiv Bajaj were part of the Forum of Young Global Leaders.

In Delhi, Rahul set up a full-fledged office at 12, Tuglaq Lane, where elite SPG guards kept a round-the-clock vigil. Here, each day, a chosen few are ushered in to hold brainstorming session with the young Gandhi. The 'experts' grooming Rahul do not wish to be named but said they were thrilled by Rahul's grasp of complex issues, his comprehension and articulation. Led by Kanishka Singh, son of the late S.K. Singh (former Governor and foreign service officer), a battery of professionals keep tab on everything that relates to Rahul. Uttar Pradesh Congress leader Siraj Mehdi learned this aspect in a rather hard way. Mehdi who heads the UP unit of the women's cricket association apparently gave a press statement saying Rahul would inaugurate a championship but without getting the young Gandhi's consent. When he sought an appointment with Rahul and failed,

Mehdi became apprehensive and checked at 12, Tuglaq Lane. He was curtly told about the 'indiscretion' which Mehdi denied. The phone attendant then advised him to check the Google search engine forcing Mehdi to search for an answer.

By April 2005, a section of Congressmen began looking at Rahul as their heir apparent, a final arbitrator in the party and the government. When he casually remarked that he was ready to take up greater responsibility, Congressmen accorded great significance to the statement. His support became crucial in the fast-changing political equations in the Delhi durbar. The prime minister's camp increasingly looks at the GenNext Gandhi for support with his thrust on reforms, foreign affairs and matters of national importance.

The old guard too counted on him. Leaders like Arjun Singh, M.L. Fotedar, Narain Dutt Tiwari, Sheila Dikshit and others felt 'duty-bound' to apprise him about the primacy of socio-political programmes to strengthen the Congress's mass base. The truth is that unlike Sonia, both camps do not enjoy proximity to Rahul. During this period, Sonia keenly observed Rahul's responses to tricky political situations that are part of his hands-on orientation for a future role. Sonia's role model and mother-in-law Indira Gandhi had adopted a similar course while grooming Rajiv Gandhi. He was given a suite at 1, Safdarjung Road, and made accessible from a separate entrance on 1, Akbar Road. He was given a private secretary, V. George, and associates Vijay Dhar and Arun Singh. Dhar's father D.P. Dhar had been in Indira Gandhi's inner circle of advisers. Rajiv's office used to be an alternative durbar where regional satraps, warring ministers, industrialists, scientists and senior bureaucrats made a beeline.

More than backroom politicking, Rahul showed greater interest in linking technology to rural areas, meeting the youth and 'discovering India' Rahul told these ticket seekers that they should realize that anybody owning a mobile phone should be considered as 'resourceful person' having an ability to connect with many.

The thrust on technology and info-tech was evident each time Rahul travelled out. For instance, in November 2010, he was in Amethi's Sarvan village near Fursatganj where the young Gandhi launched a broadband service named 'Fibre to panchayat', technically known as the GPON technology. Sarvan village became the first village in the country to have optic fibre for services like the broadband, Internet, telephonic service and cable TV. Sharing the dais with Sam Pitroda, the pioneer behind the information technology revolution in India, Rahul stressed upon the role of information technology facilities in the development of backward regions of the country. He said the employment of information technology is necessary to bridge the gap between the rich and the poor. 'Today, connectivity development in the field of transportation, electricity and information technology is the need of the hour,' he emphasized while urging people to make use of this technology readily irrespective of their age. Speaking about the growing disparity between urban and rural development, Rahul said if farmers and the poor are connected to the world through the Internet, it will open the path of development. People at the village were quite enthusiastic at the prospect. Ramchand, a college student, was much excited at the idea of making use of the facility for booking a ticket for train and air. Earlier, he had to go to a nearby town.

So when Rahul came face to face with Bill Gates in December 2005, the young MP left no one in any doubt about what was priority number one. When the IT czar expressed his wish to contribute to India's health sector through his multi-billion-dollar Bill and Melinda Gates Foundation, Rahul was quick to respond: 'Why don't you do something for Bihar?' For the next few minutes, Bill and his wife Melinda listened raptly as the young Gandhi described movingly how the deadly kala azar kills hundreds in Bihar every year. Rahul told Gates that over 14,000 fresh cases of kala azar had been reported in Bihar and that he feared an epidemic by 2007 if precautions were not taken fast. In two years, between 2004 and 2006, over 300 patients had died in Darbhanga alone. Transmitted by the bite of a sand fly, the disease can lead to an enlargement of vital organs such as the liver. Untreated, it causes death.

When he finished, the American businessman quietly said he would 'love to visit Bihar' as Melinda nodded in approval. Senior Congress leader Murli Deora, who had accompanied Gates to 10, Janpath, for a meeting with Sonia Gandhi, said the tech baron was deeply impressed by Rahul's passion to eradicate kala azar from Bihar.

Under pressure from Congressmen, Sonia appointed Rahul as AICC general secretary in September 2007, virtually taking a leaf out of her mother-in-law Indira Gandhi's book. It was in February 1983 that Rajiv Gandhi was given a similar assignment under the watchful eyes of Indira.

Rajiv was young and full of dreams. His mother, however, was in deep trouble having lost Karnataka to Ramakrishna Hegde and Andhra Pradesh to N.T. Rama Rao. Along with Gujarat, Maharashtra and Kerala, these were the states that had stood by the Nehru–Gandhi family in the 1977 general elections that had wiped out the Congress.

Under Sonia's leadership, Rahul perhaps faces a more formidable task. Apart from reviving the Congress, he has to act as an interface between party workers across the country and his mother. While most party functionaries and many others in the country see Rahul as the 'heir', the brief his mother has given him is to reorganize and revitalize the party, particularly its youth wing which has been in decay for years. The Congress, controlled from the Centre, has had its grassroots structure diminished considerably. For old-timers, Rahul's induction into the All India Congress Committee today is an emotional moment but they feel the young MP from Amethi should not be compared to his father.

For one thing, Indira was prime minister in addition to being party president. Two, between 1981 and 1983, Rajiv had built a team for himself that included highly skilled management executives like Arun Nehru and Arun Singh as well as the more down-to-earth Buta Singh. Three, Rajiv had already successfully organized the 1982 Asian Games that transformed Delhi with new roads, stadiums and hotels.

Rajiv had a lot more grey hair, having flown the Boeing aircraft for Indian Airlines and was married with two children. Rahul, a bachelor, who has worked with Monitor, a global consultancy firm, has done well looking after his constituency since May 2004, and is widely travelled but his experience at this stage is not anywhere close to Rajiv's.

Moreover, Indian politics, too, has changed a lot since February

1983. Each time Rahul travels out of Delhi, he has to keep the 'coalition dharma' in mind while speaking about parties that support the UPA. In most matters, Rahul could neither endorse nor attack whimsical and unpredictable regional satraps.

In fact, each time Rahul spoke in public, his remark kicked up a controversy. During the 2007 UP assembly polls, Rahul observed that the Babri mosque would not have been demolished had his family been active in politics in 1992. It led to a huge political brawl. But Rahul's Babri remark was a mere repetition of his mother Sonia Gandhi's identical statements made in 1992 and in 1998.

On 6 December 1992 when the domes of the sixteenth century mosque in Ayodhya were pulled down, Sonia exhibited her political colours, perhaps for the first time in the political arena. As chairperson of the Rajiv Gandhi Foundation in memory of the late prime minister, Sonia had overruled P. Chidambaram and other members of the trust and issued a very strong statement saying that had Rajiv been alive, he would not have allowed the Babri demolition.

Chidambaram, a minister in the then Narasimha Rao government, and a few others had argued that there was no need to make a comment on this political issue. A member of the trust who was present then had recalled that Sonia was uncharacteristically assertive and told them she would be belittling the Nehru–Gandhi legacy if the RGF failed to express its sense of outrage. Rao, too, being a member of the RGF had to swallow the reprimand.

In January 1998, when Sonia formally joined politics, she repeated the comment she had made in Hyderabad. Addressing a gathering of a predominantly Muslim audience in Hyderabad, she said exactly the same thing that Rahul had said in Uttar Pradesh. Apparently, a month before his assassination, Rajiv had told her that should any attempt be made to touch the Babri Masjid, he would stand in front of it and they would have to kill him first.

In 2004 Sonia had again talked about the Babri demolition in Shekhar Gupta's *Walk the Talk* on NDTV, recollecting: 'Well, I wasn't in politics. As the chairperson of the Rajiv Gandhi Foundation, we issued a very strong statement. That was again a day I shall never forget. In fact, that brought not just tears, we were all distraught . . . well, the Congress was in power in the Centre but don't forget there was a BJP government in UP.'

In electoral terms, the remark has not fetched votes since 1992. When Sonia offered a conditional apology in Hyderabad, the poll outcome of the 1998 general elections was far from encouraging and even prompted the whimsical Sitaram Kesri to comment that the party had lost in most seats where Sonia had campaigned. The successive assembly and parliamentary election results since 1998 in Uttar Pradesh too have shown little impact even in the Muslim dominated constituencies. In fact, privately most Congressmen like to avoid talking about the ghost of Babri. When Narasimha Rao's book on the Ayodhya issue came out, Congress leaders including Arjun Singh kept mum even though Rao made a dig at Rajiv Gandhi debating whether the *shilanyas* Rajiv allowed in Ayodhya in 1989 took place on 'disputed' or 'undisputed' land. Rao cited several government records and statements to indicate that it was the latter. The only person who retaliated against Rao was the family retainer M.L. Fotedar. But in the process, Fotedar sought to queer pitch for current prime minister, Dr Manmohan Singh. Fotedar, sidelined in the present party dispensation, alleged that Manmohan had supported Rao's stand on the Babri Masjid. Claiming that on 4 December 1992 when he had raised the Babri issue in a cabinet meeting, Rao said that he was looking into it. 'Dr Manmohan Singh, finance minister at the time, supported Mr Rao. I told him [Manmohan], "Kindly keep quiet, it is our duty to protect the disputed structure,"' Fotedar said.

Unlike Priyanka, Rahul has always been an enigma to the Indian media. He stays away from the Page 3 circuit and his trips to Amethi have been few and far between. But those who know him say that he is very 'thorough in whatever he does'. Points out Congress MP and family freind Rajiv Shukla: 'What impresses me about Rahul is his attention to detail. Talk to him about any constituency in UP and he'll have the caste break up on his finger tips.' In fact, some Congressmen were amazed when a chance conversation with Rahul resulted in him spouting details such as '*UP mein Kurmi, Kohli, Lodh zyaada hain.'* Not quite what they were expecting from a Harvard–Cambridge graduate. In fact, despite his foreign stint, he speaks in an unaccented Hindi which is basically *'UP vaali Hindi'*.

But according to *India Today*'s senior editor, Priya Sahgal who was in St. Stephen's at the time Rahul was around, however much he shirks the limelight, the media glare has always caught up with Rahul. 'During my interaction with Rahul I found him to be unassuming, approachable and well informed. These are important qualities in a politician,' says Sahgal.

In the Lok Sabha, during his first term, Rahul sat on the left-hand corner seat in the eighth row of the treasury benches. In Parliament the first-time MP from Amethi spoke little but his presence was eloquently felt. The other first timers had to make painfully long stammering speeches to get Sonia Gandhi to turn around and smile at them. Rahul waited for long to make his maiden speech. Despite this, every Congress MP, including the Congress president kept smiling at him. They watched him as he walked into Parliament, dressed in a crisp white kurta and exchanged jokes with the rest of the first timers. They tried to catch his eye as he waved to his friend Omar Abdullah across the hall. Some like union minister Renuka Chowdhury did more than just nod. In one session, realizing that Rahul was sitting right behind her, she craned her neck and indulged in an acrobatic twenty minutes of animated monologue. The minute Chowdhury paused for breath Rahul gave her one of his dimpled smiles, politely picked up his headphones, tuned out Renuka and tuned into the proceedings of the house.

It's not just the backbenches where privacy eludes India's most public pin-up face. Rahul has to change his gym constantly as the trainer waits for the Gandhi scion to climb on to the treadmill and turn up the speed before approaching him with a list of requests. The trainer knows that once he has Gandhi on the treadmill he has a captive audience.

The Congress too is aware of the fact that they've got Rahul on a political treadmill. He really has no choice but to complete what he's started. Somewhat like his father, Rahul remains a reluctant recruit on the Indian political scene. It's the worst-kept family secret that had Priyanka Gandhi been a boy, Rahul would still be riding his motorcycle to work at his office in the London-based Monitor Consulting. But destiny—and Sonia—chose Rahul. So he traded his bike for a staid white Ambassador and his corporate office for the Parliament of India.

Political analysts like Priya Sahgal believe that in Rahul the politician, there is a certain disconnect between his esoteric worldview and the ground reality. For instance, in Amethi, Rahul sanctioned a project for women where they were taught how to make yoga kits, candles, pottery, and stitch garments and make bamboo furniture. But the women did not have the basic raw material or a near-home market where they could sell their produce.

In Parliament, Rahul became a ring leader of sorts of a group of young MPs. The fourteenth Lok Sabha had twenty-eight fresh young faces who loved to drive white Bentleys and Pajeros. Most of these youngsters held MBA degrees from Boston and Texas, or an MPhil from Cambridge, or a law degree from Lincolns. They carried with them the promise of purpose, the earnestness of idealism and the blueprint of a fresh perspective.

The privileged and elite group of Milind Deora, Jitin Prasada, Sachin Pilot, Sandeep Dixit, Tejeshwani Seeramesh, Deepinder Singh Hooda, L. Rajagopal, Madhu Goud Yaskhi and Jyotiraditya Scindia (though he was often left out for inexplicit reasons) became core members of Team Rahul ironing out every kink.

During the Uttar Pradesh assembly polls, most of these young MPs were assigned ground duty such as setting up communication centres, coordinating with local administration and organizing election campaigns. Former MP and Gandhi family loyalist Satish Sharma was always at hand, chauffeuring Rahul's Prado. A team consisting of Kishorilal, Kanisha Singh and Girja Shankar Pandey were other members of Rahul's core team. In fact, whenever assembly or parliamentary polls were held where Rahul campaigned, Kishorilal's duty was to visit the rally venue a few hours before, assess the arrangements and size up the crowd. He then sent back advice regarding whether Rahul should start right away or wait till the crowd built up.

In the Congress organization, Rahul was given charge of reviving the youth Congress, NSUI and Sewa Dal. Initially, there were lots of hopes and expectations as party men described Rahul as 'Sachin Tendulkar' and 'M.S. Dhoni', but a few months after the September 2007 appointment, they realized that the young Gandhi did not have a magic wand to revive these defunct youth frontal organizations. Unlike the SFI or ABVP, the youth Congress had no tradition of being anti-establishment, therefore its grooming fields of leadership were non-existent.

Privately, many Congressmen called Rahul the 'Congress's Dhoni' as the day the young Gandhi took over as party general secretary in 2007, Team India lifted the Twenty20 World Cup in South Africa under Dhoni's leadership. Rahul appeared to have unwittingly taken the Dhoni comparison rather seriously. The next day, when the Congress Working Committee met at 24, Akbar Road, he suggested that the committee extol Team India. The party immediately picked up the cue, spokesperson Abhishek Singhvi telling the media: 'The spirit of youth was reflected on Monday afternoon [24 September 2007] when Rahul Gandhi took over an important position and Dhoni and his team delivered a magnificent victory to India.'

Dhoni and Rahul have known each other well thanks to a network of common friends and their shared passion for cricket, football and fast two-wheelers. A common love of bikes is said to have bonded Rahul with Dhoni and actors John Abraham and Salman Khan.

In 2009, Rahul was spotted at a specially built and carefully camouflaged racing track 25 km from Delhi, enjoying the thrills of power biking (on a Yamaha R1) and go-karting with brother-in-law Robert Vadra. On another occasion, Rahul was seen cycling in Delhi in a blue T-shirt, red shorts and sunglasses while two vehicles packed with SPG personnel tailed him.

While Rahul and Dhoni have excelled in biking, the young Gandhi has been a tad defensive on the cricket field. Each time he has captained in a friendly match, he has chosen to field first and has restricted himself to that rather than picking up the bat. In his social relationships, too, Rahul appears a little restrained despite his wide circle of friends.

On the organizational front, the parent organization however continued to make a mockery of his call to restore inner-party democracy and better representation for the weaker sections. Rahul's thrust on democracy and 'talent hunt' has taken a beating with the entire party election process in 2010 taking the 'consensus' route. Sources say the central minders and state leaders have kept in close touch with selected party delegates. For instance, most of the 502 Pradesh Congress Committee delegates in Madhya Pradesh were picked from one or the other of the six prominent regional camps, led by Digvijay Singh, Kamal Nath, Jyotiraditya Scindia, Suresh Pachauri, Arjun Singh and Subhash Yadav. Added to that the 'family' factor: the delegate list teems with the wives, sons, nephews, brothers and brothers-in-law of prominent party leaders.

Sonia's plank for a better deal for women, tribals, Dalits and minorities has been ignored. Despite her repeated appeals for a 33 per cent representation for women, the gender makes up less than 10 per cent of the delegates.

Only forty-seven out of the 502 delegates were women and even among them, there was abysmal representation of the minorities and weaker sections.

Madhya Pradesh has a sizeable Other Backward Classes population that, if clubbed with the Dalits and tribals, accounts for over 60 per cent of the population. Yet, the Brahmins and the Thakurs, less than 10 per cent of the population, occupied more than half the slots on the delegate list.

By Rahul's own admission, there are 'two Indias' within India: one urban, prosperous and on the path to development, and another struggling with poverty, want and poor delivery system. Likewise, it often appears as if there are 'two' Rahuls too. One in Delhi who is generally reticent and often diffident; and another in rural settings who is energetic, candid, charming, witty and leader-like.

Rahul has been the epitome of his rural self during his numerous visits to the tribal—Dalit belts of Uttar Pradesh, Orissa, Chhattisgarh, Madhya Pradesh, Tamil Nadu, Kerala and other far-flung areas of the country, giving candid and comprehensive replies to all queries and snubbing both opponents and 'in-house sycophants'.

In one place, he was asked how he felt being called 'yuvraj' (heir apparent). Pat came the reply: 'I feel the word "yuvraj" is insulting. India is a democratic country and this word has no meaning today.'

Rahul's comment came after a furore in the Rajya Sabha over Congress MP E.M. Sudarsana Natchiappan calling him 'yuvraj'. The BJP had risen up in protest, saying only members of the royal family could be given such 'titles'.

Next Rahul was asked what he thought about Mayawati's comment that each time he interacted with Dalits, he took a shower and washed his clothes with special soap.

The young Amethi MP, perspiring in the soaring Chhattisgarh heat, stood up and showed his kurta to the Kanker audience. 'Look, does it look like it is being washed with some special soap?' he asked.

The candid repartees did not end there. Asked about Arjun Singh and others projecting him as the 'future prime minister', Rahul sought to clear the air over Manmohan Singh's continuation beyond May 2009. 'Manmohan Singh is my leader and the most able person for the PM's chair,' he declared. Rahul also emphasized that he 'fully supported' incumbent Manmohan Singh as he was the 'most capable prime minister'.

Asked about the Naxalite problem, Rahul said the Chhattisgarh and Orissa regimes had been unable to reach the 'poorest of the poor'; the benefits of welfare schemes were not percolating down to them. To drive home the point, he added that the benefits of the National Rural Employment Guarantee Scheme and the Indira Awas Yojana had not reached the needy.

The BJP leadership however kept criticizing Rahul's visits out of Delhi. Party leader Ravi Shankar Prasad was heard commenting, 'The BJP has no objection to Mr Gandhi's study tour. The "political miracle" caused by his visits to Uttar Pradesh, Gujarat, Himachal Pradesh and some other states has already been observed.' He was referring to the Congress loss in the 2007 Uttar Pradesh assembly polls and subsequent setbacks in other states.

Rahul's sartorial taste too came under close scrutiny. When he stepped on to Kerala campuses in jeans and a shirt in October 2009, he was seen as sending out a signal to the youth that politics is not the sole province of serious-minded elders.

Rahul who had been coaxing young professionals and budding doctors, engineers and managers to view politics as a career option, was in Kerala to recruit members for the Youth Congress and the National Students' Union of India. 'The kurta–pyjama symbolizes the established political culture whereas the youth tend to be anti-establishment,' a Congress leader said, claiming Rahul had received feedback that the young view politics as a drab profession that leaves little room for privacy or time for hobbies.

According to senior Congress leaders, the idea of dressing up casually in jeans and a shirt was Rahul's way of telling GenNext that if they join him in nation building, they will not have to compromise on their appearance or style, nor give up on fun.

Politicians have for long been known to use their attire to send out a message to their audience. Some politicians like BJP's S.S. Ahluwalia and Sushma Swaraj reportedly believe in a system similar to Vaastu and numerology that advocates a particular colour on a particular day of the week for good luck, such as saffron on Tuesdays, green on Wednesdays and blue on Thursdays.

Sonia, who many perceive as having almost single-handedly resurrected the sari as a fashion statement among politicians, loves to pull out rare weaves and prints in an era of flashy synthetics. Whether it's an expensive Maheshwari or a Chanderi or a homespun Bagru, the statement is that India lives in its villages and in the homes of its weavers and printers.

Throughout his brief political career as party general secretary, Rahul seemed caught between family loyalists and the professionalism that he wished to usher into politics. The party's old guard had tremendous trouble adjusting to the corporate culture that Rahul tried to bring in.

In the Congress organization, Rahul's presence posed a piquant problem for a number of party leaders who had cut their political teeth under Sanjay and Rajiv Gandhi. They lacked a rapport with the AICC general secretary. Even an old guard like Pranab Mukherjee went public saying he did not see himself serving under a government that might be headed by Rahul Gandhi.

As the Congress celebrated the completion of 125 years on 28 December 2010, the grand old party seemed to be getting ready to accept Rahul Gandhi as its supreme leader. The Burari AICC plenary held in Delhi between 18–20 December 2010 saw general secretary Digvijay Singh calling himself and his generation of leaders as having an 'expiry date'. Digvijay's generation, or Congress leaders in their sixties, are currently calling the shots as UPA ministers, chief ministers, AICC functionaries and state Congress chiefs. Some of these leaders, who were handpicked by Sanjay and Rajiv Gandhi, are Ahmad Patel, Ambika Soni, Vayalar Ravi, Janardhan Dwivedi, Oscar Fernandes, Ghulam Nabi Azad, Kamal Nath, Sushil Kumar Shinde, Bhoopinder Singh Hooda, Ashok Gehlot, B.K. Hariprasad, Suresh Pachauri and Ramesh Chenninthala.

Digvijay was barely thirty-seven when Rajiv made him the Madhya Pradesh chief amid loud protests from Arjun Singh, Madhavrao Scindia, the Shukla brothers and others. Ahmad was crowned head of the Gujarat unit, while Hooda was picked for Haryana in spite of opposition from the old guard. But unlike Rajiv, Sonia and Rahul did not appear to have the kind of talent that was produced in the 1970s. Nowadays, Youth Congress activities include holding periodic demonstrations at Jantar Mantar. At times, the venue shifts to auditoriums where workshops and seminars are held. Street fights and social work play only a token role in its agenda.

Unlike his father or uncle who used the youth wing to counter Jaiprakash Narayan, V.P. Singh and the Bofors allegations, Rahul appears to be a reluctant leader who prefers playing cricket with the National Students' Union of India and the Youth Congress to foster team spirit. While Rahul's bid to build the Youth Congress and the NSUI on the basis of academic record and inner party democracy are not showing results, 24, Akbar Road, is contributing little in terms of either generating new ideas or sending any concrete proposal to the government. Some old-timers even wonder if the Congress has assumed a negative role, with officials acting more to kill or blunt initiative than utilizing the talent at its command.

ELEVEN

THE OFFICE OF PROFIT CONTROVERSY

On 23 March 2006, Sonia stunned everyone yet again by hurriedly stepping down as a member of the Lok Sabha and chairperson of the NAC, once more displaying an ethical bent of mind like in May 2004, when she had declined the office of the prime minister while responding to her 'inner voice'. This time she responded to the call of her conscience, tendering her resignation in the wake of the unsavoury row over 'office of profit'.

In parliamentary lexicon, an office of profit can best be defined as a position that brings to the person holding it some financial gain, or advantage, or benefit. An office or place amounts to one of profit if it carries some remuneration, financial advantage, benefit, etc. The amount of such profit is immaterial. As per Article 102 (1)(A) of the Constitution of India, an MP or an MLA is barred from holding any office of profit under the Government of India or in any state other than an office declared by Parliament by law as not disqualifying its holder.

The office of profit controversy gained currency after Samajwadi Party MP Jaya Bachchan was disqualified on the grounds that she held an office of profit by being chairperson of the UP Film Development Council. Along with her, about sixty-two MPs were said to be holding similar offices of profit, many of them from the Left parties in Bengal. Sonia stoutly denied that she was behind the campaign to have Jaya Bachchan disqualified. 'There is no question about it. My nature is not a vindictive one and is not a petty one and besides I have larger issues to concentrate on than the petty ones for which I am accused,' she told Vir Sanghvi in an interview in October 2006.

The remarkable thing about the controversy was that the entire mess was of Congressmen's own making. And the only way out of the mess was for Sonia to resign. The villain of the piece was said to be Union Law Minister H.R. Bhardwaj who mishandled an internal discussion among MPs over some kind of changes in the Members of Parliament (Prevention of Disqualification) Act of 1959.

In a bid to be one up in a no-holds-barred war between the Congress and Samajwadi Party in Uttar Pradesh, a Congressman from Uttar Pradesh who lost an election complained to the Election Commission that Rajya Sabha member Jaya Bachchan, as chairperson of the UP Film Development Council, was holding an office of profit. When the issue erupted on the national platform, the Congress pushed it to its logical conclusion without thinking of the consequences.

Mulayam Singh Yadav, then Uttar Pradesh chief minister, tried his best to save Jaya by amending the state law through an ordinance to take the UP Film Development Council chairmanship out of its purview. But the Congress didn't play ball, primarily because the Gandhis and Bachchans have fallen out and the latter are now on the side of the Congress's arch-rivals. In fact, whatever the merits or otherwise of the issue, it played itself out primarily as a sideshow of the Bachchan–Gandhi family feud which had worsened in the intervening years with the Bachchans' growing proximity to Amar Singh and the Samajwadi Party.

As the BJP-led NDA and the Samajwadi Party mounted a major political campaign against Sonia over the issue of office of profit, she sprang a surprise that would take away the sting from the Opposition's charge that the government's move for an ordinance to redefine office of profit was aimed at saving her from 'a certain disqualification' as an MP. Her resignation came on the day the BJP petitioned President A.P.J. Abdul Kalam seeking her disqualification from the Lok Sabha on the grounds that she held an office of profit as chairperson of the NAC. The TDP had already petitioned the President in this regard.

In a statement to announce her resignation, Sonia Gandhi said, 'In the last few days some Opposition parties are trying to create an impression that the Congress and the United Progressive Alliance are using Parliament and the government only to protect me. This has hurt me very much. I have stated earlier also that I am in politics and public life not for my selfish ends. I have taken a pledge to serve the people of the country and to protect secular ideals. So, in keeping with my public life and political principles and according to my own belief, I resign as member of the Lok Sabha and chairperson of National Advisory Council. I have full faith that brothers and sisters of Rae Bareli and the whole nation will understand this feeling of mine.'

Hours before Sonia's resignation from Parliament, the Manmohan Singh government tried to redefine office of profit and toyed with the idea of protecting her under the new ordinance. Congressmen were keen that the NAC should also be covered by the amendment to the Members of Parliament (Prevention of Disqualification) Act. But Sonia firmly told the prime minister that she did not want to be seen as having benefited from any legal device. 'I have done this because this is the right thing to do,' Sonia said with Rahul standing by her and Priyanka peeping from a door at 10 Janpath.

Was Sonia holding an office of profit by virtue of being chairperson of the NAC? Most independent legal experts said she was not but the Opposition parties were adamant she was. The Opposition sought her disqualification as an MP on the grounds that as NAC chairperson, she enjoyed the rank and status of a Union Cabinet minister. Congress leaders, on the other hand, argued that the post of NAC chairperson is not an office of profit as Sonia received no salary or perks, and she had a purely advisory role.

The NAC was set up in 2004 as an interface between the people and the government with regard to the implementation of the UPA's Common Minimum Programme (CMP). The NAC comprises distinguished professionals drawn from diverse fields of development activity who serve in their individual capacities. Through the NAC, the government has access not only to their expertise and experience but also to a larger network of research organizations, NGOs and social action and advocacy groups. The NAC makes detailed recommendations to the government in the areas of priority identified in the CMP.

On 31 March 2008, the NAC was finally shut down after waiting in vain for Sonia to return. Much of its weight was derived from the fact that its recommendations had Sonia's stamp of approval. Though it was touted as a key political office, the NAC largely comprised non-political, civil society activists like Jean Dreze and Aruna Roy, and other persons of eminence like C.H. Hanumantha Rao and Pratham's Madhav Chavan.

In its initial two years, the NAC took the lead in pushing through key legislation and social sector programmes like the NREGA, the Right to Information Act, tribal policy, the National Rural Health Mission and the National Rehabilitation Policy. It also sent draft legislation on the Right to Education and for setting up Gram Nyayalayas.

Having set a shining example of probity in public life, Sonia went on a resignation spree, stepping down from all socio-cultural organizations—including those connected with the Nehru–Gandhi family—that have been receiving government funding. She severed all associations with the RGF, Indira Gandhi Memorial Trust, Jawahar Bhavan Trust, Jawaharlal Nehru Memorial Fund, Indian Council for Child Welfare Trust, Swaraj Bhavan Trust, Kamala Nehru Memorial Society and Hospital, Nehru Trust for Cambridge University, Round Square (International Group of Schools) United Kingdom, Nehru Memorial Museum and Library. She also resigned from the chairpersonship of the Jallianwala Bagh National Trust.

An overcautious Sonia even removed two of her trusted lieutenants who used to often function as her 'eyes and ears'. P.P. Madhavan and S.V. Pillai, both Class II Government of India officials, who were the most visible faces at Sonia's residence, were asked to leave. Madhavan was originally from the home ministry and Pillai from the PMO. The move was significant, as way back in 1975 Indira Gandhi had suffered ignominy when the Allahabad High Court set aside her election as MP, forcing her to resign as prime minister. The order came after her aide Yashpal Kapoor, a government employee, was seen at a poll meet in Rae Bareli.

The outside world has very little idea of the importance of Madhavan and Pillai whose links with the Nehru–Gandhis date back to the late 1980s. The duo had become extremely influential since Sonia's private secretary V. George went on leave. George returned, but his detractors strove to reduce his workload. Madhavan and Pillai worked in shifts almost round the clock. They fixed appointments with Sonia. They also vetted reports from AICC general secretaries, controlled access to Sonia and even booked film tickets for Priyanka and Rahul Gandhi.

The second act of renunciation brought back the aura and restored some sheen that had been lost in the period between May 2004 and March 2006 on account of a host of issues, including the Volcker Report.

While filing her nomination papers from Rae Bareli for the by-election, Sonia submitted a list of her assets before the Election Commission. The country's most powerful person gave an account of how rich she was. According to her declaration, Sonia has no house in Delhi but her ancestral home in Italy is worth Rs 13 lakh. She owns jewellery worth about Rs 21 lakh, out of which gold is worth Rs 11 lakh. She has lent Rs 5 lakh to her daughter Priyanka Gandhi Vadra. She has Rs 85,000 in a savings bank account with UCO Bank and Rs 20 lakh in fixed deposits in the same bank. The affidavit said Sonia owns Rs 12 lakh in RBI bonds and Rs 52,800 in UTI bonds. She also has an investment of Rs 1.49 lakh in National Savings Scheme and Rs 17.88 lakh in PPF. Apart from some investments in the stock market she owns ten shares of Maruti Technical Services Pvt. Ltd, whose worth was not quoted in the declaration. She also had 500 shares of Western India Tanneries. She owns three agricultural plots worth about Rs 2 lakh in villages Dera Mandi and Sultanpur. In all, Sonia is worth approximately Rs 1.4 crore.

She got re-elected from Rae Bareli with a record margin of 417,888 votes. Despite an all-time low voter turnout of only 43 per cent, Sonia garnered the bulk of the votes, and her two key opponents, Vinay Katiyar of the BJP and Raj Kumar Chaudhary of the ruling Samajwadi Party, lost their security deposits. While her victory was a foregone conclusion, the poor voter turnout had led to speculation about a possible fall in her victory margin of 240,000 votes that she had scored in the 2004 general elections.

Sonia Gandhi's election agent Priyanka Gandhi attributed the success to Rahul Gandhi who had led the campaign in the constituency. 'All credit goes to my brother Rahul who really worked very hard and went from door to door canvassing for our mother,' Priyanka Gandhi said. Rahul Gandhi said: 'I was given a job, and I am happy that it has been done. It is the victory of my mother's dedication for her constituency and I would like to thank the party workers as well as the people of Rae Bareli for once again reposing their faith in my mother in such a big way.'

At the same time, Jaya Bachchan returned to the Upper House as an MP of the Samajwadi Party in July 2006. Her re-entry into Parliament was a great photo-op for journalists when her husband Amitabh Bachchan accompanied her to the swearing-in ceremony. Amitabh's gesture was significant as it came in the wake of whispers that the megastar was uncomfortable about his wife's political career and her penchant for taking on the Gandhis.

TWELVE

THE PRESIDENTIAL POLLS

Sonia seems to have made a habit of springing surprises and bouncing back every time her detractors appear to have her on the defensive. If it was her renunciation of the prime minister's post in 2004 and her resignation from the Lok Sabha in 2006 in the wake of the office of profit controversy, in 2007 she managed to extricate herself from a seemingly hopeless situation when she hand-picked the little-known figure of Pratibha Patil as a candidate for the highest ceremonial office in the country.

The presidential polls of 2007, marked by skulduggery, controversies and bizarre allegations, turned out to be one of the murkiest in the history of independent India. For several days before the announcement of the candidate, Raisina Hills witnessed palpable tension, hectic lobbying and high drama over the choice of the country's twelfth president.

To begin with Sonia was keen to appoint Shivraj Patil, low-key and dapper, Union home minister. Privately, many senior Congress leaders were surprised at Sonia's preference for Shivraj Patil. A few suggested that this was perhaps 'guru dakshina' (teacher's fees), for Patil had helped Sonia shape up as an able parliamentarian between 1999 and 2004. The former Lok Sabha Speaker had enlightened the then first-time MP on the nuances of parliamentary practices. He had briefed her on key issues and often acted as an intermediary between Sonia, then the leader of the Opposition, and the ruling NDA in his capacity as deputy leader of the House. Also, Patil's past, relatively free of controversies, his loyalty and his thrust on probity and procedure seem to have impressed the Congress chief. He seemed a perfect fit for Rashtrapati Bhavan by every yardstick, encouraging a master tailor to knock at 4 Janpath in case the home minister wanted a wardrobe upgrade. The Speaker himself, a staunch devotee of Puttaparthi's Sathya Sai Baba—whose 'miraculous' powers are said to be based on the principle that if you will anything, you can create it—kept counting on faith to see him through to Rashtrapati Bhavan.

However, the ways of the Delhi durbar are indeed labyrinthine.

Sonia's preference for Shivraj and the latter's faith in Sathya Sai Baba ran into unforeseen roadblocks. The UPA allies led by the Left parties vetoed his candidature. The Left parties, by now increasingly vocal on a number of policy matters, politely but firmly conveyed to Sonia that the Union home minister was unacceptable to them on account of his less-than-impeccable secular credentials. Crucial southern ally M. Karunanidhi backed the Left and Ram Vilas Paswan and Lalu Prasad, too, expressed reservations about Shivraj.

Many Congressmen were afraid that their leader might turn her personal choice of Shivraj as presidential nominee into a suicidal prestige battle, ruining the relationship with key allies. As she appeared alternately adamant about Shivraj and unsure in the face of Left opposition, several alternative names began doing the rounds, the list lengthening by the minute and threatening to become the biggest blot on the UPA's record. In the early afternoon hours of 14 June 2007, minutes before Pratibha won the UPA nomination, some Congress leaders were worried whether Sonia could salvage the situation after the allies and the Left turned down the party's three principal choices: Shivraj, Sushil Kumar Shinde and Karan Singh (who went public with his claim of being 'best qualified' for the job).

In fact, the list of probables floating in the rumour-infested capital air, and the reasons they ultimately didn't get the nomination, make for a grand theatre of the absurd. As Sonia pulled out of her hat the one person no one expected, the others, with more lustrous careers behind them, could well have asked why they weren't considered.

Sheila Dikshit, far more visible as a woman leader than the eventual presidential candidate, was ignored despite her lineage—she's from the family of Uma Shankar Dikshit, a Congress legend—and two successful stints as chief minister of Delhi. Congress leaders confess in private that Sheila's 'independence' and contempt for the 'coterie' was her undoing.

Just as his overt desire spoiled N.D. Tiwari's party. As three-time chief minister of Uttar Pradesh, the veteran had always had Delhi's eyes and ears and relished being referred to as 'New Delhi Tiwari'. But from January 2006, Tiwari got too proactive. He wanted to step down as Uttarakhand chief minister and 'rest' in one of the Raj Bhavans, the idea being to somehow slip into the queue for the 2007 presidential nomination. The durbar frowned, and Tiwari never got to within a mile. As he sulked in Dehra Dun, the Congress lost power in the hill state. The chances had vanished for a man who, many party colleagues still believe, would have made a fine President.

It was self-importance that rocked Karunakaran's boat. The proud Indira loyalist had been a veteran of many battles, including the one to dislodge Rao and then Sitaram Kesri so that Sonia could take over in March 1998. Some party leaders feel that the Kerala elder, a Congress member since 1937, took his 'senior' status a bit too seriously. The high command didn't take kindly to his protests against the importance given to his rival A.K. Antony. Karunakaran returned to the Congress in early 2008 after meaninglessly heading Sharad Pawar's Nationalist Congress Party, hardly a force in Kerala.

P. Shiv Shankar had thought his threat to quit over a minor issue would have the leadership begging him to stay. His phone never rang. The legal expert, former governor and backward class leader would have been more acceptable to the Left than Shivraj, but was forced to cool his heels in Andhra Pradesh.

Jagannath Mishra, used to playing the high command's hatchet man in the states, wouldn't have expected to ever be at the receiving end. The Bihar strongman was seen as a politician among politicians, who as chief minister had built a formidable vote bank of Brahmins, Muslims and the disadvantaged. But when the durbar got too cosy

with Lalu Prasad, Mishra lost his patience and his career. He is now a
nobody in the Janata Dal (United).

Arjun Singh's humiliations were the worst. The Union human
resource minister, who prides himself as a 'loyalist' of the Nehru–
Gandhi family, was not considered in spite of subtle hints from the
Left and M. Karunanidhi. He had even walked away from the party in
the Rao era, claiming to represent the 'Nehru–Gandhi family'. Back
after the return of 'family rule', he failed to reclaim the unofficial
'number two' tag he had held in the party and government in 1992–
94. His perceived attempts to upstage and embarrass Manmohan
wouldn't have helped his cause.

As leader of a breakaway group, Sharad Pawar was never in the
race for prime minister or President, but his history is a warning to all
Congress leaders with ambition gnawing at their hearts. In a hurry to
become 'Lokmanya Tilak II', Pawar had challenged Sonia in 1999
and left the party. Five years later, he was among the hundreds hailing
the Congress chief's 'act of renunciation'. Rao's defence minister who
would be prime minister had to settle for the agriculture ministry in
the Manmohan regime. The one presidency he will have to satisfy
himself with is that of the Board of Control for Cricket in India.

Of all the probables rumoured to be in the running, Pranab's
predicament was the most glaring: he was grounded on grounds of
efficiency. The foreign minister was told that the government could
not spare him. Privately, Pranab's colleagues launched a whisper
campaign that his friends in the Left were pushing his name in spite of
Sonia Gandhi's opinion about his value to the government. Pranab
was so alive to this campaign that he issued two statements distancing
himself from the Left and asserting that as a 'loyal Congressman' he
would do what Sonia deemed fit.

If efficiency went against Pranab, Shivraj had the 'non-performer'
tag attached to his name. The home minister's 'secular credentials'
went on to become a matter of intense debate. In the musical chair of
names bandied about, nobody in the UPA or the Left bothered to ask
a simple question: if Shivraj's credentials were questionable, why had
nobody raised an eyebrow all these years he was the home minister in
the UPA?

Sushil Shinde, another name forwarded by the party high command, was constantly ridiculed as a 'lightweight'. His background as a Dalit, a former chief minister, Union minister, governor and AICC general secretary in charge of almost all states, and his distinction of winning from a non-reserved parliamentary seat cut no ice with his detractors. The plight of the last contender, Karan Singh, was such that in the final hour the former Sadr-e-Riyasat of Jammu and Kashmir had to run from door to door with copies of his biodata. He was last heard on television ruing how the nation has missed out on the 'best candidate' (himself).

As tension mounted among senior Congress leaders and Cabinet ministers who kept a wary eye on one another, hoping that a rival would not be chosen for Rashtrapati Bhavan, Sonia, aware of the ugly mood, decided to take a fresh look instead of letting the matter fester. She accepted her mistake and climbed down—and then made the most of a bad situation through an inventive solution. If being forced to switch one Patil with another was a political defeat, springing on the country its first likely woman President was a moral victory of sorts. A first woman President was not only a political masterstroke, it also meant Sonia did not have to backtrack all the way to the Pranab Mukherjees and Motilal Voras whom some of the allies appeared to favour. With Pratibha, governor of Rajasthan at the time, winning the UPA nomination to become the first woman President of India, Sonia Gandhi's masterly gamble, coming in the face of near-certain ignominy, paid off. Speaking from Mount Abu, Rajasthan, miles away from the backroom manoeuvring and murky negotiations that marked her ascent to the top, Pratibha gave her first reaction, saying, 'I never dreamt and thought of the top constitutional post.' Most of India, too, did not think so till that evening.

Sonia's choice of Pratibha came when the inflexible 'inner voice' with its unilateral decisions was perhaps losing its sheen. Sonia found a new way to surprise and grab the initiative. At another level, once Pratibha's name rippled down the Congress grapevine, many party leaders breathed a sigh of relief. Pratibha's elevation to Rashtrapati Bhavan provided relief to many male ministers in Manmohan Singh's government. They may not have made it to the top job, but none of their colleagues and/or rivals had made it either. The also-rans chose to accept Pratibha's nomination gracefully. Minutes after she was named, Pranab appealed to all parties and members of the Electoral College to extend support to elect her as India's first woman President. Pratibha Patil met every criterion the Left and other allies could ask for. She held an MA and an LLB degree, and as Rajasthan governor had sent back a hawkish anti-conversion bill passed by the BJP regime.

In an interesting aside, the elevation of little-known Pratibha made many Congress leaders wonder if fame and fortune visit those who keep a low profile and a humble visage. Pratibha Patil knows it as well as Manmohan Singh, or the late P.V. Narasimha Rao before him. Like the two prime ministers, the President had done precious little politically to earn the job—probably just the reason it came to her on a platter. The more ambitious and active Arjun Singhs and Narain Dutt Tiwaris fell by the wayside, as the K. Karunakarans and Jagannath Mishras had done.

Pratibha's rise almost mirrors Rao's in 1991. Rao had refused a Lok Sabha ticket and packed his bags when tragedy struck the nation and the Congress, and Nehru–Gandhi loyalist M.L. Fotedar came to ask the 'retired' politician if he would be prime minister. Likewise, from January to April 2004, Manmohan had sat idle in Safdarjung Road while his party colleagues were campaigning or contesting. But when Sonia Gandhi's 'inner voice' spoke, it whispered the name of the teacher who had turned a politician of sorts.

Sonia's choice of a woman candidate threw the Opposition into disarray, at least in the immediate aftermath of the announcement. The Shiv Sena, part of the BJP-led NDA, came out in support of Pratibha as she hails from the home state of the party that thrives on the sons (in this case daughter)-of-the-soil theme. While the BJP was initially rattled by Sonia's audacity in projecting a woman candidate and the sheer difficulty of opposing the candidature lest they be seen as anti-women, they soon went on the offensive. Sonia called up Atal Bihari Vajpayee the same evening seeking support for Pratibha but the former prime minister rejected the plea. 'Atalji, main pahli baar aap ka sahyog maang rahi hoon (This is the first time I am asking for your cooperation),' she told Vajpayee. 'Aapne der kar di (You are late),' Vajpayee replied while declining to pledge support.

The BJP lost no time in raking up dirt on the presidential nominee. Both the media and the Opposition parties vied with each other to highlight certain 'unsavoury' aspects of her past, ranging from allegations of financial irregularities to her gender insensitivity.

BJP leader and journalist Arun Shourie compiled a booklet titled *Does This Tainted Person Deserve to Become President of India?*, while his party colleague Arun Jaitley launched a website, knowpratibhapatil.com, which contained various reports and documents concerning questionable financial dealings of Pratibha and her family.

A serious allegation pertained to that of shielding her brother on a murder charge. Rajni Patil, a professor of Marathi in a Jalgaon college and the widow of murdered Jalgaon Congressman Vishram G. Patil, alleged that her husband was killed by Pratibha Patil's brother G.N. Patil.

The other controversies included allegations of financial indiscretion. Pratibha Mahila Sahakari Bank, a cooperative bank set up by her in 1973, had its licence revoked in 2003 by the RBI for alleged financial irregularities. Among the reasons listed by the RBI for cancellation of the licence was the faulty loan policy of the bank and loan interest waivers given, among others, to Pratibha Patil's relatives. She was one of the chairpersons of the bank and, along with a number of her relatives, was also one of its directors. In her defence, her supporters claimed that she was not the founding president of the bank, and that she held the post of chairperson for only a month and eight days. They also pointed out that the RBI did not mention Patil's name in the report and the court had not charge-sheeted her.

A cooperative sugar factory, Sant Muktabai Sahakari Sakhar Karkhana, of which Pratibha was a founder member, was alleged to be a drug trafficking ring, and was declared a defaulter for failing to repay a Rs 17.5-crore bank loan. Pratibha had been its chairperson and director till she became governor of Rajasthan. The loan was taken in 1994 when Pratibha was its chairperson. The bank sealed the factory on 23

January 2007 after issuing many reminders. This was the second time the mill was sealed. Earlier, it had been sealed in January 2006, but was reopened after the board of directors headed by G.N. Patil—younger brother of Pratibha Patil—requested for an opportunity to improve the performance of the mill. Shourie pointed out that the bank and sugar mill were listed as achievements in Pratibha's biodata as Rajasthan governor. 'There is no mention that she has resigned or is no longer associated with them. Are we going to use technicalities to defend the President of India?' he asked.

However, Union Minister for Agriculture Sharad Pawar termed Shourie's remarks as part of a 'malign campaign' and defended Pratibha, mentioning that there was never any inquiry under the Maharashtra Cooperative Societies Act against her. He also pointed out that as many as seventy-four mills were issued notices in December 2006, and it was 'unfortunate that only one particular case has been brought up in the media'. Pawar said most of the mills had failed to repay the loans because of persistent drought affecting sugarcane production, leading these mills to go sick.

According to the *Economic Times*, a prestigious financial paper, the Shrama Sadhna Trust, a charitable trust in Mumbai of which Pratibha was the managing trustee, had allegedly siphoned off funds totalling Rs 4.16 crore between 2001 and 2003 from an engineering polytechnic run by it in Jalgaon.

It is ironical that while Sonia, the Left and the rest of the UPA leaders touted Pratibha's candidature on grounds of gender, her past record showed a penchant for making politically incorrect and gender-insensitive statements. When she was the health minister of Maharashtra in 1975, Pratibha had advocated in the Maharashtra assembly that people with hereditary diseases should be compulsorily sterilized. On 17 June 2007, while addressing a congregation of Rajputs in Udaipur, she remarked on the purdah system, 'Women have always been respected in the Indian culture. The purdah system was introduced to protect them from Muslim invaders.' Though she qualified the statement by adding, 'However, times have changed. India is now independent and hence, the systems should also change', historians took her to task for her 'ignorance' on matters of Indian history in alleging a link between the purdah and Muslim invaders.

There was more to follow. Pratibha claimed to have spoken to the spirit of the deceased Brahmakumari spiritual leader Baba Lekhraj at Mount Abu. 'Dadiji ke shareer mein Baba aye . . . Maine unse baat ki (Baba entered Dadiji's body and he communicated to me through her),' she remarked before television cameras, even as rationalists and intellectuals shook their heads in disbelief at what was a blatant reinforcement of superstition by someone nominated to the country's highest post.

Till the last date of the presidential elections, Shourie continued to describe her as 'the pious face for small local racketeers'. Her candidature, he said, was 'a powerful announcement that even the President of India can be a mediocre person'.

Pratibha's stint as first woman President of the country continued to be mired in controversies. There were many red faces in the UPA and Left when Pratibha's son was caught using a taxpayer-funded trip on his mother's entourage to Latin America to conduct personal business in the US.

Rajendra Singh Shekhawat took a detour and time off from the presidential delegation in Mexico City to travel to Florida. Minister of state in external affairs Anand Sharma made feeble attempts to defend Rajendra's indiscretion on the grounds that since he was in Mexico City, he took the opportunity to visit a university in Florida for 'academic purpose'. Archana Datta, the Rashtrapati Bhavan's spokesperson, explained Shekhawat's thirty-six-hour disappearance from the presidential entourage saying, 'There was a long-pending invitation (for him) from the University of Florida Atlantic for academic purpose. Since Shri Shekhawat was in Mexico, he took the opportunity to visit the university.'

But in Boca Raton, Florida, Kristine McGrath, press secretary at the Florida Atlantic University—whose officials Shekhawat is supposed to have met during his detour—insisted that her office was not aware of Shekhawat's visit.

According to senior diplomatic correspondent K.P. Nayar,

Rashtrapati Bhavan had asked the Indian embassy in Washington to send an official to Miami to look after Shekhawat even though he was not there for any official duties. The embassy flew its head of chancery to Florida and put the official up in Miami at public expense to look after the President's son during his brief foray into the US. Nayar says if Shekhawat had, indeed, an invitation from the Florida Atlantic University, he should have taken any commercial flight from Delhi to Miami instead of joining his mother's entourage at state expense. After all as part of his mother's entourage, it was Indian taxpayers who were paying for Shekhawat's accommodation and other expenses during the President's stay in Lisbon, Sao Paulo, Rio de Janeiro, Brasilia, Mexico City, Guadalajara, Santiago and Cape Town.

According to officials who handled the financial arrangements for Pratibha's Latin American tour, Rajendra drew a daily allowance from the government amounting to 25 per cent of the rates for officials in the delegation. He was paid in cash. The full rates for officials were Euros 47.33 in Lisbon, $75 in Brazil and $56.25 in both Mexico and Chile for each day the President was outside India. Sources at the Indian embassy in Mexico admitted that Shekhawat had drawn his daily allowance from the government even for the time he was in Florida on private business.

Though Sonia seems to have made the most of a bad situation in getting Pratibha Patil into Rashtrapati Bhavan, the disputes arising over Pratibha's candidature made the 2007 presidential polls the most contentious in the history of independent India and Pratibha the most controversial presidential candidate ever. Despite the gender-related brownie points the Congress and the UPA hope to win with Pratibha's ascent to presidency, the controversies have left a bad taste that will be hard to get rid of.

THIRTEEN

A TALE OF FRIENDSHIP

Sonia's resignation as MP and the high drama that accompanied the office of profit controversy in 2005–06 brought out into the open the Gandhi–Bachchan family feud, simmering in the background for over a decade. The office of profit issue forced actress Jaya Bachchan, wife of megastar Amitabh Bachchan, to face disqualification from the Rajya Sabha, even as it left Sonia Gandhi with no alternative but to resign from the Lok Sabha. The build-up to the controversy led to a war of words between the country's two best-known families, each nurturing a sense of having been betrayed by the other.

The 'split' has been painful for both families which have had close ties for nearly sixty years. According to Amitabh's father, the late Dr Harivansh Rai Bachchan, the Gandhi–Bachchan ties started in Anand Bhavan, the Nehru–Gandhi family home in Allahabad. Sarojini Naidu had invited Harivansh Rai and Teji to Anand Bhavan. 'This led to the beginning of a close and lifelong friendship between Teji and Indira, who was still unmarried. Mrs Naidu introduced the pair of us very dramatically as "the poet and the poem", a phrase which Indira was to remember for long, alluding to it frequently when introducing Teji to foreign visitors,' recalled Harivansh Rai in his autobiography.

In Khalid Mohamed's *To Be or Not To Be*, Amitabh elaborated further, linking the inter-caste marriage between his parents with that of Indira–Feroze Gandhi. 'The very notion of a Sikh girl marrying a

Kayasth wasn't acceptable to her father—my nana—at all. It was the first inter-caste marriage for Allahabad. It was like the Feroze and Indira marriage in a way. There was something common, then, and that's how the friendship developed with the Nehrus. Sarojini Naidu introduced my father to Pandit Nehru. Ma was extremely beautiful. I'm told that Vijayalaxmi Pandit's daughters Nayantara and Chandralekha were very excited when they heard that Ma would be visiting them at Anand Bhavan. Ma was believed to be the epitome of beauty and adab from Lahore. Mrs Indira Gandhi, too, was very excited at the prospect of meeting her. Everyone dressed up for that occasion, perhaps with the intent of comparing fashions. Lahore in those days was considered the epicentre of fashion and culture.'

In a letter to her close friend Dorothy Norman on 22 August 1982, Indira wrote about her ties with the Bachchans: 'A certain couple was introduced to my father and me way back in 1942 by Mrs Sarojini Naidu. They married a month and a half before I did and lived in our neighbourhood in Allahabad. We both had two sons of more or less the same ages, who grew up together in Delhi. Some years ago their elder son became one of our more glamorous film stars (though I cannot say that I enjoy the violence of his films). On the eve of our departure for the United States he had an accident. In Los Angeles a message came that his condition was critical. Had I been in India, our whole family would have gone to Bombay to be with them all. As it was, we decided that Rajiv should fly back and on my return to Delhi, Sonia and I also went down to Bombay for a few hours. When one is battling for one's life or indeed for anything else, it makes an enormous difference if close friends are there to help build morale.'

For Sonia, the breakdown of the relationship has been particularly heartbreaking for it has meant the loss of the first friend she made in India. Amit, as she affectionately addressed him, was the one who received her on a chilly winter morning at Palam airport on 13 January 1968. In the period leading up to her marriage to Rajiv Gandhi forty-three days later, Sonia stayed at Amitabh's house, with his mother Teji Bachchan and father Harivansh Rai Bachchan playing host. At that time, Amitabh was yet to become a superstar and Rajiv was a carefree soul. Along with the Bachchan brothers, Amitabh and Ajitabh, Sanjay Gandhi, Rajiv Gandhi and Sonia were frequently spotted on the India Gate lawns having ice cream. Rajiv had an old Lambretta scooter, which often had ignition problems. Invariably, either Sanjay or Amitabh had the 'honour' of pushing it for a few metres.

Sonia recalled in an interview with *Dharmayug* in 1985: 'Mummy [Indira] had asked me to stay with the Bachchans so that I could also learn Indian customs and culture from close up. Slowly I came to learn a lot from that family. Teji Aunty is my second . . . no, my third mother. My first is my mother in Italy, the other was my mother-in-law Mrs Indira Gandhi, the third is Teji Aunty. Amit and Bunty [Ajitabh] are my brothers.' In those carefree days, she and Rajiv seldom discussed politics. Instead the talk veered around business, music, art and, of course, flying. 'We used to get together with our friends from Cambridge, Sanjay's friends, Amit and Bunty. We would sit at home chatting, listening to music, just sitting around. Sometimes we'd go out for a dance, a movie, a picnic, a long drive . . . we'd laugh and talk and enjoy ourselves.'

Sonia's description of Teji as her 'third mother' gives an indication of the depth of the Gandhi–Bachchan family ties. When Teji died on 21 December 2007, the two families lost not only their last and most formidable link spread over four generations but also perhaps any possibility of an early rapprochement. Till her last breath, Teji remained a very special person for Sonia Gandhi. She had taken on the role of Sonia's godmother when Sonia first arrived in India, introducing her to Indian ways of life.

Even some of the rituals during Sonia's marriage, such as the mehendi ceremony, were held at the Bachchan home with Harivansh Rai Bachchan and Teji singing at the wedding and Amitabh crooning humorous songs that his father had composed. Sonia's mother Paola had come over from Italy for the wedding, but it was Teji who played the role of the mother in the rituals of a Hindu marriage ceremony.

Teji was one of Indira Gandhi's closest friends. Though she never flaunted her proximity with the Nehru–Gandhi family, she once admitted to writer Uma Vasudev that she was present with Indira when Nehru breathed his last. In Teji's own words, 'She [Indira] was suffering from intense shock as if the earth had slipped away under her feet. But she is so sincere and loyal and self-effacing that she thinks of others even in the smallest detail. She was sitting in the room holding her dead father's hand, his body hadn't even grown cold; even so, she had this sense of the impersonal demand in the midst of despair . . . and she exclaimed to me, "Oh Teji, see that a doctor is available when Padma mausi comes!" And a little later asking me again to see that a flask of juice was put in phupi's room.'

In 1973, Indira appointed Teji as one of the directors of the Film Finance Corporation under the chairmanship of B.K. Karanjia, then editor of *Filmfare*. The Film Finance Corporation of India was a Government of India undertaking whose main objective was to finance the production of purposeful films of good quality with a view to improving the general standards of the medium.

During the Emergency, when the Nehru–Gandhis were living at 12 Willingdon Crescent and the Bachchans were next door, Sonia had made a pathway between the two bungalows which enabled her and Teji to visit each other easily.

Amitabh too has fond memories of his first meeting with Rajiv when he was four years old and Rajiv was two—at a fancy dress party on Bank Road (the Bachchan residence in Allahabad). Rajiv Gandhi, Amitabh recalled, had been dressed up as a freedom fighter. 'Ma says he messed up his pants. We were all such tiny kids then, absorbed in our little games that it didn't seem such a big deal that Pandit Nehru's grandson was in our midst.'

Subsequently, the Bachchan siblings became friends with the Gandhi brothers when Rajiv and Sanjay were studying in Doon School while Ajitabh and Amitabh were in Nainital. During the holidays, which fell around the same months, the boys would hang out and swim every day at the pool of the Rashtrapati Bhavan. Later, whenever Rajiv returned home from Cambridge, they'd get together and exchange notes. When Rajiv started flying, Amitabh accompanied him to 'provide ballast at the Flying Club of Delhi'. After Mrs Gandhi became prime minister, the family moved to 1 Safdarjung Road, which was close to the Bachchan home at 13 Willingdon Crescent. Rajiv, Sanjay, Ajitabh and Amitabh formed a closely knit group of friends.

According to Gandhi family insider Nathu Ram, 'I remember the days when Panditji [Nehru] moved to the Teen Murti House, New Delhi. There were simple quarters then, not much of what's there now. Rajiv and Sanjay would come home from Doon School for the holidays. Bunty and Amitabh would come along to play along with our children. So would Mohammed Yunus's son.'

It was Rajiv and Sanjay who exposed Amitabh to avant-garde cinema at a young age when European films were specially screened at Rashtrapati Bhavan for the Nehru family. Amitabh recalls attending, with Rajiv and Sanjay, screenings of films like *The Cranes Are Flying*, and other Czech, Polish and Russian films which often packed in an anti-war message.

The Amitabh–Rajiv friendship saw many lighter moments too. When Amitabh was struggling to get a foothold in the Hindi film industry in Bombay, comedy king Mehmood was his patron. Mehmood's brother Anwar Ali shared a flat with Amitabh while his sister Zubaida was a close pal of the budding actor. In *Mehmood: A Man of Many Moods*, author Hanif Zaveri reminisces, 'Just before the release of *Bombay to Goa*, Amitabh had brought a very fair young friend to Mumbai. The friend had accompanied him from Delhi. Mehmood was on a high after taking Calmpose tablets, a drug that Mehmood was addicted to. Anwar introduced the young man to Mehmood, but in his state, he was unable to understand what was said. Mehmood took out Rs 5,000 and handed it over to Anwar to give to Amitabh's friend. A puzzled Anwar asked what the money was for. Mehmood said the young fellow was fairer and smarter than Amitabh. He would become an international star. The money was the signing amount for taking the young man on Mehmood's next project.'

Anwar then had to reintroduce Amitabh's friend—Rajiv, son of Prime Minister Indira Gandhi—to Mehmood. Mehmood quietly took the money back. Both Amitabh and Rajiv had a great laugh. Many years later when Rajiv became prime minister, Amitabh acknowledged Mehmood's good judgement saying the only difference

was that Rajiv was indeed an international star on the political arena
and not on the silver screen.

After Amitabh became a star, Rajiv would often visit him on the
sets, extremely unobtrusive, waiting patiently till he completed his
shots. According to Amitabh, 'His nature was that he would never
misuse his name or family connections. On the contrary, more often
than not, he would not disclose his surname, fearing the distance it
would create between him and the common man.'

Family friends and associates blame 'politics' for ruining the ties.
They say the first blow came when Rajiv Gandhi entered politics and
'requested' Amitabh to help him out in the wake of Indira Gandhi's
assassination. Though both of them got off to a winning start—
Amitabh humbling H.N. Bahuguna at Allahabad and Rajiv leading
the Congress to its biggest ever election victory—things started going
downhill soon after. Amitabh had a disastrous stint in politics as Rajiv
Gandhi was sucked into controversy after controversy—Bofors, Fairfax
and the HDW deal. Amitabh's name figured in several scandals in
which Rajiv Gandhi was the principal character. Libel suits, allegations
and counter-allegations followed, resulting in Amitabh quitting
politics—much against Rajiv Gandhi's wishes and according to family
friends and associates against Sonia's too.

Yet, the families had cordial enough relations even after Amitabh
left politics. The families were close enough for Rahul and Priyanka
to address Amitabh as 'mamun', Avadhi for maternal uncle. Even at
the time Rajiv Gandhi was assassinated, Bachchan was among a few
family friends on whom Sonia and her children relied upon for every
major decision. On the day of the assassination, Amitabh was in
London in connection with a hearing of the Bofors case against a
Swedish newspaper. Rahul was in Boston. They landed in Delhi
together from London. Amitabh then took charge of the funeral
arrangements with Priyanka while Rahul stayed home trying to
console Sonia and accepting condolences.

Recalling that horrific day Amitabh says, 'My first reaction was of
complete disbelief. The fact that something like this could actually
happen was unthinkable . . . I was shocked for quite a while and

remained numb and speechless. I am afraid I cannot describe it in words.'

In fact, Amitabh was at the forefront of people advising Sonia not to enter politics in 1991–92 after Rajiv's assassination. He himself resisted attempts to draft him into politics once again, this time to help Sonia out. Asked if he was considering joining politics to assist Sonia, Amitabh said that it was only because he was cutting down on films that people surmised he intended to join politics. He reiterated that Rajiv had been a very dear friend and that he was one of Sonia's genuine well-wishers and close to her family, but questioned how his entering politics would ease her concerns and her pain. 'And why should she need me or require my help? She is extremely strong, sensible, competent and fully capable of taking her own decisions. She is aware of what she should and should not do,' he said.

The Gandhis and Bachchans have been extremely tight-lipped about the reasons that caused their differences. For years, in Delhi's Raisina Hills, which houses the country's politicians, word was that the two illustrious families fell out over money. Rumours and often-unsubstantiated allegations of disputes over money and matrimonial prospects between the Gandhi–Bachchan children grew louder with both sides refusing to confirm or deny them. Close family insiders from the two sides, however, deny these factors as responsible for the break. According to them, the Bachchans' problems with Amitabh Bachchan Corporation Limited (ABCL) may have aggravated and further strained ties, but it was not the prime reason for the end of their friendship.

Family insiders say that the Gandhi–Bachchan ties should be seen as a more down-to-earth story of human failings. It was also a combination of a clash of personalities, ego and one-upmanship amid failures and tragedies. Moreover, in the context of a friendship spread over nearly six decades, the bitterness forms just about a one-sixth part of that period.

If informed and trusted sources in both families are to be believed, Sonia enjoyed close and cordial ties with the Bachchans till Teji was taken ill. For over a decade prior to her death, Teji was too ill to intervene in the family feud, and it is during this decade that the relationship came undone. Even in the past, there had been minor skirmishes and spells of aloofness. A story from Sanjay Gandhi's side of the family is that post-Emergency when Indira was voted out of power, there was a proposal to invite the Bachchans at a public rally but Teji reportedly declined, citing her son's film career. Sanjay was reportedly furious and relations between the two families snapped. On another occasion, Sanjay was said to be very upset when Amitabh did not show up to receive his friend at the airport, a job he used to greatly relish. (Though Rajiv was a close buddy, it was Sanjay who had more open and informal ties with Amitabh. In fact, it was Sanjay who represented the Gandhi family when Amitabh married Jaya in 1973.) But these skirmishes did not fester probably because of the influence of the elders who had a stronger sense of the ties that bound the two families. With the death of these elders the relationship floundered. As Amitabh himself has mentioned, the newer members of the two families could not understand the true nature of the Gandhi–Bachchan ties.

Things soured around the time Sonia took the plunge into politics. By this time, Amitabh, reeling from the debacle of ABCL, had moved close to Amar Singh—who is rumoured to have helped bail the star out from the financial mess of ABCL—and by proxy to the Samajwadi Party. But the real breaking point came with Priyanka's wedding which took place on 18 February 1997. Amitabh fixed his daughter Shweta's marriage for the 17th.

Family insiders said that while Priyanka's wedding announcement had been made much in advance, Shweta's was a 'chat mangni pat vyah', a hurried affair, with the engagement announced in December 1996. There was a view that the Bachchans chose 17 February deliberately, to overshadow Priyanka's big day. The media too was expected to give more attention to Shweta's wedding which would be more glamorous with films stars in attendance. There was much confusion among common guests like Lalit Suri. Well-placed sources who do not wish to be named say that, in looking for reasons for the souring of the relationship, the importance of the row over wedding dates cannot be underestimated. It isn't surprising then that no member of the Gandhi family attended Shweta's wedding.

Cut to 1999 when Abhishek Bachchan debuted in *Refugee*. An invitation was sent to Sonia Gandhi. But it was politely communicated to the Bachchans that the Congress president does not visit 'extravagant' five-star hotels as the party philosophy revolved around simple living and high thinking. The Bachchans did not take kindly to Sonia's 'no-show' which added fuel to suggestions that one of the most celebrated friendships in India had soured. But even then, the two families kept their cool and held their silence. The only time that Amitabh spoke on the cracks in the relationship was when he admitted in an interview to a private news channel that things were no longer the same between the two families.

But over the next few years, the two sides broke the code of silence. Social circles are abuzz and rumour mills wagging on what could have prompted them to go public after keeping mum for years. 10 Janpath insiders say that Sonia has been deeply hurt by Amitabh's one-liner to a television channel that it was she who shut the door on him. Sonia was also exercised by Jaya's tirade against the Nehru–Gandhis at an election rally in Barabanki, Uttar Pradesh. Jaya's remarks were attributed to her proximity to Amar Singh who has no love lost for Sonia Gandhi. Political circles say it is this 'Amar effect' that may have spoiled the relationship beyond repair.

Amar, blamed as a 'spoiler', defends himself by pointing out that the Bachchan–Gandhi relationship dates back to a time before he was born. 'I have no authority or competence to comment on the ties of two great families. Only they are competent to comment on each other.'

But it is no secret that over the past decade Amar Singh has been almost a shadow to the actor and his family. Given Amitabh's taciturn nature, Amar Singh has often acted as the family's spokesman when contentious issues cropped up involving the star. For example, when Bachchan was issued a flurry of tax notices by the government, Amar took it upon himself to issue a veiled warning to the authorities. The Samajwadi Party general secretary said in Mumbai that the Congress-led government should not 'torture' Bachchan and his family 'to such an extent as to force the party to use him in the Uttar Pradesh assembly elections' due in 2007. It was left to Bachchan to issue a clarification that he harboured no political ambitions. Amar had to quickly set the record straight. 'I did not say he will enter politics. I said that if you continuously keep humiliating someone, he would be compelled to join politics,' he said. Between Amar's first and second comments, the actor himself told a television channel: 'I don't know politics . . . I am never going to do politics again.'

But Jaya was a different matter altogether. Her outbursts against the 'dynasty' became increasingly strident. She had been itching to take on the Gandhi family for a while. Those who know Jaya well said that the actress had shown both her political acumen and strength way back in 1984 when Amitabh had contested the Allahabad Lok Sabha polls. In *Ten Years' File*, senior journalist Kumkum Chadha has noted several instances to show the political colours of Jaya Bachchan.

According to Chadha, Amitabh, a novice in politics, was far from impressive as a real-life hero and a politician. 'With each passing day, Amitabh mellows, a trifle sad, a great deal withdrawn and somewhat aged. Perhaps the reality of what politics is all about has gripped him and worries him.' In this scenario, Jaya entered the fray, first mobilizing women and then taking to door-to-door campaigning. Chadha, who accompanied Jaya in the busy and dusty streets of Allahabad, observed: 'Walking through the dingy, dirty lanes, she [Jaya] woos the voters in a language that they understand; and with an emotion to which they respond. She talks about being daughter-in-law of Allahabad who seeks her dues—in the form of votes. "Main bahu ke nate aap ke paas aayi hoon. Jab bahu sasural aati hai to use moonh dikhai di jaati hai. Mujhe Allahabad se meri moonh dikhai chahiye. Rupyon mein nahin par voton mein (I have come to you as daughter-in-law of Allahabad. And when a daughter-in-law visits her in-laws, she is customarily given something. It is her due. I want my due from the people of Allahabad. Not in the form of money but in votes)."'

Chadha says Jaya was impressive and confident. 'Her sentences had the correct strain; her words the right emphasis.' The apolitical strategy seemed to be working well for both Amitabh and Jaya. Their naïve politics was in marked contrast to the heavy political dose that Bahuguna was giving to the Allahabad electorate.

Two decades later, there was a complete role reversal. Jaya was leading from the front in the political arena and an apolitical Amitabh was present on all occasions, making the right noises, lamenting that the 'system' and the bureaucracy were harassing him and his family. The media, needless to say, was lapping up each and every word and sound bite.

In October 2004, Jaya targeted the Congress for its stepmotherly treatment of Uttar Pradesh and accused the Gandhi family of betrayal. At an election meeting held in the Siddhaur assembly segment in Barabanki district, Jaya remarked, 'Yeh doosri baar hai jab main aap se vote mangne aayi hoon. Pehli baar jab Amitabh ji Allahabad se chunav lade the to maine unke liye vote mange the. Jin logon ne humko rajniti mein aage badhaya, unhone beech mein hi hamara saath chhod diya. Saath tab chhoda jab hum taqleef mein the. Yeh log hamesha dhokha dete hain (This is the second time that I am asking for your votes. The first time was when Amitabh was contesting the elections in Allahabad. Those who brought us in politics left us midway. They left us when we were in a crisis. They are known to betray people).'

Though she did not take names, the reference was more than obvious. She then hit out at the Congress and said that the centre was targeting Chief Minister Mulayam Singh Yadav on the law and order issue and was deliberately not providing power to Uttar Pradesh even on payment. 'Yeh to wohi baat hui—jabra mare rone na de (This is like you hit someone on the jaw and then don't even let him cry),' she added. Jaya then praised Amar Singh and said, 'Mere devar Amar Singh sach mein Thakur hain—jo kehte hain woh karte hain. Aap Samajwadi Party ko vote dijiye—yeh log vade aur rishte nibhana jante hain (My brother-in-law is a real Thakur—he does what he says. Please vote for the Samajwadi Party because these people know how to keep promises and relations).'

This was the first time that a member of the Bachchan family had spoken so strongly against the Gandhis. Rahul Gandhi reacted sharply to Jaya's remark at the family borough, Amethi. He reiterated that the

Gandhi–Nehru family was not known for betraying anyone. He retaliated, saying, 'The Bachchans are lying. Why are they levelling the charge now after so many years? Amitabh was introduced to politics two decades ago. They have changed loyalties. Those who know the Gandhi family know we have never betrayed anyone. People know better about who betrayed whom. People also know who their loyalties are with.'

Rahul's remarks hit Amitabh badly. In his characteristic fashion, Amitabh regretted his wife's controversial remarks about the Gandhis but squeezed in a reference dripping sarcasm. Without naming anyone, Amitabh said he was deeply hurt by statements in the media that described his family as 'liars'. Recalling the relations between his father Harivansh Rai Bachchan and Jawaharlal Nehru and the ties between his mother Teji Bachchan and Indira Gandhi, Amitabh pointed out that the relationship went back to a time when neither Jaya nor Sonia, neither Rahul nor Priyanka was there.

Amitabh said he could neither forget those relationships nor tolerate any comment on them. Those relationships were between the two families. 'I have nothing but respect and goodwill for them. I am shocked by the way the relations between the two families were needlessly being scrutinized by the media and debated by the members and well-wishers of the two families.'

Then came the unkindest cut. The Nehru–Gandhi family has ruled the country, Amitabh said, adding, 'Woh raja hai, hum rank hai (They are king and we commoners).' The megastar added that only the king establishes contact with the poor and not the other way round. 'If the king says he does not want to have a relationship, what can the poor do? The poor cannot afford to say that we want to have relations with the king.' In the same breath, he tried to douse the fire by declaring that Jaya's feud with the Gandhis was a 'closed chapter'. He added, 'What I share with the Gandhis isn't meant for public consumption. Some of the media may enjoy this kind of thing. I certainly don't. Peace of mind is far too important for me to get into media-manufactured controversies.'

Jaya, however, continued her tirade against Sonia and the family.

In March 2006, she travelled to her late father-in-law's native village Babupatti in Pratapgarh district of Uttar Pradesh, about 270 km from state capital Lucknow, vowing never to quit politics like her superstar husband as it was destiny that had brought her this far. Addressing a gathering, Jaya said, 'My first experience of politics was when Amitabh contested the polls from Allahabad. I had accompanied him to some of the campaigns. He quit politics later. But I can tell you now here that I won't ever do it.'

Dressed in a pink silk sari, the 'bahu of Uttar Pradesh' inaugurated a library in Babupatti and promised help in building a college near the village. 'My father-in-law used to tell me if you think you are out to do something out of God's will, you should not go back on that,' she told the gathering, which had earlier lined up to greet her with lighted candles and blowing conch shells. 'It is God who has brought me this far,' she added. 'Even in this village. It is destiny. And I am not going to go back.'

Jaya told the villagers she had 'no words' to express what she felt. 'I am feeling restless now thinking when I will be able to share this experience with Amitabh and my son Abhishek. I will tell them every bit of it when I return to Mumbai,' she said. Jaya met some distant relatives of Harivansh Rai Bachchan who still live in the village. 'I was searching the face of Babuji [Harivansh Rai] among the present generation of Bachchans here. It is such an emotional experience for me,' she said.

Though she did not actually visit the ancestral home of her family-by-marriage (the family migrated to Allahabad some decades ago) she acted out beautifully the role of a dutiful bahu, a very different one from the saas–bahu versions currently fashionable. She spoke little, said in a soft voice that she was overcome with feelings, cried a little and appeared visibly to struggle with her emotions as she inaugurated the public reading room in Harivansh Rai Bachchan's memory.

The Gandhi–Bachchan potboiler continues to have several twists and imponderables in its script. As the Samajwadi Party and the Congress drifted closer in July 2008, the realignment's personal subplot involving the Bachchans and the Gandhis too came under the media glare, with conjectures on what it could mean for the two families, whether their would be a rapprochement. Social circles in Delhi and Mumbai waited with barely suppressed excitement for Jaya Bachchan's reaction to her party's new-found proximity with the Congress. In the wake of Jaya's comments in Mumbai about speaking in Hindi and not Marathi—which created a controversy with Maharashtra Navnirman Sena (MNS) chief Raj Thackeray calling for a ban on the films starring the Bachchans and his goons going around Mumbai defacing posters and advertisement hoardings that featured Amitabh and Abhishek—when Sonia Gandhi issued instructions to the Congress chief minister of Maharashtra to ensure that individuals are not victimized, newspaper reporters were quick to attribute it to a thaw in the relations.

But the freeze between the Bachchans and Gandhis continued with the Congress–SP ties failing to trigger warmth between Sonia Gandhi and Amitabh Bachchan, whom she once regarded as a brother. The relationship has taken quite a beating for personal grudges and issues to be resolved just because the Congress and the SP have come together due to political exigencies. Sources close to the Bachchans say that the family is a little wary of Mayawati, fearing a witch-hunt by the Uttar Pradesh chief minister, following the Congress–SP patch-up. The Bachchans chose to keep a low profile on the issue and left for the 'Unforgettable Tour' to the US for the next six weeks.

FOURTEEN

SONIA'S HANDLING OF THE CONGRESS ORGANIZATION, 1998–2008

14 March 2008 marked the tenth anniversary of an unusual event in Congress history—it was the day the Congress had, through a 'constitutional coup', ousted Kesri as its sixtieth president and anointed Sonia Gandhi, flagging off a new era for the then 113-year-old party.

The ailing Kesri, then seventy-nine, had arrived at the Congress Working Committee meeting at 24, Akbar Road, convinced that a party president could not be forced out. He did not know that before the 11 a.m. meeting, most CWC members had gathered at Pranab Mukherjee's home to endorse two crucial statements. The first was an ultimatum asking Kesri to step down; the second a resolution to replace him with Sonia.

As soon as Kesri, party chief since 1996, stepped into the hall, he could sense the mood: loyalist Tariq Anwar was the only one who stood up to greet him.

As Kesri sat cross-legged, Pranab began reading out a resolution 'thanking' him for his services and invoking clause J of article 19 of the Congress constitution. A dumbstruck Kesri listened to its provisions: the CWC could act beyond its constitutional powers in 'special situations' as long as it got the decision ratified by the All India

Congress Committee within six months.

'*Arre yeh kya keh rahe ho* (hey, what are you saying)?' was all Kesri could say when he found his voice. He looked round: his colleagues' faces were shining with glee.

Kesri railed at the 'unconstitutional' meeting and screamed that he was still the Congress chief. But Jitendra Prasada, the party vice president, was already announcing amid thunderous applause that 'Madam Sonia Gandhi' was the new leader. The axed president stormed out, followed by Anwar. He spent over an hour in his office calling up his advisers, but it was difficult to hear them amid the crackers and slogans welcoming Sonia.

When Kesri stepped out of the room, his nameplate was missing, replaced by a computer printout that said: 'Congress president Sonia Gandhi'.

Within minutes, the Special Protection Group moved into the party headquarters. By the time Sonia arrived for the day's second CWC meeting, party leaders who used to drive in had been told to leave their cars on the street and walk in.

During the two more years that he lived, Kesri would often say: '*Congress leadership tapte hue suraj ke saman hai. Bahut pas jaoge to jal jaoge aur bahut door rahoge to thand se mar jaoge* (The Congress leadership is like the blazing sun. Get too close and you'll be burnt, stay too far and you'll freeze to death).' Kesri died of cardio-respiratory failure on 24 October 2000, aged eighty-one.

Against this backdrop, Sonia's handling of the Congress during 1998–2008 offered an interesting insight and a fascinating story of success against all odds. The eventful period saw many highs and lows.

The period between March 1998 and May 2004 saw the Congress leaders initially hoping for a 'miracle' and then suffering from an utter sense of despondency. Brand Sonia was seen as Sachin Tendulkar but by 2000, even the most optimistic and vociferous supporters had started conceding that the Congress president lacked a magic wand. Some leaders like Jairam Ramesh went much further, equating Sonia with Rabri Devi, the apolitical and naïve wife of Lalu Prasad Yadav, whose tryst with destiny saw her as chief minister of Bihar for over two years.

Ramesh made an observation about Sonia in an article entitled 'Sonia—No Longer the Saviour' published in the 12 May 2000 issue of the magazine *Asiaweek*. Speaking to senior journalist Ritu Sarin, Ramesh, secretary of the party's economic wing, said, 'Two years down the line, Sonia is seen as a loser, and the morale in the party is very low,' adding, 'The hype generated when Sonia became party president has settled down. The mood has swung from one extreme to the other. People who saw her as a ticket to nirvana now see her as a ticket to narak [hell].'

What Ramesh calls a 'crisis of confidence' was reflected in the manner Sonia has been grappling with the vagaries of coalition politics. In Maharashtra, she expelled Sharad Pawar from the party in May 1999 only to later forge an electoral alliance with him to defeat the BJP in the state. In Bihar, Sonia first described the state government led by Rabri Devi as 'casteist and corrupt', but later teamed up with her after the state assembly polls. In 2000, a year after the 1999 general elections, Sonia asked senior party leader A.K. Antony to conduct a postmortem. But when Antony submitted a report, she avoided implementing it.

However, during the period that Ramesh describes as a 'crisis of confidence', senior Congress leaders like Pranab Mukherjee and Arjun Singh consistently insisted that Sonia was a force to be reckoned with. 'The mistake people are making is of underestimating Sonia, the same way she underestimates herself,' Pranab observed, adding, 'She remains the only point of consensus in the party.' But Ramesh was not so sure. He told Sarin, 'If things go the way they are, the Congress will not come back to power for another fifty years.'

This was in 2000. Ramesh had to eat his words when the Congress bounced back within four years. A sagacious Sonia laughed off Ramesh's remark and, in fact, helped him in getting the post of a junior minister in February 2006 even though Prime Minister Manmohan Singh had kept him away while choosing his first council of ministers in May 2004.

By early 2008, there were many in the Congress who were dismayed that the party organization has been neglected during its four years in power. They had reasons to be disappointed. The number of CWC meetings, the apex decision-making body, fell sharply since May 2004. The party president's visits to the state units too had become extremely infrequent.

At 24, Akbar Road, there were too many office-bearers but too few had been attending office. A senior AICC functionary like Ahmad Patel had not even bothered to have an office at the party headquarters when he served as political secretary to Sonia.

The last conclave of party chief ministers took place in November 2006. Even the six-monthly AICC sessions became passé.

This was in sharp contrast to the Sonia era (1998–2004) when she had insisted upon holding at least one CWC meeting every month. The practice continued till May 1999 when Sonia received a jolt at her residence from the Sharad Pawar–P.A. Sangma–Tariq Anwar alliance. At a meeting at 10, Janpath, the trio raised questions about her 'foreign origins' and Sonia got a little disillusioned with the CWC meetings.

Still, fourteen CWC meetings were held in the year 2000. The number, however, fell to twelve in 2001, to eight in 2002 and to seven in 2003.

The frequency of CWC meetings took a further nosedive after 2004. Between January 2005 and December 2006, only ten were held, including condolences and the customary pre-plenary session meeting in January 2006. Between January and June 2008, only two CWC meetings took place. This trend of infrequent CWC meets continued till the eighty-third AICC plenary session held at Burari, Delhi, from 18–20 December 2010. At Burari, the AICC amended its constitution to extend its party president's term to five years from the current three. Since the polls for the party president's post would now be held after every five years, the CWC elections, party plenary, etc., would also be held every five years.

Sources close to Sonia defended her, citing her preoccupation with running the ruling coalition and keeping the partners happy. They said that with the party in power, the CWC had assumed a sort of secondary role since government policies and programmes reflected the party line.

But old-timers disagreed. They said that Indira Gandhi and Rajiv Gandhi used to hold CWC meetings regularly even when they were in power. Both mother and son would insist also on having meetings of the central parliamentary board, a ten-member body that wielded supreme authority in all important matters, including the appointment of state party presidents and chief ministers, and the selection of poll candidates. The parliamentary board was not constituted even once during the Sonia era.

A series of electoral debacles followed. By the time the Congress lost Karnataka, Madhya Pradesh and Chhattisgarh in 2008, it had lost control over a large number of state assemblies. The party, however, did retain Andhra, Delhi and Haryana and snatched Rajasthan from the BJP, but continued to perform badly in Orissa, Jharkhand and Bihar.

But the role of the Congress high command, including party president Sonia Gandhi and her close associates such as Ahmed Patel, in making these mistakes and half-hearted measures did not come under scrutiny. As a senior party leader remarked, 'This is the special style of inner-party democracy in the Congress . . . You never speak anything against the supreme leader, even as the leader goes on rewarding those who led the party to successive defeats, be they in Gujarat, Himachal Pradesh or Karnataka.' It was a different matter that in spite of all his righteous indignation, he avoided saying anything openly against the number one family of the Congress.

Sonia, however, sensed the general sense of disquiet and within ten days of the Karnataka defeat in 2008, she set up a party panel under A.K. Antony to 'revitalize' the organization. But her 'pill' for the party had few takers. The report's recommendations were adopted by the Congress Working Committee but not implemented in any subsequent assembly polls.

In the thirteen years since Sonia has been Congress president, there has been a virtual panel raj with several committees getting appointed with the task of reviving the organization. But most of the recommendations are gathering dust in the backrooms of 24, Akbar Road, that houses the party's national headquarters in New Delhi.

Senior party leaders wondered at the idea of yet another panel under Antony in 2008 when the report of an earlier Antony panel formed after the 1999 general elections was still waiting for 'action taken'.

In 1999, the committee members had toured all over India and spoken to a large number of Congress workers about the reasons that led to the party getting its lowest ever number of seats (111 out of 542) in the Lok Sabha.

The committee had submitted twenty recommendations relating to party elections, inner-party democracy, party structure, candidate selection and observers for the process. Recommendations were also made on matters of party discipline, the nitty-gritties of organizational elections, media relations as well as interactions with opinion-makers, alliances, coalitions and ideology and image. The committee recommended a clean-up drive but the high command decided against it.

Apart from the comprehensive and exhaustive Antony panel reports of 1999 and 2008, Sonia was in possession of several other reports. They included the report on organizational polls by Ram Niwas Mirdha, Manmohan Singh's report on party funds, the P.A. Sangma and Sam Pitroda reports on modernizing the organization and Pranab Mukherjee's report on organizational affairs. In addition, she was handed over a report submitted by the Future Challenges Group that had Rahul Gandhi as an active member.

In a nutshell, almost all of these panels and committees had recommended sweeping changes in the organization but intrinsic compulsions prevented any concrete action. For example, both Mirdha and Antony had emphasized the need for 'democratic' organizational elections after discovering that the party had polled lesser votes in many states where the number of primary members was higher. While the Congress claimed to have over forty million primary members, the party leadership discovered that a substantial part of the membership was 'bogus'. This became evident when Congress candidates in states such as Tamil Nadu, Bihar and Uttar Pradesh got lesser votes than the listed number of primary members.

In July 2007, a party panel headed by foreign minister Pranab Mukherjee had called for scrapping Congress committees at block, city and district levels and recommended replacing them with units at polling booths and assembly and parliamentary constituencies.

The logic was to make the Congress more 'election-friendly' and eliminate the tendency of district Congress committees to be at loggerheads with candidates contesting polls. But the leadership is still weighing the pros and cons of the suggestion.

Like Antony, Mukherjee, too, had insisted on selecting assembly and parliamentary candidates at least six months before voting, but subsequent polls in Punjab, Gujarat, Tripura, Meghalaya, Karnataka, Haryana, Andhra Pradesh, Delhi, Madhya Pradesh, Bihar and other states saw no sign of the recommendation being followed.

Interestingly, Mukherjee, who was looking after the party in Bengal then, had opposed the idea of appointing central ministers as in-charge of Congress affairs in states.

Instead, between 2006 and 2010, Sonia picked over a dozen ministers in the Manmohan Singh government to look after party affairs across the country.

Some other reforms suggested by Pranab were: Selection of assembly and parliamentary candidates at least six months before voting; a mechanism where the party guides key economic and social policies of the government (when the party is in power); mandatory meetings of AICC general secretaries twice a month (at present, these meetings are not held regularly); selection of Congress legislature party leaders and state unit chiefs by a panel of senior leaders (at present, an ad hoc procedure is followed); fixed tenure for Youth Congress, Mahila Congress and other departmental heads; no truck with communal forces and the need to make conscious efforts to equate majority communalism with minority communalism; an annual brainstorming session on the lines of the Panchmarhi meet that was held in September 1998.

Pranab Mukherjee also recommended smaller state party units. At present, there is no uniformity in their size. Many of them have 200 to

250 office bearers, thus making them unwieldy. Following the old traditions of the Congress, the units could have twenty-one members, including the state president.

In private conversations, Congress leaders kept lamenting that Sonia was not assertive while taking decisions on state matters. Such conversations generally revolved around complaints like 'Madam is diffident in taking on the regional satraps in various states and is wary of offending any one of them.'

This was evident both in Gujarat and Karnataka, where in spite of putting up good electoral battles, the Congress failed to project a chief ministerial candidate. This was on account of the fear of offending one or another regional leader, but obviously the high command would have to choose one after the polls. So why not take the decision right at the beginning and face the consequences, they argued.

Another point that was discussed in low-key whispers in the party circles after the Karnataka and Bihar assembly poll defeats was the effectiveness of Rahul Gandhi in attracting votes. As part of his Discover India yatra, Rahul had extensively toured Karnataka, especially its Dalit- and tribal-dominated areas, but the results from these seats were far from encouraging. Of thirty-six scheduled caste (SC) seats in Karnataka, the Congress could win only ten as against twenty-two by the BJP, three by independents and one by the Janata Dal (Secular). Of the fifteen scheduled tribe (ST) seats, the Congress and the BJP shared seven each while the JD(S) bagged one. Overall, out of the fifty-four Assembly seats where Rahul campaigned in the run-up to the elections, the Congress won only twenty-two.

In Bihar, Rahul made several forays but the final outcome read only four out of 243 assembly seats. There were over 200 Congress nominees who had forfeited deposit in the assembly polls. (When a candidate contests Lok Sabha or assembly polls in India, they need to submit nomination papers to the Election Commission. Along with that, they are required to deposit Rs 10,000 as security for a Lok Sabha seat or Rs 5000 for an assembly seat. If the candidate fails to secure one-sixth of the total number of valid votes polled in that election, the deposit is forfeited). After 24 November 2010 Congress leaders wondered if it was bravado or Rahul Gandhi's scant regard for intelligence inputs that saw him campaigning in about three dozen constituencies that were earmarked as 'winnable seats'.

It is believed that twice during the long-drawn Bihar polls, the AICC general secretary was presented a dismal picture of the party's fortunes in the state assembly polls. But Rahul continued to play the role of chief campaigner. His close aides rubbished the possibility of the Congress getting single digit seats.

Rahul's tribal tours to Chhattisgarh and Madhya Pradesh too left many party men with a sour taste in the mouth. For instance, Rahul's two-day Bundelkhand visit in April 2008 left a trail of red faces in the Madhya Pradesh Congress.

District Congress presidents of Tikamgarh, Chattarpur and Panna ran for cover as they had no explanation as to why they were kept 'out of the loop'. As Tikamgarh district Congress chief Ravindra Adharvyuv told the author, 'I am glad he came and spent time among the tribals. But politically we have not gained because we were not told about his visit.' He added: 'My disappointment has little to do with my political aspirations. How do I mobilize votes for the party when we are not even informed about high-profile visits? What do I tell my people?'

He said he had reached the spot where Rahul was staying at a tribal house at night but was asked to leave by Uttar Pradesh Congress chief Rita Bahuguna Joshi. 'This was in sharp contrast to Indira Gandhi's visit in 1978–79 when the region suffered from acute drought. But the day Indiraji came, it rained. And the slogan, *"Indiraji aaeen varsha laeen* (Indira came, and brought the showers)"* was coined,' said Adharvyuv.

Jai Prakash Patel of Panna was more cautious in his complaints, attributing the slight to security considerations. 'Rahulji is a VVIP. I have no complaints as he is trying to directly strike a rapport with the voters,' he said. But like Adharvyuv, Patel could barely hide his disappointment when asked about the political dividends from the visit. 'Of course, in an election year [MP assembly polls of November 2008] things would have been a lot different if we were kept in the know,' he said, pointing that the party had drawn a blank in the district in the 2003 assembly elections.

Jagdish Shukla of Chattarpur had a question to ask: 'Even if someone says Rahul Gandhi is on a familiarization trip, can we deny that it was aimed at creating a favourable political climate for the party that he is leading and for us?' Shukla's poser failed to get a response from senior party leaders, including state unit chief Suresh Pachauri, who was himself kept in the dark. Pachauri rushed to Bundelkhand after hearing that Rahul was touring the region.

After staying in power for over four years, another problem that constantly confronted the ruling dispensation was that Manmohan's policy orientation did not reflect the constituency requirements of a mass-based 'aam aadmi' party like the Congress. Manmohan, however, kept insisting that the party had not done enough to take the achievements of the government to the people.

The appearance of a party-versus-government schism was evident at the Congress's chief ministers' conclave in Nainital when party general secretaries almost pounced upon central ministers P. Chidambaram and others. The Government of India came under attack. The finance minister's rarefied logic was proving a flimsy shield and the academic-turned-prime minister was looking around for support.

None came, even from Sonia Gandhi. As the Congress's general secretaries and fourteen chief ministers turned the heat up on the Centre, the party president seemed to enjoy the government-versus-party battle.

It was at this moment that Manmohan Singh and P. Chidambaram badly missed a figure in spectacles who was away in New York shaking hands with the NATO Secretary General Jaap de Hoop Schaffer. Pranab Mukherjee with his experience, abundance of anecdotes and his ability to bury critics under an avalanche of facts and figures, would have been Singh's best bet as troubleshooter.

Like a good lawyer, Chidambaram argued well, but to many in the restless audience, his dispassionate, clinical arguments lacked political savvy and sensitivity. The more the finance minister resisted a National Agriculture Credit Act and changes to the Money-lending

Act, the more he put his adversaries' backs up.

For instance, he pleaded he couldn't intervene in agriculture as it was a state subject. Haryana Chief Minister Bhupinder Singh Hooda immediately shot back: 'Then why have we been called here?' Again, when Chidambaram shot down the demand for a one-time loan waiver to the drought-affected states' farmers, an All India Congress Committee member said: 'It is this mindset that is posing problems for the government.'

The then finance minister had started with a disadvantage, anyway. Most of the criticism targeted Nationalist Congress Party chief Sharad Pawar's agriculture ministry, and Chidambaram was forced to defend decisions he did not personally support. Embattled home minister Shivraj Patil, under fire for his failures on internal security, sat grim-faced through the meeting but never tried to take on the party. The then minister of state for commerce and industry, too, found himself on the ropes when he opposed raising import duty on cotton. Even Manmohan asked Jairam Ramesh: 'Why do you not increase import duty on cotton?'

The session on agriculture saw general secretaries Digvijay Singh, Margaret Alva, Satyavrat Chaturvedi and Janardhan Dwivedi pounce on the Punjab and Haryana chief ministers. While Hooda fumbled with his replies, Amarinder Singh was sharp. Attacked for providing farmland for special economic zones, he said: 'In Punjab, I do not have an inch of barren land.' He defended setting up five SEZs, saying he needed alternatives to agriculture. 'If I do not do this, nobody will come to Punjab. Hasn't the Volkswagen project gone to Bengal instead of Punjab?'

Congress circles believed that even the two bright ideas of the UPA government, the National Rural Employment Guarantee Scheme (NREGS) and the Right to Information (RTI) Act, had been sullied by criticism that their implementation had been ham-handed and dishonest. Several prominent NAC members like Aruna Roy quit the advisory body expressing dissatisfaction with the manner of implementation of pro-people programmes they had backed.

Sources close to Sonia said that when the organization needed her time and attention, the party president was busy placating the Left or negotiating with whimsical allies. Through 2004–10, Sonia had identified key people to hold every loose plank on the UPA cart tight. During the standoff with the Left over the nuclear deal she was in constant touch with Brinda Karat, Sitaram Yechuri and A.B. Bardhan to soften their stand. She also had Rashtriya Janata Dal chief Lalu Yadav rein in the Nationalist Congress Party boss Sharad Pawar, and the late Vishwanath Pratap Singh to keep the linkages with the DMK smooth. Rather unwittingly, the Congress organization was reduced to one creaky part.

The 2004–08 period also saw Arjun Singh at work who phased out to oblivion when the UPA registered an emphatic comeback in May 2009. Arjun was dropped from the Union cabinet. Coming back to Arjun's role during 2004–08, many in the Congress believed that Arjun was working to trip Manmohan, while some felt that the Thakur from Churhat was driven by other political compulsions.

His plank for quota in educational institutions for OBCs was never allowed to derive mileage from what many saw as Mandal II. The controversy and the knee-jerk reaction of the party and the government managed to alienate the upper castes while the backward classes were not pleased to see the government constantly dithering.

Arjun showed his disenchantment with Sonia in a more pronounced manner in May 2008 when he went public saying the party's decision-making process had fallen into 'a bit of a disarray'. In the presence of Prime Minister Manmohan Singh and President Pratibha Patil at a book release, the then Union human resource development minister rued: 'Nowadays, the evaluation of loyalty is being done in a very limited context.' Instead of 'true loyalty, dikhawa (pretence) is gaining ground', he added. The prime minister, whom Arjun had tried to bait in the past, avoided making any comment. The HRD minister paid tribute to Indira Gandhi and Sanjay Gandhi, saying they never held his reservations about the Emergency against him.

Arjun's comments came at the release of *Mohin Kahan Vishram*, a collection of articles and interviews by him. A comment in one of the interviews created a flutter in the Congress. It said: 'Earlier, there were many opportunities to contribute to the decisions, and even major decisions of the Congress were taken after going through the process of consultations and people used to accept it. But now this process has fallen into a bit of a disarray and when people do not have the feeling that they have contributed to the decision-making process, they have no hassles in defying it.'

A day after Arjun's comment on the lack of internal democracy, he met Sonia Gandhi at a convocation ceremony at Jamia Hamdard in New Delhi. Though they sat side by side, the eye contact was missing. For the first time in many years, Sonia Gandhi and 'loyalist' Arjun Singh avoided talking to each other at a public forum.

But, more significantly, when Sonia spoke about the government's contribution to education, she praised Prime Minister Manmohan Singh only, overlooking the human resource development minister's role.

The Arjun–Sonia divide showed another side of Sonia, revealing her as a seasoned politician who was equipped to tackle internal factionalism and outwit astute politicians.

First, she signalled that games of one-upmanship will not be tolerated. But more significantly, she showed that as the leader of the Congress parivar, she did not resort to a purge or crack a whip whenever a party leader was seen as speaking out of turn.

Sensing that Arjun's outburst was aimed at some of her key aides, Sonia stuck to her line that the party's internal decision-making mechanism was democratic. But she ignored the clamour for his immediate exit from the council of ministers. Eventually, Arjun had to make amends. He denied any strain in his relations with Sonia.

Sources close to Sonia said her assessment of key individuals and their capacity to cause damage came in handy. Arjun's commitment to the Congress ideology and loyalty to the family did not come under scrutiny and perhaps helped ensure his longevity in Shastri Bhavan. When his initial outburst in a book hit the headlines, the Congress president was convinced that even a 'hurt' and 'angry' Arjun would not quit the Manmohan Singh government and cause more embarrassment.

Congress ministers have a poor record when it comes to resigning. Sonia must have had this in mind. Arjun had raved and ranted on 6 December 1992, following the Babri Masjid's demolition, but did not resign. His long list of supporters, including Digvijay Singh, Ajit Jogi and dozens of other MPs, kept urging him but Arjun avoided creating a 'crisis'.

In June 2007, Shivraj Patil was declared the party's presidential nominee but just as the home minister got all set to order new bandhgalas, the Left parties protested. Patil was not 'secular enough' to move into Rashtrapati Bhavan, they said. Even as A.B. Bardhan and Prakash Karat scuttled his candidature, Patil behaved as if it was business as usual. Loyalty prevented him from contemplating quitting.

Under different circumstances, Pranab Mukherjee, too, had swallowed humiliation. In July 2007, his presidential aspirations were rejected on the grounds of efficiency—Pranab was projected as 'Mr Indispensable' to the party. The then external affairs minister may not have had strong reasons to consider resigning, but in Congress circles, there was near consensus that he had been slighted.

Arjun insisted he was not snubbed by the Congress president at the Jamia Hamdard convocation, but he failed to explain why Sonia remained pointedly silent on the series of harsh statements issued by his colleagues against him. He was finally tamed, however. He pledged 'unflinching loyalty' to the Gandhi family and tried to douse the fire sparked by his rebellious comments. In a statement he cited his loyalty to the Nehru–Gandhis through five decades.

'I shall do everything to maintain the loyalty and commitment to the remaining members of the family till I live,' he said. 'This is a closed chapter as far as I am concerned.' Some senior Congress leaders, who were sympathetic to him, put his outbursts down to age and domestic problems. When the UPA returned to power in 2009, Arjun's name was missing from the cabinet.

Amidst these hiccups in the party, Uttar Pradesh, the country's most populous and politically significant state, continued to be Sonia's 'problem area' in spite of the party's rather surprising and spectacular performance during the May 2009 general elections, when it won twenty-two seats there (one through a subsequent by-elections).

Differences of opinion between leaders marred the approach to the successive UP assembly polls. Congress leaders of all hue and shade kept 'advising' Sonia to look for electoral crutches either from the Bahujan Samaj Party or the Samajwadi Party. Some old party leaders kept asking her to do it alone, but the majority of leaders favoured an alliance. In this confusion, between 1998 and 2008, the party's best scenario expectations in Uttar Pradesh remained very modest. Of the 400-odd assembly seats, Sonia and Rahul focused on 150-odd seats, hoping to win at least fifty. But this magic figure remained elusive as the tally hovered around twenty to thirty.

The Congress under Sonia kept dithering. Closer to May 2007 UP assembly polls, Rahul Gandhi planned to win back at least a section of Muslim votes in UP. A huge political brawl followed after Rahul told a gathering in Deoband that the Babri mosque would not have fallen had a member of the Nehru–Gandhi family been at the helm of the country's affairs.

The 2007 UP assembly polls results proved disastrous. The late Kesri, who had tightfistedly managed the Congress coffers for twenty-seven years, would have been appalled by the manner in which the party blew resources in the Uttar Pradesh polls without success. With no CWC meeting or AICC session convened to discuss the UP debacle, Congressmen themselves counted losses at an informal level. The losses were colossal. About fifty Congress candidates who were placed in category A by the party high command and given the best 'resources' had secured less than 5000 votes. In other words, they had forfeited the deposit. If party men are to be believed, each vote in these constituencies had cost the Congress over Rs 1000 each.

There were three other informal categories—B, C and D—which were given funds in accordance with their winning prospects. Congress sources said category D nominees were given Rs 10 lakh each as per prescribed limit by the Election Commission.

The results showed a different picture. As per definition of category D, around 280 party nominees lost the deposit against the party's pre-poll projection of fifty. Most candidates who were in category A ended up in B or C while B and C slumped to a crowded D. The outcome of the 2007 UP assembly polls resulted in the Congress netting twenty-two seats, coming second in another twenty-three.

The big question that kept doing the rounds in Congress circles was whether Sonia and Rahul Gandhi would fix responsibility and hold party managers responsible. But nothing happened as the resources had already gone down the drain.

Apart from the practice of funding, the party had requisitioned twelve choppers that were flown across the length and breadth of UP. Some non-Congress but friendly leaders like Beni Prasad Verma and Arif Mohammad Khan were also permitted to use these urankhatolas, but both performed miserably. Beni lost and Arif's wife Reshma finished a poor fourth. In fact, only one of the many nominees that 'Babuji' Beni had fielded came near to victory.

Since the weather in Uttar Pradesh remained hostile throughout the month-long electioneering, hundreds of Congress campaigners had to be provided with air-conditioned hotel accommodation and vehicles.

The actual cost of these expenses alone ran into several crores. Prior to the polls, the Congress's star campaigner, Rahul Gandhi, had gone about picking nominees in a 'scientific' manner. Several teams of political and non-political observers were sent to eighty districts to scout for 'winnable' nominees. These candidates were subsequently invited to Delhi for a screening, interview and training. After this elaborate exercise, over a hundred persons who had contested previous assembly polls on non-Congress platforms were given a party ticket, but only four of them won.

Senior party leaders said Rahul's inexperience might have contributed to the 'extravaganza' which was in sharp contrast to the stingy manners of Kesri. 'Chacha' Kesri had been notorious for his penny-pinching ways. Congress nominees seldom received the full amount that was sanctioned to them; invariably they would discover huge discrepancies between money granted and money received. Kesri would laugh at all this, saying it was part of the shagun (good omen).

Often in a serious mood, Kesri used to recall a story that perhaps

Rahul had not heard. He used to talk about a Congress candidate who sold party flags for char anna (25 paisa) during elections. When the leader's son once asked why he was selling a party flag for such a paltry sum instead of giving it out free, the leader responded, 'Beta, when they buy it, they put it up on their bicycle but if they get it free, they will use it as a shopping bag!'

Uttar Pradesh showed signs of a turnaround during the 2009 Lok Sabha elections. The dramatic comeback of the Congress in the state was not foreseen even by its own leadership. Before the verdict came out, senior Congress leaders, like AICC general secretary Digvijay Singh, were heard saying: 'We will not go below nine'—the party would not come down from its 2004 tally of nine seats.

According to political observers like Nirmal Pathak and Sharat Pradhan, what tilted the equation was a clear shift in the Muslim and Brahmin votes from the Samajwadi Party and the BJP, respectively, to the Congress.

SP chief Mulayam Singh Yadav's much-debated bonhomie with BJP renegade Kalyan Singh, who was better known as the Babri Masjid demolition man, was largely responsible for this shift in the Muslim vote. BSP Chief Minister Mayawati, who had moved heaven and earth to get what she thought was a captive Muslim vote, failed to succeed in her mission.

What made the difference was the refusal of the young Muslim voter to be guided by any diktat or fatwa of the maulana. In Lucknow, barely hours before the polling, some Muslims circulated handbills urging people not to be guided by the clergy who were alleged to have been bought off by a BSP leader.

Lucknow-based Pradhan feels the preference for the Congress also rose on account of its confirmed secular credentials, because a large section of the voters had had enough of the regional political satraps who believed in pursuing their personal agenda at the cost of the larger interests of the state and its 180 million people. The sheer numbers could rank Uttar Pradesh as the sixth largest country in the world!

According to Nirmal Pathak, political editor of the popular Hindi daily *Hindustan*, the 'political puzzle called Uttar Pradesh' needed to be understood carefully in the context of the Congress's influence over minorities, Dalits and upper-caste voters.

The success of the Congress in the 2009 general elections, Pathak says, was cemented by a return of the Muslim voters along with the consolidation of upper-caste votes. 'In UP the Congress will have to accept that its votes will come from the Dalits to be followed by Muslims, Brahmins and Rajputs in that order,' Pathak said, adding that it was actually Brahmins and Rajputs who had been doing 'tactical voting' in Uttar Pradesh since Independence. As long as the Congress was relevant and powerful, the Brahmins sided with it. In the late 1980s and 1990s, when the BJP was on the rise, the upper caste shifted to it. In between, sizeable sections moved towards Mulayam Singh Yadav when the intermediary class leader offered a 'better deal'. Then they moved towards Mayawati who tried to enforce 'social engineering', rewarding scores of Brahmins as ministers when she won the 2007 assembly polls riding on a Brahmin–Dalit–Muslim combination.

Sonia continued to face the accusation that she is surrounded by a small coterie that influences the entire decision-making process. Some called them advisers, others cronies, while the bitter ones simply described them as the cabal.

Ironically, the coterie charge was levelled by the faithful and the dissidents alike. Whenever something went wrong, loyalists blamed her advisers.

Sonia's detractors said that she had no mind of her own and was tutored by a group of party leaders who lacked mass support and had a vested interest in keeping the name of the family alive.

Sonia was acutely aware of the charges. At first, she took them as an indictment of her style of functioning. However, over time, she began to view the criticism as a professional hazard. The Congress president tried damage control first by expanding her group of advisers, but this did not help. Soon, reports had it that Sonia had several coteries, her A team, B team and so on!

For many political analysts, the coterie charge has more than a grain of truth. Even before Sonia joined politics, former prime minister

P.V. Narasimha Rao had viewed dissident leader Arjun Singh as a mole. Singh did not mind the accusation and made political capital out of it. Even as Rao went on to lose his political authority in 1995 and 1996 because of various scams, the list of Sonia loyalists swelled.

The 1995 split in the Congress formalized a select band of party leaders consisting of Narain Dutt Tiwari, Arjun Singh, Mohsina Kidwai, M.L. Fotedar, Natwar Singh and Sheila Dikshit as Sonia loyalists. They got the distinction of being part of Sonia's coterie when she took over as Congress chief, and were subsequently given prize posts in the party.

One of the key decisions that Sonia made after taking over as Congress chief was to project economic reforms guru Dr Manmohan Singh as a figurehead. It was a brilliant strategy because if there was one person in the Congress who drew nationwide respect and admiration, it was undoubtedly Dr Singh. True, he hadn't won an election, but Sonia had come across evidence of the role of some senior Congress leaders in ensuring his defeat in the South Delhi Lok Sabha seat in 1999, possibly because they perceived him as a threat to their own position in the party hierarchy.

Soon, he became an eyesore for the traditional topiwalas, who viewed the technocrat with suspicion. A committee headed by A.K. Antony that investigated the poll debacle of 1998 general elections concluded that Dr Singh's reforms had led to the downfall of the party and resulted in the Congress' worst-ever performance. Sonia did not agree.

Disregarding the Antony panel, she went on to appoint Singh as leader of the Opposition in the Rajya Sabha. The move caused heartburn for some, for they saw it as a virtual crowning of Singh as number two in the party.

The reforms man, however, quickly slipped from the number two slot primarily because he was uncomfortable dealing with traditional Congressmen, who had little or no awareness of the changing global situation and latest trends in economic thinking. At party fora, Singh hated the idea of being grilled by people who had no knowledge of the fundamentals of economics. His skirmishes with Congress leaders left him a disillusioned man. At one juncture, he even toyed with the idea of quitting to taking up academics and Track II diplomacy, but Sonia persuaded him to stay on, promising to defend his policies.

In Congress circles, Sonia was, however, constantly seen as a person who seldom interfered in the functioning of the party and the government, hated the idea of pitting one against another, and took up the cause of several politically correct issues such as gender sensitivity, women's empowerment, health and education.

During 2004–09, Sonia faced many challenges from within and outside but the trickiest part was her handling of the N-deal that showed her deftness in a crisis. Virtually cornered from all sides by rigidity and one-upmanship, Sonia saved the government between August and November 2007 when almost all political gurus and commentators had written the UPA's obituary.

In the one year between August 2007 and July 2008, Manmohan and Sonia teamed up in a shrewd and decisive manner to checkmate their opponents, discarding old and trusted friends in the Left and courting new and volatile allies like old foes Mulayam Singh Yadav and Amar Singh. Their sense of pragmatism stunned many. For weeks, Delhi witnessed rather sordid events and real politick at work with Manmohan and Sonia occupying centre stage. For a bulk of their party men, however, the end result justified the means.

The Left's support to the UPA was critical as the coalition having 237 seats in a 543-member Lok Sabha lacked a simple majority. But when the Left pulled out of UP on 8 July 2008, Manmohan and Sonia already had a contingency plan in operation. Their old foe, the Samajwadi Party, with 39 MPs came to the UPA's rescue, and by the time the prime minister won a trust vote in Parliament on 22 July, the UPA had 275 seats with 256 MPs opposing it.

The N-deal crisis was triggered off with Prime Minister Dr Manmohan Singh giving a rare and candid interview to Manini Chatterjee of the *Telegraph*. Perhaps a tad tired of the Left parties' constant barks and opposition to economic restructuring, the good doctor had finally dared them to bite after their diatribe against the Indo-US nuclear deal continued unabated.

In an uncharacteristic manner, Manmohan told Manini: 'I told them [the Left] that it is not possible to renegotiate the deal. It is an honourable deal, the cabinet has approved it, we cannot go back on it. I told them to do whatever they want to do, if they want to withdraw support, so be it . . .'

He was referring to his conversation with the CP(M)'s Prakash Karat and the CP(I)'s A.B. Bardhan hours after the Left released a statement on the nuclear deal.

Reacting to the Left's tough and inflexible posture, the prime minister said he was 'not angry but anguished' at the harsh tone and tenor of the Left's reaction, and made it clear that the UPA–Left relationship could not be a one-sided affair. 'I don't get angry, I don't want to use harsh words. They are our colleagues and we have to work with them. But they also have to learn to work with us.'

According to Manini, although he did not raise his voice, those last ten words had a hint of steel which underlined the prime minister's new resolve to take on the Left. There was no immediate response from the Left leaders. Singh added: 'They haven't thought it through.'

According to Manmohan, the Left had a 'flawed understanding' not just of the 123 Agreement but also of India's intrinsic strength and its enhanced status in the world. He said: 'It is an honourable deal which enlarges India's development options, particularly in regard to energy security and environmental protection, and it doesn't in any way affect our ability to pursue our nuclear weapons programme. We have not surrendered an iota of our freedom in this regard; not an iota of our sovereignty.'

Asked why then was the Left objecting to the deal, Manmohan Singh said: 'I don't know . . . [but] they seem to have a problem with the United States,' and then elaborated: 'I want India's relations to improve with all powers and we have been doing that—with the US, with Russia, with the EU, with France, and particularly with China. We have had a breakthrough with China, a historic agreement where we have defined the principles that will outline the border agreement . . .'

On the Left's fears that the 123 Agreement would draw India further into a strategic alliance with the US, rendering it an American satellite, Manmohan raised a counter argument: 'How can we ever become anyone's satellite? Yes, we live in an increasingly interdependent world but the challenge before us is to forge new linkages, widen our strategic options and, at the same time, guard against the negative side of the process of globalization.'

These remarks were significant in the context of the Left parties' consistent stand on why the N-deal agreement was not acceptable. They viewed the agreement in the light of the Hyde Act passed by the US Congress, and in the context of the wider implications of India being bound into a strategic alliance with the United States and its adverse consequences for an independent foreign policy, sovereignty and the economic interests of the people.

Some political analysts feel that at this point (October 2007), Karat who was repeatedly empowered by his Left allies and his own central committee and politburo to act decisively, dithered. Karat and Yechury were apparently taken in by Sonia's persona, her dispassionate way of looking at issues and a hint that she would act as arbitrator. In July 2008, reality dawned on them that like communism was deeply seeped inside them, in her heart of hearts, Sonia was a committed Congress person. She had been solely driven by her survival instincts to save the party and the government. But by then it was too late.

Though a political theoretian of repute, Karat blundered in assuming that 'other things being equal' the UPA would not be able to muster support. His closest ally and friend Mulayam Singh Yadav ditched him when he needed the Samajwadi Party the most. Karat should have known it and would have been better off had he sought advice from former prime minister V.P. Singh or any other oldie of the Janata parivar.

The tale of Mulayam's change of heart was not less intriguing. A hardcore Nehru–Gandhi family baiter, the Samajwadi Party leader remained reluctant till the very end on the idea of supporting the Congress which it had opposed for several decades. But influenced by his politician son Akhilesh and then close associate Amar Singh, Mulayam saw reason and switched sides days before a crucial vote in

Parliament on 22 July.

He had several compulsions. In heartland Uttar Pradesh, riding high on 'social engineering' arch rival Mayawati had left little political space for him. With the socially weaker sections, upper castes and Muslims providing a formidable ring around her, the Samajwadi Party's dreams of netting UP on its own appeared bleak. Since May 2007, every day Mulayam woke up to news of some or the other party associate getting arrested, beaten or wronged by the Mayawati regime. Caught between a hostile Centre and a hawkish Mayawati, Mulayam chose to make peace with those whom he considered a lesser evil.

Mulayam had strong reasons to be upset with the Left as well. He was hurt by Karat's indifference to check some of the Left leaders' constant tirade against him and Amar Singh. Gurudas Dasgupta, Bardhan and several others habitually used very strong language against Mulayam and his Man Friday Amar Singh for siding with the corporate. Mulayam is said to have repeatedly urged Karat to rein in Dasgupta and Bardhan, but it fell on deaf ears. So when the moment of opportunity came, the Samajwadi Party returned the compliment. Amar was even heard mocking the CP(M) general secretary: 'But why should comrade Karat be upset? He is the one who has been wanting us to be with the Congress all this while.'

In Rahul, Manmohan found a powerful votary of the N-deal. Unlike his mother who the Left viewed as having her heart slightly left of centre, Rahul projected himself as an unabashed supporter of the economic reforms and whatever Manmohan stood for. When the N-deal standoff reached its crescendo, Rahul stood up to be counted among those behind Manmohan, lauding the prime minister's 'bold' stand on the deal. In fact, a few days before the crucial trust vote in Parliament, he even went on to suggest that it was worth sacrificing a government to uphold 'national interest and principles'.

If the government fell because of the prime minister's stand, Rahul continued—hastening to add in the same breath 'it will not go, of course'—it was 'simply bad luck'. 'But in politics, it is more important to stand for national interest and principles,' the young MP emphasized to the CWC at Sonia's residence.

Rahul told the Congress's apex decision-making body that it was important to consider the positive effects of the deal that allowed India to separate its civilian and military nuclear facilities, pursue defence programmes and bring in the option of clean energy. He and Sonia agreed with the prime minister that the deal was a 'unique achievement'.

Post-trust vote, a new troika emerged in the Congress. When Manmohan had presented his first budget seventeen years ago, few in the Congress had thought the quiet, 'apolitical' minister would be capable of transforming into a confident leader of the country. But by July 2008, 'politician' Manmohan had arrived—and was here to stay.

The traditional sections in the Congress continued their antipathy towards the economist prime minister but after the May 2009 victory, Manmohan packed his cabinet with those he was comfortable. The exit of Arjun Singh and Shivraj Patil was a signal to others that loyalty or seniority would not suffice.

In the cabinet, ministers were judged by their acumen and performance. By 2010, Jairam Ramesh, P. Chidambaram, Kapil Sibal, Prithviraj Chavan and others won laurels while seasoned hands like Kamal Nath and Sushil Kumar Shinde struggled. Nath had a running feud with Planning Commission deputy chairman Montek Singh Ahluwalia and when he turned towards the party for patronage, the longest serving Lok Sabha member realized that his support base was not there.

Manmohan continued setting up more and more expert committees, packing them up with professionals like Nandan Nilekani, C. Rangarajan and others. Most of these experts and gubernatorial nominees were from outside the Congress. Senior party leaders like Margaret Alva and Shivraj Patil were made Governors of smaller states like Uttarakhand and Punjab, while former bureaucrats E.S.L. Narasimhan and K. Sankaranarayanan occupied Raj Bhawans in Hyderabad and Mumbai, respectively.

There were reports that Digvijay Singh and Jairam Ramesh made bids to become NAC members when Sonia began her second innings as its head, but there were no seats for politicians. The AICC chief seemed to carry a dim view of the party in terms of throwing up ideas that the government could pick for implementation.

In terms of theoretical framework, too, the party offered little. In fact, by the time the eighty-third AICC plenary was held in Delhi in December 2010, the party's political and economic resolutions lacked debatable issues. This was in sharp contrast to some of the stormy party meets held in Avadi, Bhubaneshwar, Hyderabad, Mumbai, Calcutta, etc. earlier where the ruling leadership had to fight hard to convince the AICC delegates that the ideology of the Congress 'keeps evolving in tune with the changing times' (AICC resolution adopted at Avadi, Madras, 1955).

Often, the Congress appeared as having a captain but of an adrift ship. The internal mechanism failed to perform. With the absence of a strong regional leadership, it gave vigour to its own enemy born out of its womb (dynasty culture and lack of inner-party democracy) that led to conditions where the sole aim of the party appeared to be to stay in power. The question that went almost unattended at the plenary and elsewhere was whether the party was failing Sonia in spite of her great act of renouncing power in 2004.

REFERENCES

Adams, Jad and Phillip Whitehead. *The Dynasty: The Nehru–Gandhi Story*. BBC Books, Penguin, 1997.

Alexander, P.C. *My Years with Indira Gandhi*. New Delhi: Vision Books, 1991.

Ali, Tariq. *The Nehrus and the Gandhis: An Indian Dynasty*. London: Picador, 1991.

Bakshi S.R. ET AL. *Sonia Gandhi: The President of AICC*. South Asia Books, 1998.

Bhagat, Usha. *Indiraji: Through My Eyes*. Penguin–Viking, 2005.

Bharti, Pushpa. 'Sonia Gandhi.' *Dharmayug*, 15 June 1985.

Bharti, Pushpa. *Amitabha Akhyana*. Rtugandha Prakasana, 1994.

Brass, Paul. *The Politics of India Since Independence*. Cambridge: Cambridge University Press, 1994.

Bright, J.S. *Indira Gandhi*. New Delhi: New Light Publishers, 1984.

Buckhory, Somduth. *The Call of the Ganges*. New Delhi: Vikas Publishing House, 1979.

Chadha, Kumkum. *The Ten-Year File*. New Delhi: Sanchar Publication House, 1992.

Chandra, Pradeep. *AB—A Photographer's Tribute*. Rupa & Co, 2006.

Chatterjee, Manini. '"Anguished" PM to Left: If You Want to Withdraw,

So Be it.' *Telegraph* (Calcutta), 11 August 2007.

Chatterjee, Manini. 'PM Integrity Unquestioned, No Reason Govt Should Not Last Full Term: Karat.' *Telegraph* (Calcutta), 31 October 2007.

Chatterjee, Rupa. *Sonia Gandhi: The Lady in Shadow*. New Delhi: Butala Publications, 1998.

Chatterjee, Rupa. *Sonia Mystique*. South Asia Books, 2000.

Chowdury, Neerja. 'Power Play: Sonia Set for a Poll Vault.' *Indian Express* (New Delhi), 18 March 2002.

Dé, Shobhaa. *Selective Memories: Stories from My Life*. Penguin Books India, 1998.

Deep, Mohan. *Eureka: The Intimate Life Story of Rekha*. Mumbai: Shivani Publications, 1999.

Dhar, P.N. *Indira Gandhi:The Emergency and the Indian Democracy*. NewDelhi: Oxford University Press, 2000.

Dua, H.K. 'It Is Sonia Gandhi Versus India.' *Pioneer* (New Delhi), 1 June 1999.

Elliott, John. 'In Asia, the Dynasties Still Rule.' *New Statesman* (UK), 8 November 1999.

Frank, Katherine. *Indira: The Life of Indira Nehru Gandhi*. London: HarperCollins, 2001.

Gandhi, Indira (in conversation with Pupul Jayakar). *What I Am*. New Delhi: Indira Gandhi Memorial Trust, 1986.

Gandhi, Indira. *My Truth* (as Told to Emmanuel Pouchpadass). New Delhi: Vision Books, 1981.

Gandhi, Indira. *Letters to a Friend 1950–1984. Correspondence with Dorothy Norman*. London : Weidenfeld & Nicolson, 1986.

Gandhi, Sonia. *Rajiv*. New Delhi: Penguin Books India, 1992.

Gandhi, Sonia. (ed.) *Freedom's Daughter: Letters between Indira Gandhi and Jawaharlal Nehru 1922–39*. London: Hodder, 1989.

Gandhi, Sonia. (ed.) *Two Alone, Two Together: Letters between Indira Gandhi and Jawaharlal Nehru 1940–64*. London: Hodder, 1992.

Gill, S.S. *The Dynasty: A Political Biography of the Premier Ruling Family of Modern India*. New Delhi: HarperCollins India, 1996.

Godbole, Madhav. *Unfinished Innings: Recollections and Reflections of a Civil Servant*. London: Sangam Books Limited, 1996.

Goldenberg, Suzanne. 'Gandhi Assassination.' *Guardian* (UK), 22 May 1992.

Government of India. *White Paper on Misuse of Mass Media During the Internal Emergency*. August 1977.

Grover, Rajeev. 'Notes from B School.' *Mid Day* (Mumbai), 10 October 2006.

Gupta, Bhabani Sen. *Rajiv Gandhi: A Political Study*. New Delhi: Konark, 1989.

Gupte, Pranay. *India: The Challenge of Change*. New York: Mandarin, 1989.

Harding, Luke. 'Gandhi Family Fortunes, Despite the Numerous Failings of India's Coalition Government, the Likelihood of the Opposition's Sonia Gandhi Becoming Prime Minister Remains Small.' *Guardian* (UK), 20 August 2001.

Hasan, Zoya. 'The Prime Minister and the Left.' In *Nehru to the Nineties*.

Hines, Jessica. *Looking For the Big B: Bollywood, Bachchan and Me*. Bloomsbury, 2007.

Jain, Sandhya. 'Double Speak, Dubious Intentions.' *Pioneer* (New Delhi), 2 February 1999.

Jayakar, Pupul. *Indira Gandhi*. New Delhi: Penguin Books India, 1992.

Kang, Bhavdeep. 'Educating Sonia.' *Outlook*, 6 July 1998.

Khilnani, Niranjan M. *Four Diamonds of Anand Bhavan (Motilal Nehru, Jawaharlal Nehru, Indira Gandhi, Rajiv Gandhi): A Perceptive Analysis of Indian Political Experience from 1929 to 1987*. New Delhi: Raaj Prakashan, 1987.

Malhotra, Inder. *Indira Gandhi: A Personal and Political Biography*. London: Hodder and Stoughton, 1989.

Manor, James. (ed.) *Innovative Leadership in Modern India: M.K. Gandhi*. Albany, New York: State University of New York Press, 1993.

McGirk, Tim. 'That Gandhi Magic.' *Time Asia*, 2 March 1998.

Merchant, Minhaz. *Rajiv Gandhi: The End of a Dream*. New Delhi: Penguin Books India, 1991.

Mishra, Dina Nath. (ed.) *Sonia: 'The Unknown'*. New Delhi: India First Foundation, 1991.

Mishra, Sumant. *Main Amitabh Bol Raha Hoon: In Candid Conversation*. Egmont, 2003.

Mishra, Vijay. *Bollywood Cinema: Temples of Desire*. New York & London: Routledge, 2002.

Mitra, Ashok. *A Prattler's Tale: Bengal, Marxism and Governance*. Translated from the Bengali by Sipra Bhattacharya. Kolkata: Samya, 2007.

Mitra, S.K. 'India, Dynastic Rule or the Democratization of Power?' *Third World Quarterly*, 10 January 1988.

Mohamed Khalid. *To Be or Not To Be*, Saraswati Creations, 2002.

Naravane, Vaiju. 'In Maino Country.' *Frontline*, 25 April–8 May 1998.

n.a. 'Fight with Rajiv was not worth it: V.P.Singh.' *Times of India*, 23 February 2005.

n.a. 'Here is Ramola Bachchan!' *Society Magazine*, January 1994.

n.a. 'Readying for Race Course Road.' *Times of India* (New Delhi), 17 November 2002.

n.a. 'She stands remarkably alone.' *New York Times Magazine*, March 1966.

n.a. 'Sonia—No Longer the Saviour, Dissent against Her Leadership Is Growing.' *Asia Week*, 12 May 2000.

n.a. 'Sonia's Silence and the Importance of Being Vincent George.' *Asia Week*, 29 November 1997.

n.a. 'TV Asia needs . . .' *Asian Age*, 9 January 1995.

Nehru, B.K. *Nice Guys Finish Second*. New Delhi: Penguin Books India, 1997.

Nehru, Jawaharlal. *Letters from a Father to His Daughter*. Allahabad: Kitabistan, 1938.

Nugent, Nicholas. *Rajiv Gandhi: Son of a Dynasty*. London: BBC Books, 1990.

Paul, Swraj. *Indira Gandhi*. London: Robert Royce, 1985.

Philipose, Pamela. 'Centrestage, Interview of the Week. Khushwant Singh "Mrs Gandhi–Maneka Spats Will Do Well on TV. A Political 'Tu Tu, Main, Main'"!' *Sunday*, 23 September 2001.

Prakash, A. Surya. 'What A.C. Gupta Commission Had Said about Sonia's First Scandal: Gupta Commission Report.' *Pioneer* (New Delhi), 10 May 1999.

Rao, P.V. Narasimha. *Ayodhya: 6 December 1992*. New Delhi: Penguin Books India, 2006.

Rao, P.V. Narasimha. *Insider*. New Delhi: Penguin Books India, 1998.

Sahgal, Nayantara and E.N. Mangat Rai. *Relationships: Extracts from a Correspondence*. New Delhi: Kali for Women, 1994.

Sanghvi, Vir. 'Looking Back at the Bofors Scandal.' <*http://www.rediff.com*>, 23 September 1999.

Sarvepalli, Gopal. *Jawaharlal Nehru: A Biography*. New Delhi: Oxford University Press, 1975.

Sarin, Ritu. 'Breaking the Silence: Sonia Gandhi Grows More Vocal,

INDEX